# An Elizabethan Assassin

# An Elizabethan Assassin

## THEODORE PALEOLOGUS

*Seducer, Spy and Killer*

# JOHN HALL

*In memoriam*
*John Herbert Adams*

Front cover image: Shutterstock

First published 2015

The History Press
The Mill, Brimscombe Port
Stroud, Gloucestershire, GL5 2QG
www.thehistorypress.co.uk

British Library Cataloguing in Publication Data.
A catalogue record for this book is available from the British Library.

ISBN 978 0 7509 6261 2

Typesetting and origination by The History Press
Printed in Europe

# Contents

# Author's note

Except when quoting directly from a source, I have used the spelling Paleologus rather than one of its many variants as this is how it appears on my subject's memorial. However, I call him Theodore rather than Theodoro because the longer he lived in England, the more frequently this spelling appeared in official records. Similarly, I call his youngest son Ferdinand instead of Ferdinando.

I have kept to the original spelling and punctuation of quoted documents where this gives a flavour of the period without the risk of tiring or puzzling the reader with chunks of archaic language, otherwise I have opted for a modernised form of words.

For the crucial period covered in these pages England lagged behind Europe by observing the Julian calendar rather than the Gregorian, so the English year ran from 25 March instead of 1 January. A document of the affected months would be dated, for example, February 1689/90. Except when quoting directly from such a document, I have adjusted dates to the modern style, in this case February 1690.

I hear new news every day, and these ordinary rumours of war, plagues, fires, inundations, thefts, murders, massacres, meteors, comets, spectrums, prodigies, apparitions, of towns taken, cities besieged, in *France, Germany, Turkey, Persia, Poland, etc.*, daily musters and preparations and suchlike, which these tempestuous times afford, battles fought, so many men slain, monomachies, shipwrecks, piracies, and sea-fights, peace, leagues, stratagems, and fresh alarms … Now come tidings of weddings, maskings, mummeries, entertainments, jubilees, embassies, tilts and tournaments, trophies, triumphs, revels, sports, plays: then again, as in a new shifted scene, treasons, cheating tricks, robberies, enormous villainies in all kinds, funerals, burials, deaths of Princes, new discoveries, expeditions; now comical, then tragical matters.

Robert Burton, *The Anatomy of Melancholy*, 1621.

# *Claimed Descent of the English Paleologi*

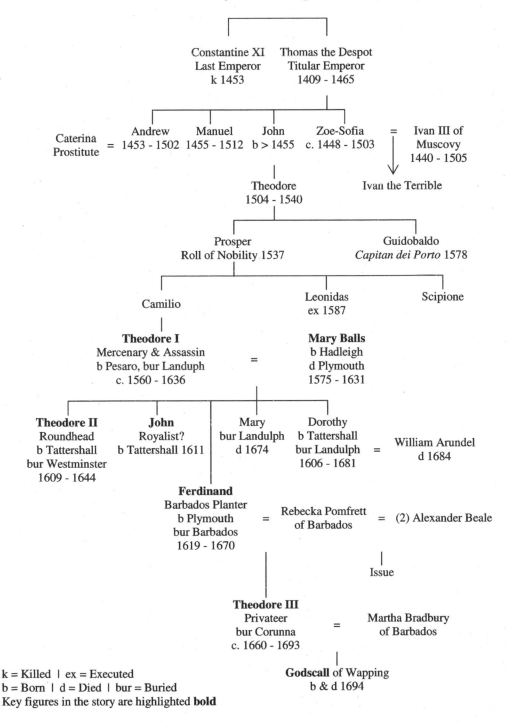

Constantine XI
Last Emperor
k 1453

Thomas the Despot
Titular Emperor
1409 - 1465

Caterina
Prostitute
=

Andrew
1453 - 1502

Manuel
1455 - 1512

John
b > 1455

Zoe-Sofia
c. 1448 - 1503

=

Ivan III of
Muscovy
1440 - 1505

Ivan the Terrible

Theodore
1504 - 1540

Prosper
Roll of Nobility 1537

Guidobaldo
*Capitan dei Porto* 1578

Camilio

Leonidas
ex 1587

Scipione

**Theodore I**
Mercenary & Assassin
b Pesaro, bur Landuph
c. 1560 - 1636

=

**Mary Balls**
b Hadleigh
d Plymouth
1575 - 1631

**Theodore II**
Roundhead
b Tattershall
bur Westminster
1609 - 1644

**John**
Royalist?
b Tattershall 1611

Mary
bur Landulph
d 1674

Dorothy
b Tattershall
bur Landulph
1606 - 1681

=

William Arundel
d 1684

**Ferdinand**
Barbados Planter
b Plymouth
bur Barbados
1619 - 1670

=

Rebecka Pomfrett
of Barbados

=

(2) Alexander Beale

Issue

**Theodore III**
Privateer
bur Corunna
c. 1660 - 1693

=

Martha Bradbury
of Barbados

**Godscall** of Wapping
b & d 1694

k = Killed | ex = Executed
b = Born | d = Died | bur = Buried
Key figures in the story are highlighted **bold**

# Prologue

Mighty, indeed, were these Paleologi: mighty in
power, dignity, and renown; yet within less than
two centuries from the heroic death of the Emperor
Constantine, their direct descendant, Theodoro
Paleologus, was resident, unnoticed and altogether
undistinguished, in a remote parish on the Tamar.

Sir Bernard Burke, *Vicissitudes of Families*.

Remember that what you are told is really threefold:
shaped by the teller, reshaped by the listener,
concealed from both by the dead man of the tale.

Vladimir Nabokov, *The Real Life of Sebastian Knight*.

It has become commonplace to describe any new study of a historical
character as a detective story. This investigation of Theodore Paleologus is
the first biography of an exotic yet elusive figure who surfaced in mysterious
circumstances in Elizabethan England. It is certainly a detective story of
sorts, and one that brims with murders, treasons, revels, battles, sieges,
tournaments, forgeries, piracies, cheating tricks, burials and much more
that we find listed among the Anatomist of Melancholy's 'enormous
villainies in all kinds'. But proof positive of the crimes of Theodore
Paleologus is now beyond mortal grasp and we might as easily call his life a
legend, morality tale or horror story.

Let us start with the legend.

At the fall of Constantinople on Tuesday, 29 May 1453, an event
which burst like a thunderclap over the Christian world, the last

emperor of Byzantium died valiantly sword in hand, defending his capital against the Muslim invader. Constantine XI, of the ancient family of
Paleologus, left no direct heir, and his only brother to reach safety in the
west was Thomas, known by his resounding Byzantine title of Thomas
the Despot. Recognised by the pope as emperor-in-exile, Thomas died
in Rome twelve years later, and of his sons – there were two, three or
four of them, depending on which authority you believe – only the
youngest, John, left heirs male. The single family of the bloodline to
survive into the next century made their home in the Adriatic port of
Pesaro, but during the 1570s they were embroiled in a disastrous vendetta. The sole survivor was the subject of this history, the then teenaged
Theodore Paleologus, last of the legitimate imperial blood.

Banished from Pesaro, Theodore wandered round Europe and after a
spell as a soldier of fortune ended up in England. Here he married a gen-
tlewoman who bore him sons, three surviving into adulthood. A revered,
white-bearded figure in old age, Theodore Paleologus died in 1636 at a
manor house in Cornwall leaving his illustrious pedigree recorded on a
small memorial brass in the parish church. The bloodline of Paleologus
must have seemed secure, so far as those tempestuous times allowed.
But all three sons fought in the English Civil War, one dying in the king's
cause and one in Cromwell's. The surviving brother fled to the new
colony of Barbados, married there and left a son, another Theodore,
who returned to England and became a sailor. This Theodore, the third
generation to marry an Englishwoman, died in 1693. His only child was
a posthumous daughter who died in infancy, the last representative of
the imperial line.

There is a poignant postscript to this tale. Over a century later, during the
Greek War of Independence, the provisional government in Athens sought
vainly in Cornwall and Barbados for a descendant of Theodore who would
accept the crown of Greece and chase the infidel from Constantinople.

Thus far the legend, yet it is also essentially a factual account of the
English dynasty of Paleologus which was accepted by respected historians until recent times. As late as 1940 Sir Stanley Casson wrote
of Theodore as 'the last recorded heir to the throne of Byzantium',

and similar assertions are scattered through scholarly works dating back two centuries and more.[1] Disobligingly, historians of the present day tend to dismiss Theodore's claim out of hand, though so far as I am aware without benefit of original research. Chief of the iconoclasts is Sir Steven Runciman, in whose famous book on the fall of Constantinople a single reference to the English family occurs in a footnote: 'The pathetic double eagles carved (*sic*) on the tomb of Theodore Palaeologus in the church of Landulph in Cornwall have, regrettably, no business to be there.' The clinching evidence for the modernists is that no son of Thomas the Despot called John is mentioned by the contemporary chronicler George Sphrantzes, a survivor of the Ottoman conquest. Alone among recent writers, the philhellene and arch-romantic Sir Patrick Leigh Fermor sounds a sympathetic note. Although admitting a 'shadowy' quality about the youngest son of Thomas, he says that if the authenticity of John is accepted, there are no grounds for doubting our Theodore's ancestry: 'Among his compatriots and contemporaries, at any rate, his Imperial descent was never questioned.' It is an argument that leaves the sceptics unmoved.

The Landulph monument has excited much curiosity over the years. The bold statement that 'Here lyeth the bodye of Theodoro Paleologus of Pesaro in Italye descended from ye Imperyall lyne of ye last Christian Emperors of Greece' comes as an unexpected, not to say stirring, sight in a lonely Anglican church. And while no life of Theodore has been published before, his legend has inspired a remarkable number of works of fiction from the early nineteenth century to the present day. The Edwardian author Sir Arthur Quiller Couch penned a novel based on a local tradition that Theodore sired a race of dashing Cornish squires; he also wrote a weird novella with a plot revolving around Theodore's progeny, occult secrets and rebirth over many centuries. Thomas Hardy visited Landulph Church in the 1880s and carefully copied the tomb inscription into the notebook in which he jotted ideas for novels, stumbling on the germ of the plot for *Tess of the D'Urbervilles*. Several romantic novels and a murder thriller have appeared in recent times in which Theodore features either as a protagonist or the ancestor of the principal character. I have also traced a lengthy Regency ballad and a First World War play about him. A complex mythology continues to evolve and the Paleologus story has even been identified as the source of the Magic Realism genre in modern literature.

These are some of the many afterlives of Theodore Paleologus, a chain of ever more fantastic reincarnations. Like Dr Who, the same man can be endlessly rearranged in time and space. To a novelist or poet, he can be a once and future king, a swashbuckling adventurer, a demon lover, a son of prophesy awaiting the appointed hour, or a kind of Wandering Jew or Flying Dutchman figure; in one recent book he is revealed as the ancestor of the rightful, black-skinned queen of England. His spirit strays deep into *Da Vinci Code* territory, wafting in and out of the Priory of Sion and the Rosslyn Chapel, whispering of global conspiracies, hermetic numbers, the bloodline of Christ and the End of Days. He is a kind of all-purpose *deus ex machina*.

My initial aim in writing this book was to separate fact from fiction. Was the man buried in that quiet spot in Cornwall a genuine heir to the Byzantine emperors or an imposter? As my researches progressed, I grasped that much which seemed fanciful in the legend is firmly rooted in fact. Searches in Italian archives, following the discovery of a long-lost box of Paleologus papers in an English university storeroom, were added excitements to my quest. So far as his imperial lineage goes, a fair body of documentary evidence can now be presented which should help decide the issue in the reader's mind. Yet the more I unearthed of my subject's story, the more beguiling his personality appeared and the wider the focus of my investigation. For if the man was an imposter, fraud would be among the lesser offences on the charge sheet against him.

Briefly stated, the Theodore Paleologus I shall portray here is a multiple murderer, mercenary, apostate, seducer and spy – a real-life figure with all the sinister glamour of the fictional characters inspired by his legend. Yet the defence may easily present him in a sympathetic light, stressing his roles as paterfamilias, asylum-seeker, freedom-fighter, expert linguist, acclaimed horseman and classical scholar.

His years in England bridge the late glories of the Elizabethan age and the chronically unsettled times before the Civil War, and among the *dramatis personae* flitting in and out of his story are some of the most dazzling characters of the times, from Sir Philip Sidney to the Duke of Buckingham, from the poet-diplomat Sir Henry Wotton to Prince Maurice of Nassau. We meet two ill-starred Earls of Essex and assorted Bacons and Cecils; we see Theodore reading Machiavelli with the colonist Captain John Smith; we picture him in the company of the historical Tom Thumb and the leading candidate as Shakespeare's Dark Lady.

But all his life he felt a magnetic pull towards very bad men, for time and again we find him intimately involved with some of the most notorious, vicious and corrupt figures of the age. And as he disappears from sight on frequent occasions, almost certainly under an alias, it seems perfectly possible that Theodore is also known to history with a completely different identity, with deeds known only to the Recording Angel. As it is, this story must be an epic assembled from scraps.

What we can trace of his wanderings show him as a restless soul. Following the banishment from Pesaro, we have fleeting glimpses of him pursuing a double career throughout Europe as soldier of fortune and contract killer. There is a claimed appearance on the Aegean island of Chios, where he may or may not have married another woman before taking his English wife. Once he emerges in England, he ranges north, east, south and west – popping up in Yorkshire, Lincolnshire, London, Devon and finally Cornwall – though with frequent absences supposedly spent fighting for the Protestant cause in the Low Countries. In between are blank periods when we simply do not know his whereabouts. Now you see him, now you don't, and all that lingers is a faint whiff of sulphur. Yet even his Cornish burial, in the honoured place next to the altar, is not our final sighting, for there is the macabre touch of the opening of his coffin a century and a half after his death, revealing the body in a perfect state of preservation.

Theodore's story is still running. On 18 April 2007, a large coach cautiously negotiated the narrow country lanes leading to Landulph, halted outside the ancient granite church and disgorged fifty black-robed Greek

Orthodox priests. Inside, the Paleologus monument was draped with silk ribbons of the Greek colours with the Byzantine eagle flag displayed above it. Led by Archbishop Gregorios, head of the Orthodox community in Britain, senior clerics exchanged their sober garb for sumptuous embroidered vestments to celebrate vespers in honour of the heir of the Paleologi. Candlelight flickered on golden icons on the altar, chants rose and fell, and clouds of incense drifted past the massed bushy beards.

This strange evocation of Byzantium in a simple Cornish church was witnessed by a handful of bemused locals squeezed along the rear pews, peering over rows of black stovepipe hats. It was explained to me afterwards that the ceremony was not technically the full Orthodox memorial rite, in deference to the imperial scion's conversion to the Church of England. I suspected the shade of Theodore was chuckling softly at such scruples, and it was then I knew this book had to be written. For here was a most striking demonstration of how the name Paleologus continues to exert its power over the imagination.

Byzantium has a deep spiritual significance for the Greeks and the Eastern Church, but there is a strong English interest in the vanished empire. Constantine the Great, founder of Constantinople, was proclaimed Caesar by the Roman army at York, and in the deep layers of ancient British myth Constantine's mother was an Englishwoman, daughter of the King Coel immortalised in the nursery rhyme. King Arthur was the claimed grandson of Constantine and was himself the claimed ancestor of the Tudors.

There is no lack of present-day pretenders to the imperial bloodline. Anyone with access to the internet is free to roam their airy realms. Paleologus is a brain-turning name, and as claimants in cyberspace range from the mildly delusional to the barking mad it is a dreamlike experience to wander through their mazy pedigrees, only to find each and every claim of descent ridiculed by some spoilsport genealogist on a rival website. There is also a recurring element of the criminal. Now and then a self-declared imperial heir will materialise to offer you a Byzantine coat of arms or title for a financial consideration, only to exit fast when the police or press come knocking.

Others have at least a half-respectable claim to Paleologus blood and some of these will be examined later. The Constantine link with the British royal family may be risible, but the future King Charles III inherits Paleologus blood twice over, from his mother's forebears and his father's. My chapter on Victor Paleologus, the only living, breathing bearer of the name to feature in this book, does not yet present a formal claim, as Mr Paleologus is currently researching his imperial descent from a cell in Chino State Prison in California, where he is serving a term of twenty-five years to life for murder. Mr Paleologus tells me of a strong family tradition of 'intricate connections' with the dynasty, though he accepts that establishing 'the constructive link' will demand further investigation.

With the single exception of Victor Paleologus, claims of imperial descent are traceable through female lines. The pedigrees of all other pretenders twist and turn and shift sideways in the ingenious manner of the Windsor descent from William the Conqueror. If we seek the last heirs of the imperial Paleologi in direct male line, it is Theodore's English family or nothing.

This book examines the strange and sometimes shocking history of Theodore Paleologus, his pedigree from the mysterious John and of his own descendants up to their extinction — or supposed extinction — a century after his arrival in England. Before tracing these generations in detail, however, we must begin with an overview of Byzantium's last ruling line, a dynasty founded on assassination, heresy and treason. A chronicle of cruel deeds and dark secrets, it seems a fittingly lurid backcloth to the tale of Paleologus of Landulph.

# 1

Talk to me, my lords,
Of sepulchres and mighty emperors' bones.

Thomas Middleton, *The Revenger's Tragedy*.

For most of us Byzantium is a hazy concept. Anyone of my own post-war generation might easily envisage an Egyptian or Roman of ancient times, if only by courtesy of Cecil B. De Mille, but the Byzantine was a figure shrouded in mystery. Many must have heard the name of his empire's great capital for the first time when taxed with the simple playground riddle:

*Constantinople is a very long word – if you can't spell it you're the biggest dunce in the world.*

The Byzantines were absent from history lessons at my grammar school; John Julius Norwich, best-known of the modern historians of Byzantium, has made the same point about his schooling at Eton. For a teenager, a next fleeting brush with the civilisation might have come on reading *Sailing to Byzantium*, with Yeats's sensuous lines offering an illusory moment of empathy where history had failed, in images of hammered gold and gold enamelling, a drowsing emperor, and an artificial bird singing on a golden bough:

*To lords and ladies of Byzantium
Of what is past, or passing, or to come.*

Our present use of the word byzantine as a synonym for the excessively complex, tortuous or duplicitous serves to distance us further from a proud Christian empire that lasted over 1,000 years. It may not be too fanciful to discern the origin of this detachment in a collective Western guilt over the conquest of Constantinople by Islam.

Constantinople was founded in the year 330 by Constantine the Great, the first Roman emperor to convert to Christianity. For the site of his New Rome he chose an established Greek settlement called Byzantion, located on the Bosphorus where east meets west. Like Old Rome, his city was built on seven hills. Drawing on legacies of the classical world, it became the centre of an empire which at its zenith was by far the greatest power on earth, ruling over present-day Greece, North Africa, Egypt, the Holy Land, the islands of the Mediterranean, much of Italy, the Balkans and Asia Minor – in all, the empire encompassed the territories of thirty-four of today's nation states. Constantinople was renowned for its fabulous wealth, sublime art and unrivalled tradition of learning; above all, from the seventh century to the fifteenth, it was Christendom's bulwark against an ever-expanding Islam. The city survived repeated sieges by the Arabs and the empire's most formidable foes of latter centuries, the Ottoman Turks.

Constantine ruled both Old and New Rome, but in 395 the empire was divided between his descendants. Less than a century later, Rome was overrun by barbarians. The emperor in Constantinople was sole ruler of what remained, and during the next golden age, the reign of Justinian the Great, many lost territories of Old Rome were regained. But the empire was constantly assailed by enemies on all fronts – not only Ottomans, but Persians, Slavs, Normans, Huns, Bulgars, Venetians and a host of others – and repeatedly fragmented by civil wars. In the meantime the empire's character changed from essentially Latin to Greek, though to the end its subjects persisted in calling themselves Romans.

The vast all-powerful Byzantine Empire was a distant memory by the time of Michael Paleologus, founder of the last imperial line and claimed ancestor of the man buried in Landulph Church. In 1204, twenty years before Michael's birth, Constantinople had been captured and sacked, not by Turks but by so-called crusaders – Latins, as the Byzantines called everyone from Western Europe. Dazzled by the enormous wealth they saw en route to the Holy Land, which like so much of the former empire was now in Muslim hands, they realised that Constantinople offered easier pickings. With the great city in ruins and its treasures plundered, a Latin usurper was proclaimed emperor; much of the Greek mainland was carved up between rapacious followers who proceeded to call themselves counts, dukes and princes.

With their empire on the verge of total collapse, the Byzantine emperors-in-exile retreated to the ancient city of Nicaea across the Straits of the Bosphorus, forty miles from the old imperial capital. The short-lived dynasty of that period, the Lascaris, was soon supplanted by the Paleologi. And it must be said that all our negative and sensational associations with Byzantine history – assassinations, plots, arcane ceremony, unbridled greed, cruelty, treachery, hypocrisy and love of ostentatious display – may justly be linked with the Paleologan era.

Though a usurper, Michael Paleologus was no upstart. The Paleologi were among the empire's great aristocratic families, counting among their ancestors no fewer than eleven emperors of earlier times. The theoretical succession from the Caesars was maintained. Paleologus – the Greek name means *ancient word* – was the most talented general serving the Lascaris, but their relationship was always fragile.

Emperor John III, an epileptic, managed to recapture considerable territory from the Latins, but grew jealous of Michael's prowess as a soldier. John's son and successor, Theodore II, was even more suspicious of the general. At one time Paleologus was so convinced he was in mortal danger from the emperor that he defected to the Turks, then busily mopping up yet more sorry remnants of the empire. But again the quarrel between emperor and general was patched up.

When Theodore II died leaving an eight-year-old successor, John IV, the looming thundercloud burst. During a memorial service for the dead ruler, the child emperor's appointed regent was hacked to pieces at the high altar. The outrage was almost certainly on the orders of Michael Paleologus, who soon afterwards proclaimed himself co-emperor. The fate of a child monarch was rarely a happy one and on Christmas Day 1261 the wretched boy's eyes were put out – along with castration, blinding was a favourite Byzantine method of dealing with rivals – and he was locked up for the rest of his life. As Michael VIII, the first Paleologus ruler assumed the sonorous title of his predecessors, *Basileus Basileon Basilieuon Basileonton*, King of Kings ruling over Kings, and signed his name in royal red ink: 'in Christ, true Emperor and Autocrat of the Romans, Vice-Gerent of God on earth, Equal of the Apostles'. He is known to history as Michael the Crafty. The first emperor to adopt the emblem of the double-headed eagle which looks east and west, he was by far the ablest of his line and is best remembered for recapturing Constantinople.

In 1261, following a series of victories against the Latins, Michael entered the Queen of Cities by the Golden Gate. With a display of piety calculated to impress the citizens, he is recorded as appearing humbly on foot behind Byzantium's holiest icon. However, it is axiomatic that any Byzantine source is contradicted by the next, and another account has him entering in triumph on a magnificent white horse. Either way, Michael's popularity was short-lived. Taxes rose steeply to finance a lavish rebuilding of the city and an imperial navy. Disgusted by the fate of the boy emperor, the patriarch of Constantinople excommunicated Michael, who responded by deposing the patriarch. But it was a more radical act which turned the majority of Byzantines against their ruler.

The schism between Orthodoxy and the Roman Catholic Church dated back to 1054. The mutual hatred between the Eastern and Western traditions intensified during the Latin reign in Constantinople, where many of the emperor's subjects regarded the rival Christian faith as a worse enemy than Islam. Once in power, Michael schemed for a reunion of the two churches – not through religious conviction, but as the means of winning papal support against his Catholic foes. Michael's promised submission to Rome enraged the powerful Orthodox clergy, but protest in Constantinople was crushed without mercy. Michael was not a man to cross and opponents escaping death faced exile, imprisonment, torture or mutilation. The simmering resentment of the Orthodox hierarchy was to dog the emperor for the rest of his reign, and in the end all his machinations came to nothing. Negotiations with Rome dragged on for twenty years with one pope after another until a newly elected pontiff, Martin IV, finally lost patience. He pronounced a sentence of excommunication on Michael, to add to that issued by the patriarch.

'The usurper Paleologus' was now fair game to any Catholic rival who wanted the Byzantine crown for himself.

The most serious challenge came from the French king's brother, Charles of Anjou. A huge French army was assembled in Sicily, formerly Byzantine territory but now one of the many possessions that Charles ruled with a rod of iron, along with the armada needed to carry it to Constantinople. The army was on the point of sailing when, on the evening of Easter Monday, 1282, outside the church of the Holy Spirit in Palermo, a tipsy French soldier molested a local girl. As the bells tolled for vespers, an infuriated crowd fell upon the soldier and his companions and killed them all. It was a strike of lightning that set the entire island on fire. Soon every Frenchman in Sicily had been slaughtered by the vengeful Sicilians, excepting a handful who managed to scramble on board Charles's ships. The greatest threat to Michael's reign was wiped out overnight.

How far Michael was responsible for the extraordinary incident known as the War of Sicilian Vespers is disputed, but he was not slow to claim the credit: 'If I dare to say that God did it by my own hands,' he wrote, 'I would only be telling the truth.'[2] For months his secret agents had been diligently at work among dissidents in Sicily, freely dispensing Byzantine gold.

But within a year Michael VIII was dead. Exhausted by a life of campaigning, excoriated as a heretic by both churches, he left a near-bankrupt empire. Doubly damned, denied Christian burial, he was laid in a shallow grave at dead of night by his son and successor, Andronicus II. Only years later did Andronicus dare to give his father a quiet burial in holy ground, and when the body was dug up it was found in a perfect state of preservation. The scene strangely foreshadows the discovery of the body of Theodore Paleologus some 500 years later in Cornwall. In popular belief – though a paradox – it was only the most saintly and most evil whose bodies were incorruptible. After Michael's exhumation, the legend arose that the earth itself had refused to take back a man so wicked.

The reign of Michael the Crafty set the tone for generations to come and would find echoes in the lives of Theodore Paleologus and his English brood. Recurring motifs in the family's history are conspiracy,

murder, treachery, apostasy, enforced abdication, denied burial, perjury, seduction, forgery and extortion. And, almost constantly, there was
war between the generations – father against son, grandfather against
grandson, brother against brother.

The strife between Michael's successor Andronicus II and his grandson serves as an illustration. Andronicus II was the longest-reigning of
the Paleologi and perhaps the unhappiest. No soldier like his father,
he would have made a better monk, and during his forty-six years as
emperor most of Asia Minor was lost forever. But it was the family that
proved the curse of his life. When his grandson and heir, the even-
tual Andronicus III, suspected his mistress of infidelity, he decided
to trap his rival by stationing thugs in an unlit passage near her door.
Unfortunately the man they pounced on and beat to death in the dark
was Andronicus's younger brother, Prince Manuel, the emperor's
favourite, whereupon Emperor Andronicus disinherited his namesake.
Years of costly civil war ensued until the humiliated emperor, at the age
of seventy, was forced to abdicate and beg his grandson for his life.

Family hostilities resumed when Andronicus III died in 1341 leaving an eight-year-old heir, John V. A bitter six-year power struggle
was waged between the regent, Andronicus's widow Anne, and the
dead ruler's bosom friend and cousin, John Paleologus Cantacuzenus,
who declared himself 'spiritual successor' of Andronicus and therefore
rightful co-emperor as John VI. Aided by the empire's wily enemies,
the Turks and the Serbs, Cantacuzenus eventually proved victorious.
To consolidate his claim he agreed to share the throne with the legitimate heir, now fourteen, who was married off to one of Cantacuzenus's
daughters. In the meantime thousands had died in clashes between the
contending Byzantine armies or at the hands of foreign mercenaries.
Part of the price Cantacuzenus paid for Turkish aid was the despatch of
another daughter to the sultan's harem.

On entering Constantinople the conqueror discovered the imperial treasury contained 'nothing but air and dust'. Desperate for funds,
Empress Anne had pawned the crown jewels and imperial plate to
the Venetians. So at their solemn joint coronation as Johns V and VI

in 1347, the co-emperors' crowns were of gold-painted leather studded with bits of coloured glass. The ceremony could not be held as tradition demanded at the Church of the Divine Wisdom, Haghia Sophia, because the great dome had collapsed during a recent earthquake. That same year, as a crowning misery, the Black Death made its European debut in Constantinople, wiping out half the population.

Inevitably, war broke out again between the two emperors, young John V gaining the upper hand with the aid of the Genoese. There now occurs one of the few uplifting episodes in the Paleologus saga. John V allowed his defeated father-in-law to live on condition he took monastic vows, and the former John VI entered the most enriching period of his life. Finding his true vocation in the cloister, he filled a fruitful retirement with meditation and theological studies, though he was frequently called back to court as elder statesman and counsellor to his former rival. He was to die peacefully in his bed aged eighty-eight.

However, there was one hiccup. The three-decade idyll in the monastery was interrupted when the ex-emperor was seized as a hostage by his own grandson, another Andronicus – son of his daughter Helena and John V – and cast into prison. Andronicus was the latest Paleologus to rebel against his father, and with Turkish and Genoese help he took John V prisoner and locked him up. The hapless John had brought about his own downfall by touring Christendom in a fruitless search for allies against Islam. In Rome, he followed his ancestor Michael the Crafty in announcing his conversion to Catholicism, to the horror of Constantinople.

The next emperor of significance was Andronicus's brother, the intellectual Manuel II, who has demonstrated that the name Paleologus can invoke fury across the Islamic world to the present day. As Manuel's reign saw the Turkish conquest of most of his remaining lands, an agonisingly long if unsuccessful siege of Constantinople, and the slaughter, enslavement or forced conversion of countless thousands of his subjects, he might not be expected to take a rosy view of the founder of Islam. 'Show me what Mohammed brought that was new,' he wrote to a Persian scholar, 'and there you will find things only evil and inhuman such as his command to spread by the sword the faith he preached.'[3]

Quoted by Pope Benedict XVI in 2006 during a university lecture, the fourteenth-century emperor's musings led to mass street protests and riots, calls for the pope's assassination and a unanimous condemnation by the Pakistani parliament, along with murders of Christians and the firebombing of churches.

Manuel was the first Byzantine emperor since Constantine the Great to visit England, during his own futile begging tour of Europe. In 1400 he met the new king, Henry IV. The chronicler Adam of Usk recorded the spectacle of the dignified but impoverished emperor at King Henry's court: 'I thought within myself, what a grievous thing it was that this great Christian prince from the farther East should perforce be driven by unbelievers to visit the islands of the West, to seek aid against them. My God! What dost thou, ancient glory of Rome? Shorn is the greatness of thine empire this day.'

The scholarly John VIII, Manuel's son and successor, is the only Paleologus emperor of whom we have reliable portraits. A bronze medal by Pisanello shows him in profile, and in Gozzoli's famous fresco in the Medici Chapel at Florence he is one of a trio of contemporary grandees represented as the Magi. Here John is the image of a Renaissance prince, though with a dash of the exotic: astride a magnificent white horse in gold trappings, he wears a sumptuous tunic of gold-embroidered green and the traditional red boots of the Byzantine emperors, while on his head is a fantastic crown of gem-studded gold enclosed by waving feathers. Whether his crown was mere paint and glass we do not know. The fresco dates from around twenty years after John's visit to Italy, but if Gozzoli did not himself set eyes on the emperor he would certainly have cross-examined many who did, and may well have studied portraits then extant. Gozzoli's John is a strikingly handsome man of kingly bearing, his long face framed by thick curly hair and neatly trimmed beard of auburn. Pisanello's profile shows an older, careworn man with the kind of long aquiline nose which would be observed at the opening of Theodore Paleologus's coffin in Cornwall.

Other portraits of Paleologus emperors follow Byzantine tradition, and instead of studies from the life we have icon-like images representing the essence of royalty rather than human beings. One beard may be a little longer or greyer than the next, but otherwise the emperors are a row of solemn look-alikes, each in his stiff bejewelled robes and the elaborate semi-spherical crown which distinguishes a ruler of Byzantium. The late flowering of Byzantine art under the Paleologi did not extend to a new take on portraiture as pioneered in contemporary Italy.

Discussing the physical appearances of these imperial figures brings me to a central challenge in writing a biography of this kind. Readers want to put a face to any character claimed as worthy of their interest. Alas, I have no portrait to offer: bizarrely, the only detailed description of my subject's appearance dates from long after his death. Nor do I see any prospect of his long-forgotten picture turning up in some dusty corridor of a country house, no *Unknown Man circa 1600* whose identity will be revealed as layers of grime are wiped from a coat-of-arms or riddling motto. The mind's eye must fill the void, taking as a starting point an uncommonly tall soldierly figure and a long-nosed, fine-boned face owing something to the ancestral line.

Despite the glamorous image reflecting his youthful visit to Italy, John VIII was one of the few emperors to inherit none of the obvious characteristics – vaunting ambition, cruelty, martial prowess and cunning statesmanship – of the founder of the dynasty. He was worthy and a little dull. His younger brother and successor Constantine XI, destined to be the last of the ninety emperors of Byzantium, was a man of a very different stamp.

History has not been kind to the name Paleologus. The dynasty is inescapably linked with the empire's decline and fall, though the die was cast long before its founder's time. But the tragic and heroic figure of Constantine XI[4] redeems the Paleologi, and to the present day his legend is an inspiration to countless Greeks. He is the sacred emperor, not dead but sleeping, the figure of prophecy who will reappear at the appointed hour.

Constantine took pains to avoid the deadly family quarrels which had blighted his forebears. Long before succeeding John VIII, he promised to be the longed-for leader who would reclaim the empire, and in early years had successfully waged war on the petty Latin rulers clinging on in mainland Greece. But the victories ended in 1444 when the Italian duke of Athens allied himself to the Byzantines' nemesis, the Ottoman sultan. Thereafter Constantine was constantly on the defensive. As well as his outside enemies, he had much to contend with from his two remaining brothers, Demetrius and Thomas, who shared the title of despot of the imperial fiefdom called the Morea, better known today as the Peloponnese. Of Thomas, there is more to be said later.

For eight centuries Muslims dreamt of conquering Constantinople, 'the bone in the throat of Allah', yet though they overran virtually every corner of the empire, all their previous twenty-three sieges of the city had ended in failure. They had never equalled the feat of the crusaders. But a ruthless new sultan, Mehmet II, was obsessed with taking Constantinople, and at the age of twenty-one he made his bid.

After a five-week siege the final assault began in the early hours of 23 May 1453. The advantage swung back and forth between attacker and defender as desperate fighting shifted to different points around the city walls, and the moment of crisis came when the leader of the Byzantines' Genoese allies was grievously injured and carried from the ramparts. His loss caused panic among the defenders and the Genoese rushed for their boats. Byzantines who followed the emperor into the gap tried to hold off the invaders but were quickly overwhelmed.

Estimates of the combatants involved differ wildly though no one has ever doubted that Mehmet's forces vastly outnumbered Constantine's. The emperor's chancellor survived the fall of the city and recorded the total number of defenders – Byzantines and their allies – as less than 8,000. The Muslim host has been calculated as anything up to 400,000, though modern historians trim this down to perhaps 200,000 including camp followers. Whatever the odds, the outcome was inevitable. The fall of the city brought to an end not only the Byzantine world dating from the fourth century but an empire whose origins could be traced to the founding of Rome in 753 BC.

All accounts of Constantine's death were based on hearsay, though the Greek world has never doubted his end befitted a hero and martyr. Several reports say that when he realised all was lost, the emperor threw off everything that could identify him, hurled himself into the enemy ranks, and was cut down instantly. However, he had forgotten about his red boots embroidered with golden eagles, and these gave him away when the bodies of the dead were looted.

According to one story, the sultan had his head cut off and paraded around the city on a stake, then sent as a present to the sultan of Egypt. One highly suspect source has Mehmet weeping at the sight of his dead adversary and ordering an honourable Christian burial at Haghia Sophia, while another says Constantine hanged himself the moment the Turks broke through the city's defences. One of the surprisingly few Ottoman accounts claims he was fleeing in terror when felled by a Turkish marine. One or two sources even say he made his escape from the city by boat. But the most persistent theme is that Constantine displayed sublime courage, unhesitatingly choosing to die rather than abandon the imperial city.

No one really knows what happened to his body. The legend quickly arose that an angel snatched him away to sleep in a deep cavern under the Golden Gate until the day he will rise again to free his people. It is a variant of the universal legend of the sleeping hero, a Greek equivalent of Britain's Arthur, Owen Glendower or Fionn mac Cumhaill. All appear to derive from the ancient tale of the Seven Sleepers of Ephesus, the Christian youths who fell asleep in a cave during the Roman persecution and woke centuries later in the Christian empire.

All surviving tombs of the emperors were destroyed. Their favoured burial place was not Haghia Sophia but the Church of the Holy Apostles where Constantine the Great himself was interred. Crusader knights had smashed and looted their resting place two and a half centuries before, departing with a great haul of gold and jewels. Among the treasures of St Mark's in Venice is a gold crown torn from one of the bodies cast out like so much rubbish. The Turks evicted the last scraps of imperial dust, determined that no place of pilgrimage would remain; Mehmet demolished the church itself to make way for the mosque which would house his own tomb. All that remain today are a few empty battered sarcophagi carved from the porphyry reserved for imperial use, transported to the environs of Haghia Sophia or the Istanbul Archaeological Museum, inevitably recalling the words of Hamlet:

*To what base uses we may return, Horatio! Why may not imagination trace the noble dust of Alexander, till he find it stopping a bung-hole?*

More fortunate than the emperors, the English Paleologi have left us three tombs to visit, though none has remained undisturbed. The earliest and historically most important is that of Theodore at Landulph with the ancestral names set out on the monument like an incantation: besides those of the commemorated man, his wife and father-in-law, the others are of six direct ancestors and five descendants.

In full, the inscription reads:

HERE LYETH THE BODY OF THEODORO PALEOLOGVS
OF PESARO IN ITALYE DESCENDED FROM YE IMPERYALL
LYNE OF YE LAST CHRISTIAN EMPERORS OF GREECE
BEING THE SONNE OF CAMILIO YE SONNE OF PROSPER
THE SONNE OF THEODORO THE SONNE OF JOHN YE
SONNE OF THOMAS SECOND BROTHER TO CONSTANTINE
PALEOLOGUS THE 8th OF THAT NAME AND LAST OF
YT LYNE YT RAYGNED IN CONSTANTINOPLE VNTILL SVB-
DEWED BY THE TVRKS, WHO MARRIED WITH MARY
YE DAUGHTER OF WILLIAM BALLS OF HADLYE IN
SOVFFOLKE GENT: & HAD ISSUE 5 CHILDREN THEO-
DORO, JOHN, FERDINANDO, MARIA & DOROTHY, & DE-
PARTED THIS LIFE AT CLYFTON YE 21st OF JANVARY 1636.

Tracing down the generations to the man buried at Landulph, we begin with an account of the last emperor's brother Thomas, last of the despots.

# 2

They are the abstract and brief chronicle of
the time: after your death, you were better have a
bad epitaph than their ill report while you live.

Shakespeare, *Hamlet.*

Sometime late in the summer of 1460, seven years after the fall of
Constantinople, a Venetian galley tied up in the Adriatic seaport of Ancona
with a party of weary, seasick and impoverished Byzantine exiles on board.
The remnants of the imperial family, they had fled before a Turkish
onslaught against the last imperial outposts on the Greek mainland, brav-
ing waters infested with enemy warships to reach this place of safety.

The leader of the fugitives was Thomas Paleologus, brother of the
slain emperor, and among his companions were his young sons: how
many he fathered has long been disputed, but if the John named on
the Landulph brass is no fiction there must have been at least three.
During his futile defence of the Morea, the last despot had fought not
only Turks but his treacherous brother Demetrius. Having thrown in
his lot with the sultan, Demetrius forfeited any claim to the succession.
Contemporaries who were fond of seeing living characters as the incarnation of figures of antiquity would call Demetrius and Thomas the new
Cain and Abel, though the new Abel's destiny was a living martyrdom.

Thomas was now the sole survivor of five brothers of the emperor.
He arrived in Italy, as a sorrowful Pope Pius II observed:

> … a prince who was born to the illustrious and ancient family of the Paleologi,
> the son of an emperor, the brother of an emperor, himself the first in line and
> so destined to become an emperor … wise, magnanimous and full of courage,
> a man who has been robbed of his empire, of his every kingdom … a man

who is now an immigrant, naked, robbed of everything except his lineage, so poor and so needy.

But Thomas did not arrive empty-handed. Though penniless and in rags, he had brought a gift for the pope wrapped in a white silk shawl – a grisly object, yet one of the most precious relics of Christendom. It was the head of the Apostle Andrew, brother of St Peter, patron saint of the Byzantine Church. It was removed by the fleeing heir from the basilica at Patras, the great city port of the Peloponnese where Andrew had been martyred. The head was venerated there for many centuries, but under Ottoman rule would certainly have shared the fate of Constantinople's fabled collection of relics, among them an icon of the Virgin supposedly painted from life by St Luke. All were defiled and destroyed at the fall of the city.[5]

Delighted with his present, Pius awarded Thomas a much-needed pension of 6,000 ducats a year, a palatial residence in Rome and the coveted papal order of the Golden Rose. Of all the pontiffs of the period, Pius II was the most sympathetic to the Byzantine cause, toiling constantly to persuade western monarchs to back a new crusade against the Turks. But Europe was now hopelessly divided, with France and Spain split by internal dynastic conflicts, England convulsed by the Wars of the Roses, and most of the German principalities and Italian states locked in venomous disputes of one kind or another. With Pius's death in 1464 all realistic hope of restoring Byzantium seemed at an end.

Thomas's landfall of Ancona, in the region of Marche, nominally belonged to the Papal States, and ancestors of Theodore Paleologus were to live hereabouts for more than 100 years. Marche boasted a long association with Byzantium. Occupied by Goths after the fall of Rome, it was recaptured by the great Byzantine general Belisarius and ruled from Ravenna, not far to the north. The region's other major cities were Pesaro, the birthplace of our Theodore, and neighbouring Urbino. Both were seats of the ducal Rovere family whose patronage was enjoyed by Theodore's forebears. Other powerful pro-Byzantine nobles seated in the area were the Gonzaga, the Este and the Malatesta. One of Thomas's dead brothers had married a daughter of the Malatesta who was a previous lord of Pesaro.

However, Thomas himself lingered in Rome, the better to plead the case for his restoration. Everyone who saw Thomas in the flesh seemed to be hugely impressed, and several contemporaries recorded impressions of his dignity, refined manners and noble demeanour. His appearance was captured by several painters and sculptors, not only as himself but in the guise of various saints – for instance, he was the model for a marble statue of St Paul executed by Paulo Tacconi di Sezze, the pope's favourite sculptor, and for one of the figures in Piero della Francesca's *Flagellation*.

The last of the despots died within a year of Pope Pius. Apart from the John named on the Landulph brass, it is generally asserted that Thomas was survived by his heir Andrew, then aged twelve, his brother Manuel, ten, and a daughter Zoe, later called Sofia, aged seventeen. In addition to the children accompanying Thomas into exile, there was a well-documented elder daughter, Helena, who married a minor Serbian royal but failed to produce an heir; there is some evidence of a third daughter who died with her name unrecorded. So how many children there were in all has long been a matter of controversy. Varying numbers of both sons and daughters are offered in early documents, even those dates a few years from Thomas's death. As well as Andrew, Manuel and John, mention of a fourth son called Rogerio has been found in archives in the Cilento area south of Naples, and the possibility of a fifth son, also called Thomas, has been mooted on the strength of an Italian history published in 1602. But enough is enough; the causes of Rogerio and Thomas the Younger have never attracted scholarly support and we shall concentrate on John.

Of contemporary authorities, the Byzantine statesman George Sphrantzes was traditionally regarded as the most reliable. Born in 1401, Sphrantzes served both Manuel II and Constantine XI, and his chronicle of the fall of Constantinople is a vivid telling of the catastrophe. It is also a painfully detailed account of the fate of Sphrantzes's own family at the hands of the sultan, for his son and daughter were both taken into the seraglio where the son was killed and the daughter died of an infectious disease at the age of fourteen. Sphrantzes shared Thomas's exile, and nowhere in his chronicle does he mention a John among the despot's progeny. This silence is at the heart of the case against the authenticity of the English Paleologi. Yet Sphrantzes's testimony has been questioned by scholars in recent times since it transpired that what had always been considered entirely his own work was virtually rewritten by a later editor. The accuracy of Sphrantzes has also been queried on the grounds that, working on the dateline he gives, Thomas the Despot's wife gave birth to one of her children at the age of sixty-five.[6]

Thomas's marital status has never seriously been questioned. He married Catherine Zaccaria, daughter of the last Latin prince to rule the Greek island of Chios, in 1430, and she died at Corfu in 1462 aged fifty. She was the mother of all the claimed children of Thomas except Rogerio, the proposed issue of an alleged earlier marriage of Thomas which has been widely ridiculed by historians.

The earliest printed reference to a son of Thomas called John occurs in *De ecclesiae occidentalis atque orientalis perpetua concensione*, which translates as 'The Western and Eastern Churches in Perpetual Agreement', a work published in 1648 by the Greek scholar Leo Allatius. This names 'Andrea, Manuele et Ioanne' as Despot Thomas's sons. What may be of crucial importance is that Allatius was custodian of the Vatican Library and so enjoyed unfettered access to one of the world's greatest collections of books and manuscripts. Born in Chios in 1586 and educated at the Greek College in Rome, he gained a solid reputation as a historian and philosopher and won the confidence of Popes Gregory XV and Alexander VII. His works include the first methodical discussion of vampires. Among acquisitions he oversaw for the Vatican were the magnificent Palatine library presented to Pope Gregory and the manuscript collections of several great Italian dynasties, among them the Rovere dukes of Urbino.

This being the time of the Counter-Reformation, entry to the Vatican Library was jealously guarded. Access to the archives became so restricted that no one was allowed in except the staff, on pain of excommunication. Following the French occupation of Rome in Napoleonic times, much of the great library was looted and carted off to France, along with the captive pope. Most of the collections were returned to Rome in 1815 and a few detained in France, but an unknown quantity was lost. So although the first known mention of John Paleologus comes in Allatius's book, there is a possibility of the loss of earlier documents known to the librarian which supported the legitimacy of an English line descending from John. Harder to explain is why a world-famous scholar like Allatius would simply make him up.

Of Andrew and Manuel Paleologus much more is known, but little to their credit. Andrew's appearance is known from several portraits including Pinturicchio's fresco in the *Appartmento Borgia* in the Vatican. The heir to Thomas's title of emperor-in-exile has the familiar long face, high cheek bones and aquiline nose of the Paleologi.

Andrew is dismissed in Gibbon's *Decline and Fall of the Roman Empire* as 'contemptible to his enemies and burdensome to his friends' and 'degraded by the baseness of his life and marriage'. The Victorian historian George Finlay, in his *History of Greece*, remarks that Andrew would hardly merit attention 'were it not that mankind has a morbid curiosity concerning the fortunes of the most worthless princes'. And while kindly old Pope Pius provided the heir with a generous pension, his successor Sixtus IV seems to have had less time for Byzantine hangers-on, and Andrew's marriage to a common streetwalker of Rome called Caterina – not even her surname is known – offered an excuse to cut off the money. Sixtus, the builder of the Sistine Chapel, eventually reinstated the pension and even raised funds for a military expedition to restore Andrew as despot of Morea, but the money leaked away without a blow struck against the Turks.

Once more cold-shouldered by the pope, Andrew hawked himself round the courts of Europe offering to cede his rights to the throne of Constantinople to the highest bidder. He even made a vain journey to London to tempt Henry Tudor. In the end Charles VIII of France outbid the king of Naples and the duke of Burgundy for the imperial title in return for an annual pension of 4,300 ducats. Four years later, in 1498, Charles's death left Andrew penniless but once again in possession of the phantom crown which he proceeded to sell off to Ferdinand of Aragon. Between times he travelled to Russia to sponge off his sister Zoe, now married to

Ivan III, Grand Duke of Moscow, and succeeded in relieving her of all her jewels. Like one of the bogus Paleologi of today, he traded honorific titles to gullible snobs for cash in hand. When Andrew died in 1502 his widow had to beg the pope for the money to bury him. Or rather, this unseemly picture has long been the received wisdom about Andrew and his wife. Scholarly efforts to rehabilitate the pair have been made in recent years and it has been pointed out that the first printed reference to the wife as a prostitute dates from the seventeenth century.[7]

Yet to contemporaries Andrew's failings paled into insignificance compared with those of his brother Manuel. Despised as he was, Andrew at least made feeble attempts to reclaim his birthright, but Manuel quickly despaired of squeezing more money out of the pope and returned to Constantinople. There he threw himself on the mercy of the sultan and was rewarded with a pension and a pair of concubines. Manuel was survived by a son, named after his brother Andrew, who in the words of Gibbon 'was lost in the habit and religion of a Turkish slave'. This is how far we have departed from the 'power, dignity and renown' of the mighty Paleologi lamented by Sir Bernard Burke.

In submitting to the sultan, Manuel was following in the footsteps of his uncle, the perfidious ex-despot Demetrius, who died there in 1470 after seeing his wife join their daughter in the sultan's harem. Some sources say Demetrius converted to Islam, others say he died a monk. Some say he had no male heir, others say a son called Manuel became a fervent Moslem with the nickname *El Ghazi*, or Holy Warrior, who was given command of the Ottoman forces. The constant repetition of given names, especially Andrew and Manuel, causes much confusion over the descent of the Paleologi, and there are even published family trees which make *El Ghazi* the father of the John named on the Landulph brass.

There are other theories as to John's true identity. Among the more persuasive is that he was an illegitimate son of either Thomas or one of Thomas's undisputed sons, a status which would still secure him illustrious patronage. The favours heaped by popes on their own bastards have filled dozens of books – Pope Julius himself had a pampered daughter – and a natural offspring of one of the imperial Paleologi would certainly possess the *bona fides* to satisfy the Rovere affinity. Some sources mention an illegitimate son of Andrew who was appointed a captain in the Pontifical Guard, but his name was Constantine.

A more beguiling conjecture is that John was the *legitimate* offspring of Andrew and his wife Caterina, and therefore the true heir. Yet whereas discreet support for an imperial bastard would appear a laudable act of charity, there was surely no question that an alliance of Christian powers – the only conceivable means by which the empire might be restored – would unite beneath the banner of the streetwalker's son, even overlooking the fact that his father had twice sold off the imperial honours. Here is reason enough why John would become 'shadowy' even in his own lifetime. But we shall return to these theories later.

The later descent of the English Paleologi according to the Landulph pedigree – Theodore, Prosper and Camilio – has provoked no controversy and is amply supported by the archives at Pesaro, so our focus must remain on John. The name Leone is sometimes given in contemporary documents instead of John, the two names being liable to confusion in Latinised form when an initial *I* is employed in place of the non-existent *J* of the Latin alphabet. The Allatius reference to 'Ioanne' as a third son of Thomas suggests how the names might be muddled, especially when taken from a handwritten source. A Pesaro document dated 1535 refers to the long and faithful service of Leone Paleologus to the papal captain Giovanni della Rovere, lord of Senigalli, whose son was to become the first Rovere duke of Urbino. This is presumably the John of the Landulph inscription.

The Rovere were one of the great families of Renaissance Italy, producing two popes – Sixtus IV and Julius II – and intermarrying with the likes of the Gonzaga and Este. The first duke's father died in 1501, so if we subtract such a span of years as might reasonably constitute 'long and faithful service' we go back to a date when it would be impossible for an imposter to charm his way into this exalted circle. The fall of Constantinople and arrival of the emperor-in-exile would still be within living memory; the first duke, Francesco Maria I, was the nephew of Julius II to whom the imperial refugees would be known personally.

Next in line according to the Landulph pedigree is the earlier Theodore Paleologus, who also entered the ducal service. A Pesaro pedigree gives this Theodore's year of birth as 1504 and date of death as 1540; Theodore's son, named on the Landulph brass as Prosper, was the third generation to serve the Rovere. And by service we mean military service, for these Italian Paleologi were fighting men like their Byzantine forebears. The Rovere themselves had come to prominence as *condottieri*, and in the early years of the sixteenth century John Paleologus would have taken part in his patron's private war against the Borgias. After 1509, when Duke Francesco Maria was appointed commander-in-chief of the Papal States, it is probable that John also fought in wars against Ferrara, Venice and Bologna. We do not know in which of the duke's many wars the son Theodore first saw action; in this generally long-lived family, his death at the age of thirty-six may well have occurred on active service, whether in combat or as victim to one of the diseases that commonly ravaged military camps – a fate reserved for a later Theodore Paleologus during the English Civil War.

The Rovere were a good long-term prospect for followers, at least when their arch-rivals the Medici or the Borgia were not in the ascendant. Sixtus IV was notorious even among Renaissance popes for his shameless nepotism, while the bellicose Julius, known as 'the Fearsome Pope', successfully wrested back substantial temporal powers lost by previous pontiffs, and enthusiastically endorsed the papal tradition of rewarding relations and supporters. But the Paleologus family's patron suffered major setbacks under the two Medici popes who followed Julius. The duke was excommunicated and ignominiously ejected from Urbino during the papacy of Leo X, the first pope to face the full blast of the Reformation; he continued in disfavour under Clement VII, best remembered in England for refusing a divorce to Henry VIII. However, Urbino was regained by force in 1522, and Theodore Paleologus may well have been present at the moment of triumph when the papal governor was flung from a palace window.

The duke's reputation had been severely dented by an incident during the Bologna war of 1511 when, in an act worthy of his foe Cesare Borgia, a cardinal was stabbed on his orders – there is no record of a Paleologus being present at the murder – and the Rovere name suffered again in 1527 when the Sack of Rome was blamed in large part on the duke's ineffective defence. However, his Byzantine adherents proved loyal in bad times as well as good and the fact they remained in Pesaro, by then favoured over the capital of the duchy, demonstrates an abiding mutual reliance.

But there was an aspect of life at Urbino which would be of special importance to our Theodore. This was the remarkable range of stables which formed the centrepiece of a vast subterranean network of buildings beneath the ducal palace. Here, where Theodore would learn the more respectable side of his future career, the dukes spent lavishly on the care of their horses and riders. Here too were workshops which rang with the hammers of armourers and smiths who equipped the duchy's private army. Here was the school of war where the young Theodore would follow in his forebears' footsteps, learning to buckle on both fighting and tilting armour, to angle a twelve-foot lance at the barrier, and to perfect his skills with rapier and dagger.

Prosper Paleologus is found enrolled among the nobility of Pesaro in 1537, a year before Duke Francesco Maria met his death at the hands of a poisoner.[8] Prosper appears to have enjoyed a long life as he is twice listed in the records of the *Consiglieri di Pesaro*, first in the register kept from 1531 and 1551, and again in that maintained between 1569 and 1580. In the second manuscript his name is spelt Prospero. This later roll also includes a Guidobaldo Paleologo, probably a younger brother of Prosper, and the two names also appear together in a document dated 1560. The term *consigliere* is widely known today thanks to gangster movies like *The Godfather*: the title was adopted by the Mafia in imitation of the states of Renaissance Italy and generally signifies the third most powerful figure at a court or within a crime family.

In 1578, the year which would see disaster strike the Paleologi, Guidobaldo was also recorded as *Capitan dei Porto*. He was surely named after Guidobaldo, son of Francesco Maria, who succeeded as second duke of Urbino. Prosper, and probably Theodore until his death in 1540, continued in the employ of Duke Guidobaldo. Here was another

Rovere in frequent need of seasoned soldiers, not only against outside enemies but inside Urbino: a revolt by citizens protesting over excessive taxation was bloodily put down in 1573.

The glories of the court of Urbino, renowned as a centre of patronage and learning, can still be vividly pictured thanks to Baldesar Castiglione's *The Book of the Courtier*, the most reprinted literary work of the Renaissance. Taking the form of a series of imaginary conversations between courtiers in the ducal palace, its extravagant praise of the virtues of the first Rovere duke helped to soften his image as an incompetent general and cardinal-killer. Like the Paleologi, Castiglione served Duke Francesco Maria I as a courtier and soldier, and had earlier served under the great Federico da Montefeltro, last duke of the previous dynasty. Though Castiglione did not regain his place after the temporary expulsion of the Rovere from Urbino, he would almost certainly have fought in the earlier wars alongside John Paleologus and very probably knew the young Theodore also.

*The Book of the Courtier* became required reading for anyone with pretensions of gentility, not only in Italy but throughout Europe, setting the standard for courtly manners up to modern times. By the end of the sixteenth century around 100 editions had been published. Its influence was especially strong in Elizabethan England, informing the works of, among others, Sir Philip Sidney, Shakespeare and Ben Jonson. The Elizabethans' hero-worship of Sidney was based largely on his perceived likeness to Castiglione's perfect courtier; Shakespeare pinched some jokes from the book; Jonson plundered it for *Every Man out of his Humour*.

Castiglione's model courtier masters the fighting skills and horsemanship of the medieval knight, and to these he adds fluency in Greek and Latin, familiarity with the classical authors and social accomplishments such as poetry, music and drawing. He writes and speaks well and dresses with understated elegance. He serves his lord faithfully and protects and reveres women; in matters of love he always deals honourably. He is naturally of noble birth and ideally good-looking. In all things he must excel without apparent effort, for nonchalance is the surest mark of the gentleman. As our story progresses, we can measure this paragon against the man buried in far-off Cornwall.

Next in line from Prosper Paleologus is his son Camilio, father of our subject. Of Theodore's mother we know nothing, not even her name. Just as the monument at Landulph refers only to male ancestors, the scant Italian records do not yield a single name of a wife belonging to the four generations who followed Thomas the Despot, nor do they suggest any detail of domestic life beyond the all-important court connection. Castiglione may have exhorted his courtiers to honour women, but the notaries who drew up the Pesaro documents saw no occasion to disclose anything about the women these Paleologi married. But I think we can take for granted that these generations would have had no difficulty in adopting the Catholic faith.

We know little about Camilio either, though as he lived in Pesaro it is reasonable to assume he followed forebears who had now served the Rovere family for the best part of a century. It may or may not be significant that he bore the same name as Castiglione's only son, though it is possible a friendship between the families influenced the choice. But we do know that Camilio had brothers called Leonidas and Scipione, because the Pesaro records show the arrest of the two of them in 1578 on a charge of attempted assassination. Detained at the same time was their nephew Theodore, described in the court documents as a minor. And so the principal character of our story finally makes his entrance.

Theodore Paleologus was probably named after his great-grandfather, the son of John. Several Byzantine saints called Theodore included two fourth-century Greek military martyrs and the name was frequently used by the imperial family; the variant Teodoro was popular in Italy. St Theodore the General was the original patron saint of Venice, only to be supplanted by St Mark when the apostle's relics were smuggled out of Egypt hidden from prying Muslim eyes under a cargo of pork. There is another possible reason for the choice of name. A fourteenth-century kinsman of the exiled family was a celebrated warrior who wrote a treatise on the art of war, one of the most influential of the age. This Theodore inherited the Italian marquisate of Montferrato and our Theodore's family may have decided on the name not only because of its soldierly credentials but to underline their connection with this recently extinct Italian branch of the imperial line.

Given the turbulent times in which he was born, the duchy of Urbino was as good a place as any in which to grow up, indeed a paradise compared with most corners of the world. Urbino's illustrious reputation may have begun to fade but it was still possible to bask in the afterglow of the world of Castiglione as Theodore learned the ways of the court, polished his languages and enjoyed expert tuition in his chosen business of war. This was the idyll which came crashing down when he joined his uncles in a family blood feud.

Here I must digress briefly to introduce two long-dead rectors of Landulph, born over 100 years apart, who both fell under the spell of their mysterious former parishioner. They are Francis Jago Arundell, who arrived in the parish in 1805, the year of Trafalgar, and John Herbert Adams, born in 1897 and instituted as Landulph's rector in 1930. Both traced descent from old Cornish families and were sons of doctors; both were graduates of Exeter College, Oxford, a college traditionally associated with West Country scholars. And both belong in that English tradition of clerical amateurs who, from the peace and quiet of a country parsonage, contributed to the world of letters and such fields of knowledge as natural history, folklore and archaeology. These antiquarian rectors of Landulph were men of the stamp of Gilbert White, Charles Kingsley, Francis Kilvert and R.S. Hawker.

Between them, Jago Arundell and Adams served this small parish for over seventy years, and neither passed many days without pondering on what strange circumstances brought Theodore Paleologus to live out his last years in their quiet corner of Cornwall. The curious brass at Landulph had been noted in published histories since at least the mid-1700s, but only with the advent of these two rectors does any record of serious research come down to us. Each in his time delved among old records, collected folk memories, swapped speculations with learned men, gave lectures and noted their discoveries in academic journals. Each laboured to rescue the historical Theodore Paleologus from oblivion, so each in a sense became part of his story.

At the time I began this book, virtually everything known about Paleologus can be credited to these two men, though it is only with

Canon John Adams in the 1930s that we find the first critical scrutiny of the legend. I was obliged to turn detective myself to trace Adams's lost papers on Paleologus, which after being bequeathed to the Institution of Cornish Studies somehow ended up unrecorded in a dusty storeroom of an outlying campus of Exeter University. The trial of the brothers and nephew at Pesaro, to take one example, came to light thanks to persistent enquiries by Canon Adams more than three and a half centuries after that murderous assault was carried out.

The target of the attack was another Greek by origin, one Leone Ramusciatti, who held the rank of colonel. So much was known to Adams, but a lengthy document of 1578 in legal Latin, only recently unearthed from the Pesaro archives, paints a picture of the Paleologi as a desperate gang who barricade themselves inside a church to avoid arrest, to the consternation of the duchy authorities: a tantalising section of the manuscript appears to refer to a successful murder being committed by the gang in addition to the attempt on Ramusciatti's life. Written closely over eight sides of decayed parchment in a crabbed legal hand, the document sets out a judgement that the civil powers will be within their rights to snatch the malefactors from the church without formally seeking ecclesiastical permission.

Other manuscripts show that the trial of the Paleologus brothers ended with Leonidas's execution, though Scipione's fate is unknown. Theodore is referred to as a minor, though clearly he was old enough to be party to the crime. At this date the age of majority varied from state to state throughout Italy and how the law stood in Urbino is unclear, but it would have been between sixteen and eighteen; the older age would place the year of Theodore's birth as 1560.

Escaping the death penalty because of his youth, Theodore was banished from the duchy. He was fortunate, for even at his tender age he might have been despatched to the galleys. We do not know if the reigning duke, Francisco Maria II, made any kind of intervention in view of the long service of the Paleologus family; nor indeed is it certain whether any of the assailants or the victim was a ducal retainer at this time. A melancholic figure of far less substance than his forebears, this duke had succeeded to the Urbino title only four years before. He had been raised at the court of Spain and may not have felt the same sense of obligation to old retainers as earlier generations; certainly he never achieved their eminence in Italy's affairs. In any case, the Rovere reign in Urbino was hastening to a close. Failing to sire a male heir, permanently harassed by lack of money, Francesco Maria II was soon to bequeath his duchy to the papacy.

So Theodore had started out in life as he would go on, for the next certain news we have of him comes nearly twenty years later when he slips into England in his professional capacity as contract killer. England is to become the nearest thing to home he will ever know. There he will meet and inspire the future colonist John Smith, and will become the henchman of perhaps the most hated aristocrat in the country. And it is in England he will marry and raise a family.

# 3

The same vice committed at sixteen, is not the same,
though it agree in all other circumstances, at forty,
but swells and doubles from the circumstance
of our ages, wherein besides the constant and
inexcusable habit of transgressing, the maturity
of our Judgement cuts off pretence unto excuse
or pardon: every sin, the oftener it is committed,
the more it acquireth in the quality of evill.

Sir Thomas Browne, *Religio Medici.*

Nineteen years have passed and the year is 1597. As in a new shifted scene,
Theodore Paleologus arrives in England. If his later claim is true, the period
of exile from his homeland has seen him employed as a soldier in the Low
Countries, shedding his blood in the Protestant cause alongside the great
general of the day, Prince Maurice of Nassau. Yet our theme of murderous
intrigue continues. He has come to London to find and kill a man.

Theodore's target is a compatriot, a noble citizen of the Tuscan
republic of Lucca. Allesandro Antelminelli is aged twenty-five and,
in his desperate efforts to evade his stalker, will soon be passing himself off under an alias and claiming to be a Florentine. One year earlier,
Allesandro's father and three brothers had been seized, tortured and put
to death on a charge of treason against the state. As we have seen in the
affair of Theodore's uncles, sudden arrest and execution was no uncommon fate in the Italy of the time.

Fortuitously absent from Lucca at the critical moment, Allesandro was
now summoned home to stand trial for complicity in the crime. Aware of

the certain outcome of complying he fled for his life, ending up in London. Here he assumed the identity of Ambergio Salvetti, the name by which he would be known for the rest of his life. It was in the guise of Salvetti that he attached himself to the poet-diplomat Sir Henry Wotton, best remembered today for his quip that an ambassador is an honest man sent abroad to lie for his country. At this early stage of his career Wotton was acting as a secretary-cum-secret-agent for Queen Elizabeth's reckless favourite the Earl of Essex, and on the point of leaving England to travel the Continent. Salvetti was placing himself in dangerous fellowship, however. As we shall see, Wotton would prove perfectly amenable to betraying his Italian companion so long as the price was right.

Now nearing his fortieth year, Paleologus is well established as an assassin. At some point during the intervening years his youthful indiscretion has been forgiven and the banishment from the duchy revoked. By one means or another he has made his peace with the ruling clique, and we know this because of an important letter addressed to Signor Teodoro Paleologo at Pesaro in 1597.

When we hear of a contract killer today, we do not expect the term to mean that the individual engaged to carry out a murder is actually in possession of a written contract. But this was sixteenth-century Italy and what is as good as a written contract does exist. Assassination was so far interwoven in the fabric of political life that the authorities would record arrangements for murder as a routine matter of official business, and the letter sent to Pesaro was signed by the senior magistrate of Lucca, Francesco Andreotti. The noble status of Paleologus explains the grandiloquent form of address:

Very Magnificent Signor

I have heard with much pleasure that you keep me in your remembrance as I do you, and to show my confidence in you I take the opportunity of employing you in my affairs. By the bearer of this you will be informed what it is that I require, and I beg and request that you will place entire confidence in him. I on my part shall not be ungrateful for besides the usual reward of your work I think of securing you a pension.

Written in the Tuscan dialect, this document was discovered in 1881 by Heath Wilson, an English resident in Florence, during a search of the city archives. Wilson's translation into English was among the papers collected by Henry Duncan Skrine, a wealthy Somerset squire with antiquarian tastes, and these were later published by the Historical Manuscripts Commission. The Skrine manuscript refers to the man addressed in this remarkable letter as 'Teodoro Paleologo the Bravo', the latter word being defined in the *Oxford English Dictionary* as an Italian term meaning 'a daring villain, a hired soldier or assassin; a reckless desperado'. The *bravi* were indispensable retainers of an Italian potentate of the time, protecting their lord from enemies and obeying any order to intimidate, kill or maim.

Various theories have been put forward as to why our reckless desperado came to England in the first place, and why he chose to settle here. An explanation based on my own researches follows in due course. The earliest scholarly account of Paleologus and his travels was the work of the Landulph rector of Regency times, the Revd Francis Jago – he had not yet added the Arundell to his name, for reasons to be clarified later – in a paper read to the Society of Antiquaries in 1815, the year of Waterloo. (Jago had a knack of synchronising his personal milestones with momentous battles.) His paper was published two years later in the respected journal *Archaeologia*.

Ignorant of the trial at Pesaro, Jago advocates several possible grounds for Theodore leaving Italy, the first and least convincing being Pope Sixtus V's decree of 1585 which prohibited foreigners from living in Rome. If the Paleologi still depended on papal goodwill, Jago conjectures, 'perhaps Sixtus might enforce this decree to rid himself of a family whose high descent he possibly regarded with a jealous eye, recollecting the meanness of his own origin' – this pope being whispered to be the son of a swineherd.

Another possibility is that Theodore volunteered for the long war against the Turks which was waged by Emperor Rudolf II from 1593. This centred on Hungary and Transylvania, and serving in the imperial army were Englishmen who might happily befriend the Italian of exalted ancestry: Jago mentions in particular Sir Thomas Arundell of Cornwall, for it was a Thomas Arundell who then owned the manor called Clifton in the parish of Landulph, the very house where Theodore would end his days. Here is a theory which has the advantage of neatness at the expense of credibility. In any case, Jago strongly prefers the notion that it was another Cornishman who influenced Theodore into coming here. This was Sir Henry Killigrew, Queen Elizabeth's ambassador to the Venetians and Genoese, whose daughter was married to the owner of this same manor house at the time of Theodore's arrival in Cornwall. This is not at all a bad idea, though one might add an overlooked West Country candidate in Sir Arthur Gorges, poet, scholar and soldier, who spent his youth on the Devon side of the Tamar, a stone's throw from Landulph. Gorges will figure in a later chapter of Theodore's story.

One contemporary of Jago's, the Scottish writer John Galt, suggested that it was actually Theodore's father Camilio who made the break with Italy, being forced to flee with his son after making himself obnoxious to the pope because of his adherence to Greek Orthodoxy. This notion, at variance with all we know of the religious scruples of the Paleologi, was to be put out of court by later discoveries.

Others took up Jago's idea that Theodore was either a pitiable victim of persecution by the pope, or else was enticed to England by a comrade-in-arms in the continental wars. The historians of Cornwall, Daniel and Samuel Lysons, assured their readers that 'the descendant of Prince Thomas who lies buried in Landulph sought asylum in consequence of the hostility shewn towards the Greeks by Pope Paul V and his successor Gregory XV'[9], while the theory preferred by Thomas Maule, in the Cornish section of *The English Counties Delineated* published in 1838, took up the idea that Paleologus 'came to England with Sir Thomas Arundell, after the battles in Hungary, and was induced to prefer Landulph for his residence, as from its vicinity to the sea, and the warmth of climate, it more nearly resembled Pesaro than any other place in the kingdom'.

Not until the 1930s would Jago's successor at Landulph realise that it was the killing ways of Theodore which first brought him to England. Canon Adams had the simple idea of asking an Italian-speaking lady parishioner to write to the librarian of Pesaro, and the librarian's response to his queries filled in several missing pieces of the Paleologus puzzle and pointed in the direction of the Skrine Archive. This enabled Adams to patch together that murky episode in Theodore's life, the Salvetti affair.

The Lucca authorities had first commissioned another assassin to track down their fugitive. This was a man by the name of Marcantonio Franceotti, who having taken an oath to kill Salvetti was paid 200 lire on account. Franceotti appears to have kept close on the trail for some considerable time, but with a cunning born of desperation Salvetti contrived to stay always one step ahead. And once Franceotti had used up his advance expenses, he seems to have despaired of running the quarry to ground. Reporting back to Lucca that the job required a more seasoned practitioner in the art of murder, his recommendation fell on Theodore Paleologus. The tone of the magistrate's letter to Paleologus indicates that Lucca was well aware of his reputation, and the dangled prospect of a pension strongly suggests the city had made use of his talents on at least one previous occasion. Franceotti was evidently 'the bearer of this': who better to brief Paleologus on the target?[10]

To anticipate our story, Paleologus's attempts to liquidate Salvetti would also eventually end in failure, though the fugitive would then face a new threat to life or liberty from his supposed friend and protector, Sir Henry Wotton. As it turned out, the hunted man was to beat all the odds by outliving every other actor in his drama, Theodore Paleologus included, despite the Lucca authorities persisting in their efforts to eliminate him until at least 1627. This was thirty years after the contract with Paleologus, whose inability to honour the bargain must have been a keen disappointment – not least because of the longed-for pension over and above the 'usual rewards' of his work. Chronic lack of funds was a common occupational hazard for spies and assassins of the time, and everything we shall learn of Paleologus says he was no exception.

So an unmistakeable pattern emerges. Our first documentary proof of Theodore's existence discloses his role in an attempted murder; this second document is a commission to commit murder; a third we shall consider shortly is a letter which tells of 'divers murders' committed by Paleologus, and of fears he is about to murder an English countess. Theodore in his prime must have been a pretty scary character. Yet tellingly, evidence of his crimes is always hearsay or circumstantial. Paleologus is never to be caught red-handed.

So what of Henry Wotton's later role in the protracted Salvetti affair? Fear of being implicated in the botched Essex revolt kept him out of England for the rest of Elizabeth's reign – his fellow-secretary Henry Cuffe was hanged, drawn and quartered at Tyburn – but in 1602 a golden opportunity arose to ingratiate himself with the queen's likely successor, James of Scotland. Wotton happened to be living in Florence when the reigning Medici grand duke of Tuscany, Ferdinand, got wind of a plot to murder King James. The resident Englishman was entrusted with a letter of warning and a casket of Italian antidotes against various poisons. A perfect command of the Tuscan language enabled Wotton to make his way to Edinburgh in the guise of an Italian. Gratefully welcomed by the Scottish king, who kept his true identity a secret from the court, he was rewarded with a knighthood on James's accession the following year.

By 1607 Sir Henry was English ambassador at Venice when he became personally involved in Lucca's efforts to do away with Salvetti. James had by this time fallen out with Grand Duke Ferdinand, who was sheltering an English refugee called George Elliot, a declared traitor. Exchanging letters in cipher, Wotton and the Lucca magistrates wove a plot to have Elliot abducted and traded for Salvetti, then living fearfully in London. Once again the wily Italian evaded capture, however, and thereby deprived Wotton of a promised bounty of 2,000 ducats. He was to die peacefully in bed aged eighty-five.[11]

But to return to Paleologus. At the time he was shadowing Salvetti, was he already a widower with a child, as recorded by several Victorian historians and accepted well into the twentieth century? According to a version of his story long given credence, Theodore was married on

6 July 1593, on the island of Chios. His bride was a noble lady of eighteen called Eudoxia Comnena, the daughter of Alexius Comnenus and his wife Helen Cantacuzene. Both surnames are of imperial dynasties of Byzantium. By this account, Eudoxia died in childbirth on 6 July 1596 – three years to the day after her wedding – leaving a daughter Theodora, and in 1614 this Theodora was married in Naples to 'Prince Demetrius Rhodocanakis'.

The trouble is the story is a complete fiction. It was concocted as late as the 1860s by a rich London-based Greek merchant, also named Demetrius Rhodocanakis, who claimed descent from the supposed princely bridegroom. Obsessed with proving his Paleologus blood, Rhodocanakis bribed an Italian genealogist to compile a false pedigree which was then backed up by assorted ancient-looking documents, the handiwork of a skilful Greek forger, and various references to non-existent antiquarian books. The pedigree was convincing enough to take in the likes of the Papal Court and the British Foreign Office, a success which emboldened the merchant to start signing himself 'His Highness'. By his reckoning, Theodora's marriage to his namesake conferred the imperial rights to him, 'there existing no legitimate male descendant of the emperors'.[12]

Rhodocanakis sought to beef up his connection with the Paleologi by laying claim to a more plausible ancestor, this time a real historical character. This was Dr Constantine Rhodocanakis, an eminent physician – otherwise, a brazen quack – who became a personal friend of Charles II during his exile in Holland. Accompanying Charles to England at the Restoration, he published a number of medical books, among them a collection of remedies of his own invention based on antimony, which were dutifully swallowed by the king and his brother the Duke of York. The doctor was pleased to publish a testimonial from the Civil War hero Prince Rupert: 'I have found the Spirit of Salt prepared by Dr Constantine Rhodokanaces very good for the stomach, and it maketh sauces to have a very excellent taste.'[13] The remedy also warded off the plague, acted as an antidote to assorted poisons and cured dropsy, scurvy, ague, cancer, wind and stone, spleen, jaundice, falling sickness and worms. According to the fake pedigree, the inventor of this marvellous medicine was the grandson of Theodore Paleologus.

The impostor finally overreached himself by penning a biography of his invented ancestral namesake. Published in Athens in 1872, its frontispiece was captioned as a portrait of the physician by Sir Peter Lely, but this was later exposed as a doctored photograph of the merchant himself in fancy costume.

Prior to the discovery of Rhodocanakis's forgeries, the Chios marriage was duly given its place in Theodore's story by a number of historians such as WH Hamilton Rogers, who included it in his chronicle of the West Country in medieval and Tudor times. For decades scholars accepted the 1593 wedding without investigation. In his early days as rector, Canon Adams himself was taken in, dutifully relating the story in a guidebook to Landulph Church published in the 1930s.

Rhodocanakis had been unmasked by a German researcher in 1908, though it appears to have taken many years for the news to reach England and historians continued to report the Chios marriage as fact. The scam has since figured in several books on remarkable fakes and fakers. But a by-product of this affair was to taint the name Theodore Paleologus with the whiff of fraud. There is irony here since the false pedigree ignored the well-documented English family of Paleologus sired by Theodore, which Rhodocanakis claimed was the result of a bigamous marriage: indeed, to acknowledge a legitimate Cornish line would fatally undermine the Greek merchant's pretence to the imperial honours. However, the Rhodocanakis red herring succeeded in muddying the waters, and no doubt contaminated Theodore in the minds of later scholars. Yet this is one crime of imposture of which our man must be immediately acquitted.

Even Theodore's real marriage in England is the subject of confusion. Early accounts wrongly state that this took place at Hadleigh in Suffolk, the birthplace of his bride Mary Balls, on 27 May 1617. The blame here rests with yet another clerical antiquary, the Revd Philip Parsons – the first I know of to make a study of Theodore Paleologus – who mistakenly believed he had stumbled on evidence of a cover-up of the ceremony. In a book on church relics published in 1794, Parsons speculated that an erased entry in the Hadleigh register for 1617 arose from 'resentment, or the desire of concealment' of the match by Mary's family, then in ignorance of Theodore's starry lineage. The line was taken up by Jago Arundell and reproduced in the *Archaeologia* article. Among others to repeat this misinformation was the distinguished biblical scholar George Tregelles, one of the authors of the *Victoria County History* volume on Cornwall.

When Adams had the Hadleigh registers checked, no obliterated entry could be found for the year 1617. He noted that a single mutilated line discovered in the search was for 1591, when Mary could have been no more than fifteen years old, but neither day nor month matched the date given in Parsons's book. Adams charitably attributed the error to 'muddle' caused by an inability to read old writing or an over-active imagination. But yet another layer of cloud was added to the Paleologus story.

As we shall see, the marriage to Mary Balls actually took place at Cottingham in East Yorkshire on May Day, 1600, and the bride was no Byzantine lady of imperial extraction but a young Englishwoman of humble, if not lowly, background, who was heavily pregnant on the day of the wedding. The later months of 1599 and the millennial year were a pivotal time for Theodore Paleologus, and by good fortune this period is the best documented of his life. But before examining his courtship of Mary, and what fraught circumstances surrounded their nuptials, we need to ask why this hardened mercenary and assassin suddenly decided his fortune lay in an altogether new occupation, in an isolated corner of another country, and in the household of a deranged nobleman.

# 4

Oppression, fraud, cozening, usury, knavery,
bawdry, murder, and tyranny, are the beginning
of many ancient families: one hath been a
bloodsucker, a parricide, the death of many a
silly soul in some unjust quarrels, seditions, made
many an orphan and poor widow, and for that he
is made a lord or an earl ... Another hath been
a bawd, a pander to some great men, a parasite,
a slave, prostituted himself, his wife, daughter,
to some lascivious prince, and for that he is exalted.
Now may it please your good worship, your
lordship, who was the first founder of your family?

Robert Burton, *The Anatomy of Melancholy*.

Theodore's new employer was Henry Clinton alias Fiennes, second Earl
of Lincoln, whose principal seat in Lincolnshire would be home to the
Italian for many years to come. The great tower of Tattershall Castle,
brooding over the flat windswept landscape of the fens, remains an outstanding landmark in this part of England, denounced by Henry VIII as
'one of the most brutal and beastly of the whole realm'.[14] Dominating a
town that had suffered a drastic depopulation shortly before Theodore's
arrival – Tattershall was now scarcely more than a village – the draughty
medieval castle must have seemed a far cry from sunlit memories of
Urbino or golden dreams of Constantinople.

In Lord Lincoln, a man at this time approaching sixty years of age, one seeks in vain for any trace of a redeeming feature. He confronts us as a figure of almost heroic iniquity. Here was a throwback to the over-mighty barons of feudal times whom the Tudors are commonly credited with having tamed. No one informed Earl Henry of this, however, and his vendettas had first attracted the censure of Elizabeth's Privy Council some twenty years before Paleologus appeared on the scene. An unknown number of men were killed and maimed on both sides in the peer's private wars against his neighbours. In a typical case among the countless 'horrible outrages' reported to the Privy Council, sixty of Lincoln's retainers from the castle descended 'most riotously' on the house of a close relation of his, Sir Edward Dymoke, armed with guns, crossbows, longbows and cudgels. Another relation subjected to violent attacks was Robert Savile, who complained that Lincoln forced his way into his parlour where 'after great threatening wordes' he struck down Savile's son with a cudgel. The property was then invaded by three-score of Lincoln's men armed with 'gunnes crosbowes long bowes and such like'.[15]

A torrent of pantomime villainies followed. Besides frequent pitched battles, we find that riots, arson, abduction, sabotage, extortion, per-jury and the suborning of juries are regular features of the story. At Tattershall the earl annexed part of the churchyard to extend the castle moat, 'so that divers people were digged up, some green and lately buried, and thrown into the moat to fill up'.[16]

Despised by his fellow peers, feared and loathed by the local gentry, a notorious swindler of his tenants and servants, above all a mon-strous tyrant to his own wife and children, the earl combined a soaring arrogance towards the common run of humankind with a grovelling sycophancy towards the handful who wielded power at court. Above all he sucked up to the Cecil family headed by Lord Burghley, the queen's chief minister. Despite every opportunity conferred by rank and wealth, Lincoln utterly failed to make a mark in public life beyond exciting universal contempt for his ungovernable temper, spite, ava-rice, miserliness, profound lack of tact and judgement and grotesque self-pity. Alarming signs of madness had been noted from his youth and succession to the title fifteen years before tore away the last checks on a cruel and sadistic nature. This he habitually indulged by violent assaults on all who crossed him, and by slandering them as traitors, thieves, cowards and papists.

As his long-suffering son-in-law, Sir Arthur Gorges, declared to Sir Robert Cecil: 'His wickedness, misery, craft, repugnance to all humanity, and perfidious mind is not amongst the heathens to be matched. God bless me from him.'[17]

The earl's forebears had not always been great men. The founder of the family fortunes was one of the 'men of ignoble stock lifted up from the dust' as a contemporary chronicler branded the unpopular tax-gatherers of Henry I, but by the sixteenth century the Clintons could hardly be called parvenus. Though the earldom had been created as recently as 1572, Paleologus's patron was also the tenth Baron Clinton. So the Clintons had been country lords for as long as Theodore's ancestors had been emperors.

Edward Clinton, the first earl, was the *ne plus ultra* of Tudor toadies, performing the remarkable feat of finding favour with every monarch from Henry VIII to Elizabeth. Then known as Lord Clinton, he secured his place in Henry's good books by marrying Bessie Blount, the king's discarded mistress. The second earl was not the son of Bessie, however, but of the second of his father's three wives. As a favourite of the king Edward Clinton profited hugely from the dissolution of the monasteries with the grant of two monastic properties in Lincolnshire and a third in Kent, along with numerous manors and other land holdings; he benefited also from the confiscated estates of less canny nobles who fell foul of the unpredictable Henry.

In earlier years the first earl had secured his heir important posts such as vice-admiral of Lincolnshire. In 1559 he briefly represented the Cornish pocket borough of Launceston and in 1571 secured a Lincolnshire seat. But in parliament as elsewhere he miserably failed to distinguish himself. The single record of his attendance in the House of Commons is predictably self-centred, to press a claim of privilege of rank following the arrest of one of his henchmen. The grander court appointments dried up as his mental instability became clear, though he managed to cling to his post as one of the county's commissioners of sewers. Even in this innocuous-sounding role he aroused deep resentment, sparking complaints to the Privy Council for gross overcharging for repairs to the drainage system and other deceptions.

In 1585, shortly before succeeding to his father's title, he had turned on his stepmother, the third wife of the first earl, accusing her of poisoning the queen's mind against him. In a hysterical letter to Burghley, he claimed his own wife was in league with the countess 'to blow innumerable slaunders into her hyghnes eares'.[18] This wife, Catherine Hastings, was not long for this world. The date and cause of Catherine's death remain obscure but only one year later the new peer was already terrorising his unfortunate wife number two. But he was a belted earl, and in Elizabethan England an earl got away with almost anything.

In all, the Privy Council would be inundated with complaints by or against Lord Lincoln for well over thirty years, and law suits without number bore his name as either plaintiff or defendant. In many of these actions he called himself Henry Fiennes instead of Clinton, in pursuit of a claim to a title belonging to that name, even though a Clinton forebear had renounced all rights to the Fiennes peerage as long ago as 1448.

It was this unhinged and highly dangerous individual who welcomed Theodore Paleologus to Tattershall Castle sometime in 1599, when his crimes against kin, neighbours, servants and tenants were about to scale new heights. For the earl, recruiting a henchman of the Italian's sinister reputation clearly had attractions over and above his skills as a horseman. Then again, Italy was the land of the vendetta, as one might say the spiritual home of Henry, Earl of Lincoln. And to judge from what evidence remains to us, the pair of them got on like a house on fire.

✥

The England of 1599 was a country in the grip of paranoia. The year saw a new Armada scare, a disastrous war in Ireland to add to the draining conflict in the Low Countries and a terrible quarrel, soon to prove fatal, between the aged queen and her former favourite Essex. A rash of murder plots against Elizabeth ignited rumours she was already dead, heightening fears of war over the succession. The faction-torn court feared foreign invasion and insurrection from Catholics at home. To the poor and weak it was above all a time of pestilence, failing crops and exorbitant prices. That summer a false report of a Spanish landing in the Isle of Wight led the panicky government to raise an army of 25,000. It was not a good time to be a newly settled alien.

Then, as ever, immigration stirred strong popular resentment, but hostile acts against outsiders were savagely suppressed by the Elizabethan establishment. A few years before Paleologus's first visit to England, the Privy Council had assumed unprecedented powers to put to torture anyone suspected of libelling 'strangers'. Among those to suffer was the dramatist Thomas Kyd, the suspected author of an anti-foreigner poem, who under torture implicated his fellow playwright Christopher Marlowe. Not all leading courtiers backed the government line that England benefited economically from migrants and was duty-bound to give asylum to political or religious refugees. Throughout the 1590s a few important figures such as Sir Walter Raleigh and Sir Nicholas Bacon protested at the granting of privileges to foreigners that were denied to the native English, such as freedom of worship, but official policy was dictated by the pro-alien Cecil party.

Distinguished scholars were not exempt from the deep popular prejudice against foreigners, and Italians in particular. This was not only because Italy was the nest of popery. Roger Ascham, the queen's venerable tutor, warned travellers against visiting the country lest they be corrupted by 'plenty of new mischiefs never known in England before; for manners, variety of vanities, and … filthy living'.[19] Typically among contemporary authors, William Harrison in his *Description of Britain* praised the English yeomanry as 'merry without malice, and plain without inward Italian or French craft and subtlety', while Thomas Gainsford, in *The Glory of England*, dismissed all Tuscans as 'buggerers and blasphemers'.

The Italian had long been seen as a figure of dangerous sensuality. The musician-cum-private secretary David Rizzio, ambitious favourite of Mary Queen of Scots and rumoured father of her son James, had been stabbed to death in the palace of Holyroodhouse in 1566 at the instigation of Mary's jealous husband, Lord Darnley. In 1571, in one of innumerable conspiracies blamed on Italians, a Florentine called Roberto Ridolfi had allegedly plotted the assassination of Elizabeth and her replacement by the Scottish queen. Every theatre-goer knew the Italian assassin as a stock character in Elizabethan drama, with special renown as a poisoner. The real-life murderer of Dowager Queen Jeanne of Navarre went under a variety of names, the only certain fact about him being that he was Italian and had been shadowed by Walsingham's spies on his arrival in England. He appears as the character Pothecarie in *Massacre at Paris*, Christopher Marlowe's take on the St Bartholomew's Day bloodbath of 1572, in which he despatches the dowager 'with a venomed smell of a pair of perfumed gloves'.

On the other hand, Italians enjoyed international prestige as horsemen, and the admiration accorded to horsemanship in Elizabethan England would be hard to overstate. Sir Philip Sidney pokes gentle fun at the Italians' high reputation on the opening page of his *Defence of Poesy*, reminiscing about a stay at the Holy Roman Emperor's court where he and a friend placed themselves under a riding master called John Pietro Pugliano:

> And he, according to the fertileness of the Italian wit, did not only afford us the demonstration of his practice, but sought to enrich our minds with the contemplations which he thought most precious … He said soldiers were the noblest estate of mankind, and horsemen the noblest of soldiers. He said they were the masters of war and ornaments of peace, speedy goers and strong abiders, triumphers both in camps and courts. Nay, to so unbelieved a point he proceeded, as that no earthly thing bred such wonder to a prince as to be a

good horseman … if I had not been a piece of a logician before I came to him,
I think he would have persuaded me to have wished myself a horse.

Elizabeth's great favourites, the Earls of Leicester and Essex, were both
appointed her master of the horse, a more or less ceremonial office so far
as the horseflesh was concerned but hugely rewarding in financial terms.
Yet the royal stables offered coveted posts promising power and wealth
for lesser souls. One Robert Alexander, who in 1588 was gentleman rider
to the Earl of Northumberland, later became equerry of the stable to the
queen and was honoured with a knighthood. In fact he had been born
in Italy as Roberto Zinzano and began his career as a riding master in
Naples before anticipating Theodore Paleologus by trying his luck in
England. Sir Robert not only earned a salary plus bed and board, but took
a cut from the sale of horses trained in the royal stables at £100 apiece.

Every great household in England appointed officers variously known
as master of the horse, gentleman of horse or gentleman rider, with non-
commissioned assistants called yeomen of the horse who supervised the
grooms. Our Theodore would have been some distance removed from
any chores like mucking out in the Tattershall stables. And there would
have been a lot of muck. Not long before this date the Willoughby stables at nearby Grimsthorpe Castle were recorded as housing 135 horses,
and the Earl of Lincoln is unlikely to have been outdone by a lower-rank-
ing neighbour. What a great nobleman of the time demanded from the
head of his stable might owe something to the horse's service in war and
everyday matters of travel, but had far more to do with cutting a fine figure
and winning the plaudits of his peers and monarch, above all in the lists.

Yet a whiff of danger hung about the post, and from the beginning
there is a sense of complicity in the relationship between Lincoln and
Paleologus. There is something strongly atavistic about the pair of them.
On the contemporary stage the horse master or gentleman rider was
frequently a key figure, and commonly portrayed as an individual high
on ambition and low on scruples. Bosola, the principal villain in the
archetypal tragedy of the period, *The Duchess of Malfi*, fatally worms
his way into his mistress's confidence after he is named her gentleman

of horse. And real life presented parallel examples. Robert Dudley, Earl of Leicester, selected as his own master of horse a pushy young blood called Christopher Blount. In 1589, eight months after Leicester's death, Blount married the widowed countess, thereby acquiring immense wealth and influence. However, in Blount's case the fall came as suddenly as the rise and he went to the block for his part in the Essex revolt.

The sinister intimacy which could grow between a great man and his master of horse is exemplified by Richard III and Sir James Tyrrell, who by tradition procured the murder of the Princes in the Tower as foreshadowed in Shakespeare's lines:

| | |
|---|---|
| KING RICHARD: | Dar'st thou resolve to kill an enemy of mine? |
| TYRRELL: | Please you, but I had rather kill two enemies. |
| KING RICHARD: | Why there thou hast it … |
| | Tyrrell, I mean those bastards in the Tower. |
| TYRRELL: | Let me have open means to come to them, |
| | And soon I'll rid you from fear of them. |

Or consider this exchange, slightly abbreviated, between Duke Ferdinand and the arch-villain in *The Duchess of Malfi*, and the Earl of Lincoln's new gentleman of the horse looks chillingly cast as a real-life Bosola:

| | |
|---|---|
| FERDINAND: | There's gold. |
| BOSOLA: | So: |
| | What follows? Never rained such showers as these |
| | Without thunderbolts i'the tail of them: |
| | Whose throat must I cut? |
| FERDINAND: | Sir, I'll take nothing from you that I have given: |
| | There is a place that I procured for you |
| | This morning: the provisorship o' the horse. |
| BOSOLA: | What's my place? |
| | The provisorship o' the horse? Say, then, my corruption |
| | Grew out of horse-dung: I am your creature. |

After so many perilous years as a mercenary, spy and assassin – probably even now evading vengeful pursuers of his own – it is not unlikely the ageing Theodore craved a spell of safer and ostensibly respectable employment. He was now around forty, 'at which year begins the first part of the old man's age', as lugubriously noted by the Tudor diarist Thomas Peynel.[20] Possibly he entered the earl's household hoping that a stint as retainer to a high-ranking noble would attract the attention of a greater one, perhaps even of the queen herself: there was Roberto Zinzano as a precedent. On his part the earl must have been expecting to call upon the lethal talents of Paleologus from the start; as we shall see in reports, an alarming plan was now festering in his mind.

Whatever the case, the new gentleman rider quickly proved indispensable to his patron. The most striking fact about Lincoln is that he fell out with virtually everyone he knew – family, neighbours, servants, the great ones at court, even the sovereign herself. The exception was Theodore Paleologus, for the domicile of the Italian and his family at Tattershall over the next sixteen years or so – for the rest of the earl's life – indicates that he rubbed along with his employer very well, or else had some hold over him. As the volatile peer and the self-reliant exile had so little in common, one must ask what kind of hold this might be. Was Paleologus tolerated at the castle because he knew where the bodies were buried, if only because he buried them himself?

The common people of Tattershall had long had reason to hate and fear their lord, and we can only guess their thoughts at the sudden appearance of this exotic creature. But we know he cut an irresistibly glamorous figure in the eyes of one young woman. For Mary Balls, the newcomer was the answer to a maiden's prayer.

# 5

The stranger within my gates
He may be evil or good
But I cannot tell what powers control,
What reasons sway his mood;
Nor when the Gods of his far-off land
Shall repossess his blood.

Rudyard Kipling, 'The Stranger Within my Gate'.

In the annals of Mary's birthplace, the wool town of Hadleigh in Suffolk, the family name appears under various spellings of Ball and Balls. On the Paleologus tomb at Landulph her father is called William Balls and described as 'gent', but this is a significant departure from the truth. My researches show the family came from far humbler stock, for Mary's father was almost certainly the younger son William who is mentioned in the 1568 will of Roger Ball, miller, of Hadleigh Bridge.

However modest their origins, the family were on the up-and-up by the 1570s when parish records present 'William Balles' as one of the well-to-do coterie of citizens who ran the town. The Balls diversified into the cloth-making business that had brought great prosperity to Hadleigh and William acquired further prestige as sub-collector for the market. This unpaid post marked its holder as an affluent and trusted individual with the running of the town's almshouses among his duties. Subsidy lists, which give a snapshot of relative wealth, regularly place one or more of the Balls menfolk among the better-off townspeople from this time well into the seventeenth century, though the Thomas Balls who ran Hadleigh Bridge Mill in King James's time was twice fined for illegal brewing.

There is no hint in the surviving town records that Mary's father or any of the family aspired to be recognised as gentry and the highest they would have classed themselves is as yeomen. But in far-off Cornwall by the 1630s, out of sight of those who knew the Ballses as millers, brewers and clothiers, no one was likely to challenge the assertion of gentle rank.

So does the fiction of Mary's gentility cast doubt over the larger claims made in her husband's name? That Theodore should gild his wife's rank does not compromise his pedigree: the more certain he was of his exalted origins, the touchier he might have been over a misalliance with a miller's granddaughter: we have already considered a number of disgraceful attachments of earlier Paleologi which later generations preferred to forget. Yet perhaps it is inevitable that the sceptic will discern here a further shadow over Theodore's imperial pretensions.

How a Hadleigh girl with no known family or friends outside Suffolk came to be in Tattershall in 1599 has puzzled former researchers into Paleologus's life. Canon Adams could find no Tattershall link with the Balls family, though he speculated that a Nicholas Ball buried in 1618 at Cottingham – the Yorkshire village where Theodore and Mary were married – might possibly be a relation. Yet as this form of the name is and was a common one, his suggestion was never more than tentative.

However, my own random searches of Tattershall records brought to light a document which appears to connect Mary's father to the village, and even to the Earl of Lincoln's household. This is an inventory of the goods and chattels of a John Atkin of Tattershall, musician, deceased, appraised on 9 March 1585. Atkin's worldly possessions, valued at a grand total of £8 0s 2d, include the dead man's instrument – *item, his harpe* – with a valuation of 3s 4d. One of the witnesses to the document signs himself William Balles. This is and was an uncommon form of the name. Now, the only likely employer of a harpist in such an out-of-the-way spot as Tattershall is the resident noble, and the fact that the name Balles seems to be otherwise unrecorded in the village strongly suggests that this is indeed William of Hadleigh, and that he is attached, at least temporarily, to the Lincoln household. That he should be asked to witness a legal document argues that the miller's son was now accorded relatively high status.

It was in 1585 that the second earl succeeded to the title and, on inheriting the bulk of his father's estate, embarked on a headlong rush to acquire more properties the length and breadth of the land. One possibility is that the entrepreneurial Balles came to his notice around this time, acted as an agent and in that role was invited to stay at the castle. Another thought is that Lincoln, as a ruthless encloser, was chiefly interested in Balles's expertise in the cloth trade. Whatever business the pair were involved in, it must have sufficiently gratifies the earl to explain the presence of Balles's daughter Mary at Tattershall some fifteen years later, though in exactly what capacity remains unclear.

He must have been an exciting new force in Mary's life, this exceptionally tall and imposing foreigner of whom disturbing and dangerous things were whispered. Perhaps she witnessed the gentleman rider's first appearance on the tilting ground next to Holy Trinity churchyard, infamously despoiled to widen the castle moat. On a choice mount from one of the finest stables in the land, armed cap-a-pied, Paleologus must have looked like the ideal image of royalty on a coin or seal, pictured by convention as a mounted hero in armour, though with little resemblance to any real king of Theodore's day. In *Henry IV, Part I*, Shakespeare caught his contemporaries' admiration of the consummate equestrian with his picture of Prince Hal vaulting into the saddle, witching the world with noble horsemanship. For Mary, the cavalier in the Clinton colours of blue and white was surely all the more alluring for the rumours swirling about him.[21]

Canon Adams, whose notes on Paleologus so often bear the stamp of a man of cloth of his day, wrote that he 'regretted to record' that Mary was pregnant before marriage, just as he 'regretted to state' his discovery of Theodore's profession as assassin. Judging from the date of her child's delivery, it is most likely Mary conceived sometime late in September 1599. So she may well have conceived during or soon after Harvest Festival, one of the hallowed English customs that Puritans of the day were striving to outlaw. Though other revels of pagan origin were succumbing to killjoy pressure, the traditions of harvest-time were still enjoyed throughout the country, a last excuse before Christmas for bucolic fun and games. But harvesting in 1599 had been disrupted by panic over the supposed new Armada, with a nationwide call-to-arms stripping farms of their labour. Peers like Lincoln were ordered to send all available forces south to face the non-existent invaders, and not until early September was the crisis declared a false alarm and the bands allowed to depart.

With the added anxieties caused by the delay, end-of-harvest celebrations when they came must have been all the more hectic. The last load of corn would be trundled out of the last field to the sound of pipe and drum, the signal for the giving of presents and feasting, drinking and singing. By convention it was a time when the barriers between masters and servants were relaxed, and kissing beneath the harvest moon tended to follow. For some like Mary there were riskier pleasures, and cheeks must have reddened as the familiar lesson from Deuteronomy was read out in church:

> Thou shalt observe the feast of tabernacles seven days, after that thou has gathered in thy corn and thy wine; and thou shalt rejoice in thy feast, thou, and thy son, and thy daughter, and thy manservant, and thy maidservant, and the Levite, the stranger, and the fatherless, and the widow, that are within thy gates.

Theodore Paleologus had been the stranger within the gates many times since his exile, but the encounter with Mary Balls changed the course of his life for good. Perhaps we should be charitable about his purposes at this juncture. Now well past the midway point in the allotted threescore years and ten of Scripture, he may have longed to leave the Dark Wood of Error remembered from his readings of Dante. He had escaped the galleys or worse for attempted murder in his teens. For twenty years or more he had dodged sabre and shot on the battlefield and every epidemic attendant on camp life. And how many times in his parallel career as assassin and spy had he risked a stiletto in a dark alley, and rope or axe on the scaffold? As I surmise from a letter we will consider shortly, Theodore's life was now at hazard in the Netherlands: after so many years in war-ravaged regions the prospect of a settled family life in a distant backwater must have had its charms. An Italian descended from Greeks who thought they were Romans would try his hand at being an Englishman.

But why was the wedding such a desperately late affair, no more than six weeks before Mary bore his son? When did Mary reveal she was pregnant, and what was Theodore's immediate reaction? Had she exaggerated her family's status? Did he misconstrue her dowry prospects? What was the reaction of his patron, the ever-unpredictable Earl of Lincoln?

A distinct possibility is that Theodore had been in London with his master, who spent a great deal of time in London because of his endless lawsuits. Perhaps Theodore was hoping to be put forward for the Ascension Day tilt at Whitehall Palace, one of the major events in the Elizabethan calendar. Age was no barrier to taking part – Sir Henry Lee, Elizabeth's master of the armoury, competed in Ascension Day tilts until nearly seventy years old – and to see a skilled exponent like Theodore Paleologus tilt in the Clinton colours would have given the earl great satisfaction, even when weighed against the considerable cost involved, for as ever Lincoln's parsimony would have struggled with the yearning to cut a dash like his fellow earls.

If this is the case the earl and Theodore were to be disappointed. The great celebration held each year on 19 November was first delayed due to bad weather then deferred until the spring of 1600 because of the illness of the Earl of Cumberland, the chief challenger. But if her lover was delayed, what was Mary's state of mind during his absence?

Terrible penalties threatened a pregnant spinster. The minister of a parish church could prosecute those of loose morals through the ecclesiastical courts and anyone found guilty faced humiliating public confession to 'the vile and heinous sin of fornication' or even excommunication. Yet in practice such sanctions were confined to the lower orders, for even church leaders turned a blind eye to transgressions committed by the better sort. A Jacobean bishop of Lincoln, John Williams, attempted a cover-up when his registrar – a man already charged with extortion – fathered a bastard. Bishop Williams bribed the registrar's accusers to withdraw their evidence but, most unusually, was later hauled before the Star Chamber, found guilty of subordination of perjury, and not only imprisoned in the Tower but fined a staggering £10,000. As a rule such scandals never saw the light of day but Williams had made powerful enemies because of his puritan sympathies.

Many aspects of Mary's plight are unclear and likely to remain so. Was her status within the earl's household sufficient to shield her from degrading public exposure? Did the earl favour William Balls enough to protect his daughter? Did a friend or relation remove her from wondering eyes, offering sanctuary somewhere outside Tattershall? Most intriguing of all, was Paleologus a willing bridegroom or the subject of irresistible pressure from family or patron? Besides being a sadist and hypocrite, the earl was a puritan in all negative senses of the word, and it is not difficult to picture him affecting moral indignation over Mary's seduction under his roof and insisting that Theodore make her an honest woman.

It is no wonder the couple preferred to marry far away from prying eyes, but why the church of St Mary in Cottingham? Today the journey from Tattershall to this East Yorkshire village is nearly seventy miles if the Humber is crossed but far longer if one skirts the river, as one might well choose to do if dependent on Elizabethan transport and accompanied by a heavily pregnant woman. All we know for certain is that the St Mary register for 1600 records the marriage of *Thedorus Palelogu* and *Maria Balle, primo die May*.

There is a Cottingham connection with Tattershall and the Clintons which offers a possible explanation why the vicar might refrain from asking awkward questions of the giant foreigner and his bride. Many years before, the lordship of Cottingham with nearly 2,500 acres had been granted to Henry Fitzroy, Duke of Richmond, the only bastard acknowledged by Henry VIII. The mother of this duke was Bessie Blount, subsequently married off to the first Earl of Lincoln. When Richmond died young, Cottingham went to the Duke of Suffolk along with the Tattershall lands.

Mary remains a shadowy figure, but the fresh beauty of English womenfolk was commonly remarked on by foreigners, among them the German merchant Samuel Kiechel who visited England in 1585 and wrote in his journal: 'Item, the women here are charming, and by nature so mighty pretty as I have scarcely ever beheld, for they do not falsify, paint or bedaub themselves as in Italy or other places.'[22]

She was about twenty-four at the time she met Paleologus. Curiously, there are two baptisms of a 'Marey Ball' recorded in the Hadleigh register for 1575, one on 6 May and another on 19 August. As there are five sons named in the will of her grandfather Roger the miller, the other Mary was probably her cousin. Beyond that, we can only sketch in the life of Theodore's wife from marriage, baptismal and burial records and the line concerning her parentage on the Landulph tomb. We can assume she was healthy as she would regularly bear children to a surprisingly advanced age, five of whom survived into adulthood. But what she looked like we have no idea, whether fair or dark, plump or slender: all we know is that something about Mary proved fatefully attractive to Theodore Paleologus.

We do, however, have a romantic vision of Theodore's bride thanks to a Regency poet called Nathan Drake, whose ballad *Mary of Hadleigh* achieved considerable popular success in the nineteenth century, appearing in numerous literary and ladies' magazines in Britain and America following its first publication in 1820. This somewhat overwrought composition was clearly inspired by the Revd Philip Parsons's belief that the Balls family vehemently opposed Mary's union with Paleologus, and it imagines the couple's secret marriage and elopement to Cornwall.

As pictured by Drake, Mary is a dark-haired beauty with 'cheeks that shame the rose' who first sees Paleologus as he is carried into her father's house by moonlight, a handsome stranger 'speechless and cold, and pierced with thrilling pain' who has been left for dead by treacherous servants:

Ah! What defence could Theodoro boast,
When o'er his couch as evening breezes die,
He saw the blushing daughter of his host
In languid sorrow bend the tearful eye.
First of the forms that ever poet drew;
Was Mary graceful as the bounding roe;
On her ripe lip sate love embath'd in dew
Or ambush'd close where heaves the living snow.
Profuse and rich her raven tresses fell;
While dark and full, and thron'd in humid light,
How many a tear those eyes of sweetness tell!
Nor was her mind less lovely than her frame;
For all that suffer'd she had learnt to grieve;
A lily shrinking from the noontime flame,
But pouring perfume on the gale at eve.

And so on for a total of thirty-one verses. The poem's climax describes William Balls's unrelenting search for his lost daughter throughout the land until one dark tempestuous night he steals into the dimly lit Landulph church and discovers a white-robed Mary kneeling by a tomb with an infant clinging to her bosom. In anguish he reads the inscription on the brass:

For there with pangs no utterance could make known,
With wonder mingling, and with shuddering awe,
Theodoro, heir of the Imperial throne,
Commix'd with Mary's humble name he saw!

The ballad ends with Mary turning towards her father with a ghastly look and instantly dropping dead.

In reality there was no romantic elopement with Theodore. We have seen how they married in Yorkshire and raised a family in Tattershall; my research has shown where Mary died, and it was not at Landulph.

# 6

Who lives past ninety-nine
Shall afterward speak of a blessed time.

John Weever, 'A Prophesy of This Present Year, 1600'.

Tattershall was a queer sort of place. A moated castle built long after the heyday of the castle, it would never be called upon to withstand a siege in earnest for the simple reason it was incapable of doing so. A determined attacker would have made short work of its walls of bonded brickwork and enormous tracery windows. Though the seat of a great nobleman, it must have struck Theodore as a primitive class of residence, but then he had known the magnificent ducal palaces of Urbino and Pesaro. Here were no Titians, Uccellos or Bellinis to ravish the senses: perhaps only a handful of portraits of Lincoln's forebears or their royal patrons, crude daubs by the standards of Renaissance Italy. Even to English eyes Tattershall was undeniably old-fashioned compared with the kind of prodigy houses being built by new men like the Cecils, whose enormous mansion of Burghley lay in the gentle rolling countryside in the south-west of the county. So like its owner, the castle had outlived its time, but it gave an impression of impregnability, a useful illusion for a man with as many enemies as Lord Lincoln.

Built the previous century by Ralph, Lord Cromwell, the grasping lord treasurer of Henry VI, its great tower was constructed of more than a million bricks, reaching a height vying with the cathedrals. Today the tower gives the impression of being a solitary landmark but in Elizabethan times it was the centre of an extensive complex of ancillary buildings, bridges and defensive walls. In Cromwell's day the household servants exceeded 100, and surviving household accounts of noble neighbours from Tudor times show this was still about the average

number. Among neighbours, the Earl of Rutland had ninety-four servants at Belvoir Castle and the Willoughby family at Grimsthorpe just
over 100. However, it is hard to picture so many mouths being willingly
fed during the tight-fisted rule of the Clintons.

The long-abandoned tower was saved from demolition in 1911, so we
can still explore the lofty chambers frequented by Paleologus and examine the vast crenelated fireplaces of the state rooms with their curious
carved panels of heraldry, badges and mottos. We can even peer into the
privies, built into the thickness of the wall on each floor of the corner tur-
rets and designed to discharge into the inner moat below. We can tread
the 150 steps up to the parapet walk round the battlements – the same
steps Paleologus would have climbed on countless occasions – taking
in the wide prospect from that windy spot, the monotonous fen landscape stretching away to the east with Tattershall's great collegiate
parish church in the foreground and the small town beyond. What
have vanished from the scene are the many ranges of service buildings
of Elizabethan times, the kitchens and gatehouses, the lodgings for the
earl's retinue – in all probability these would have included apartments
set aside for Paleologus as his family grew. However, we can still look
down on the ruins of the commodious stables, among the finest in the
land, and the site of the tilting ground can still be made out, a green
space to the right of the churchyard.

It is easy to picture the furnishings and tapestries of the principal
rooms, especially the great hall where Lincoln would have dined,
the air pungent with smoke from the wood fires and candles. In the
castle, honoured guests and favoured retainers would take their place
at his lordship's table while other senior servants ate at a separate
table. But what exactly was Theodore's status within the household?
In the rigidly stratified Elizabethan society, what precedence would
be allowed to this foreigner who, whatever his pedigree, possessed
neither formal rank nor landed property? At least, no record survives to show otherwise, and these were times when ownership of the
smallest parcel of land in England was better documented than most
human life.

No doubt it tickled the earl to have an imperial scion at his beck and call, and to judge from the whining claims of victimhood which recur in his letters, this was a man who needed constant lifts to his self-esteem. Depending on his mood, his lordship might summon Theodore to the top table or wave him away. His uncontainable rages make it likely there were times he offered terrible affronts to his retainer, and the fact Theodore survived in this atmosphere tells us something of his self-control. This was a thin-skinned age when any perceived insult might demand satisfaction in blood, as we see in the violent lives of such as Marlowe and Ben Jonson. On the other hand, perhaps our mad earl had enough sense to be a little afraid of his gentleman rider.

The earl's table would have seemed a poor thing to one who remembered the liberality of a duke of Urbino, yet foreigners were shocked by the sheer quantities of food and drink consumed by the English. The fork, long in use in Italy, was still a rarity in England, and people of all degrees still used a knife and fingers. But after years of campaigning Theodore knew what hardship was like, and the rude fare on the table or the uncouth manners of his neighbours would be taken in his stride.

And in the stables Paleologus was master. Italian methods of horse breeding, learnt in his Urbino days, were copied by leading English nobles who competed to acquire the best Italian expertise. The second Earl of Lincoln's legendary meanness did not extend to his stables, for whatever else might be said against the man, no one questioned his knowledge of horses, the exceptional quality of those he bred or his willingness to open his purse to uphold this reputation. As events will show, James of Scotland himself acknowledged the excellence of the earl's stables.

❖

However, Lincolnshire at the end of the sixteenth century was a backwater, and a notorious one. Lincoln itself was at least three days' horseback journey from London by the Old North Road or Ermine Street, a disintegrating relic from Roman times, now little more than a muddy track. Travellers dreaded not only the county's lonely roads and repeated flooding but its highway robbers and hostile, ignorant natives. The ill-drained fenlands had the blackest name of all, adding the ague and malaria to the perils facing the outsider. For how could any man stay healthy there, asked the antiquary and traveller Sir William Dugdale, 'the air being for the most part cloudy, gross and full of rotten Harrs [sea mists], the water putrid and muddy, yea, full of loathsome vermin, the earth spungy and boggy, the Fire noisome by the stink of smoaky Hassocks?'[23]

In *The Anatomy of Melancholy*, Burton wrote in echoing terms of Lincolnshire's 'bogs, fens, mists, all manner of putrefaction, contagious and filthy noisome smells'. Even a century later, when drainage had begun to transform the fenland, its enduring ill-fame was summarised by a writer who shuddered to think of 'the grim rustics of this motley place … a strange half-human and ungainly brood'.

The county had troubled the crown since Henry VIII's time. The revolt known as the Pilgrimage of Grace started in Lincolnshire, and was savagely suppressed by royal forces ordered to 'cause such dreadful execution to be done upon a good number of the inhabitants of every town, village and hamlet that have offended in this rebellion, as well by hanging them on trees as by the quartering of them, and the setting of their heads and quarters in every town'.[24]

The county's impoverishment worsened during the late sixteenth century due to frequent outbreaks of plague. In the years 1586 and 1587, when the plague combined with crop failure and catastrophic floods, the city of Lincoln had been so overrun by refugees from the countryside that all outsiders were forbidden entry, while the fearsome pestilence of 1590 was commemorated by a printed ballad, *A Mournfull Dittee on the death of certain Judges and Justices of the Peace and divers other gentlemen, who died immediately after the Assizes holden at Lincoln*. In the spring of 1599, the year of Paleologus's arrival at Tattershall, the plague struck once again.

Over the previous decade Lincolnshire had suffered its most disastrous harvests in living memory. Men still shivered at the memory of the devastation twenty years before when a freak tide and high winds wiped out entire coastal villages. Further, the prosperity of East Coast ports such as Boston declined dramatically in the late sixteenth century as the new Atlantic trade gave pre-eminence to the likes of Bristol and Plymouth. For the common folk, the rack-renting and illegal enclosures of land by grasping landlords – chief perpetrator, the Earl of Lincoln – added a simmering sense of grievance to a short and brutish life.

For the government in London, the long bleak coastline beyond the fens was a constant concern. Here were any number of lonely creeks and inlets where a boat could land and bring in a smuggled cargo or anyone who wished his comings and goings to pass unobserved. One guesses from the absence of official records of his travels in and out of England that Theodore Paleologus was not infrequently among them. The county's coast had already figured in several Catholic schemes against the queen, and continued to challenge her officials with its pick of quiet landing places for a lone would-be assassin, spy or seminary priest, or even a possible first foothold for a Spanish invasion.

Over time many of Lincolnshire's nobility and higher gentry chose to move to gentler, more sheltered countryside. Not so the Earl of Lincoln. Despite inheriting a huge number of valuable properties throughout the realm, despite his acquisition of many new ones by fair means or foul, he retained the isolated castle as his main residence outside London. Possibly he believed that a menacing physical presence was required to discourage open rebellion.

After all, had not his own tenants had the temerity to forward an official complaint when he took away their highway and enclosed their common land, then imposed heavy fines and put them in the stocks as trespassers? Had not Tattershall's townsfolk united in protest over what they called unjust taxes? Had not the Privy Council struck his name from the roll of justices of the peace 'in regard of the complaints of diverse poore men that have bin hardly used by him'?[25] Had he not been castigated by the Council in 1592, as the senior noble responsible for Lincoln gaol, when many of the prisoners locked up there died of starvation? The stern reprimand from the queen's chief advisors stated:

> We therefore, pitying the miserie of the poore men and sorrie to understand
> of so little charitie among those that ought chiefly to have the care thereof,
> have thought good to recommend unto your Lordships espetiallie the speedie
> reformacion of this so uncharitable a negligence.[26]

Even the vicar of Folkingham, another of the earl's manors in the county, had petitioned the Privy Council. The Revd John Hoskin 'maketh complaint of verie manye wrongs done unto him by your Lordship,'[27] Lincoln was warned.

Yet as Theodore quickly realised, in the earl's mind it was always he who was the victim of some shocking injustice, and a suspicion that the Cecils might be turning against him drove his persecution mania to new heights of frenzy. In letters to Burghley he repeatedly called on 'the lyvying god' to avenge his wrongs, portraying himself as being 'used lyke a vyllanous devle' and 'desolate and voyde of comfort or frend to procure me indifferent iustyce'.[28]

What Lincoln did not know was that as long ago as 1587, as he was angling for the office of lord lieutenant of Lincolnshire, Burghley had advised the other key figure in Elizabeth's administration, Sir Francis Walsingham, to block the earl's petition. This was to be done secretly, as even England's most powerful men were circumspect in their dealings with the Earl of Lincoln. As another great landowner in the county, the chief minister wrote: 'Some men of my County of Lyncoln have sent to me to prevent that my Lord of Lyncoln, be not their lieutenant. They all fear his government.' What prompted Burghley to send the warning was 'my Lord of Lyncolns coming to work underhand for his appointment'.[29]

The men of Lincolnshire had reason to fear. In Elizabethan times a lord lieutenant had far-reaching powers including the right to muster and arm the men of the county, to lead them against enemies of the crown and 'to repress, subdue, slay, kill and put to execution of death these enemies by all ways and means'; he also had at his beck and call every justice of the peace, sheriff, constable and other local official whosoever. The thought of such powers in the hands of this relentless monster alarmed the county, and Burghley neatly solved the problem by engineering his own appointment for life. To the earl, it added insult to injury that Burghley proceeded to name his deadly enemy Sir Edward Dymoke as a deputy lieutenant.

Tattershall Castle had been one of the prize acquisitions of the first earl. It had descended through heirs of Ralph Cromwell to Henry VIII's brother-in-law and arch-crony, the Duke of Suffolk, passing then to Suffolk's two young sons. Falling victim to the sweating sickness, these boys died within an hour of each other in 1551. This was during the minority of Henry's heir, the sickly boy king Edward VI, at which time Lord Clinton – the first earl's title before his elevation – was one of the greedy, self-serving council who ruled the land. Sidestepping lawful heirs, the council granted Tattershall to Clinton along with other plum estates. By the end of his life he was a major landowner in at least nine counties, with no fewer than thirty-six landed estates in Lincolnshire alone.

Yet despite vast wealth Clinton was extremely averse to paying bills. In the same year Tattershall fell into his lap a bill was taken out against him for the then gigantic sum of £2,265, whereupon the council issued a pardon for all his debts. On King Edward's death he made the near-fatal blunder of declaring for Queen Jane Grey, the Protestant candidate, only to quickly trim his sails to gain favour with the Catholic Mary Tudor. On Philip of Spain's arrival in England as Mary's husband, he netted a Spanish pension of 1,000 crowns a year. To demonstrate his neutrality he also accepted 1,000 crowns from Philip's rival, Henri II of France. Clinton declared himself a Protestant again immediately on the accession of Elizabeth, crowning his long career with elevation to the earldom – an extraordinary achievement given the queen's notorious reluctance to confer peerages. As under Henry, Edward and Mary, he continued to scoop up lucrative royal appointments and grants of land for the rest of his life.

Earls were now top of the heap. Conscious of their shaky legitimacy, the Tudors had systematically eliminated all possible claimants
to the throne among the higher aristocracy with their problematical
Plantagenet blood. The last remaining duke, Norfolk, was executed
for allegedly plotting with Mary Queen of Scots in the same year that
Edward Clinton was raised to his earldom. Lincoln was one of the
Tudors' replacements for the old nobility.

Whatever his failings, the first earl was an achiever, a successful general and admiral who satisfied each royal master. Clearly he also had a
nagging conscience over the character of his heir, then known by the
courtesy title of Lord Clinton. In his will dated 11 July 1584, the earl
left his soon-to-be widow a group of manors and lands for life, including
the second most important Lincolnshire seat, a mansion he had raised
on the site of Sempringham Priory, and carefully added penal clauses
aimed at protecting her possessions from the heir to his title.

Anticipating a ferocious backlash over the terms of the will, the earl
decreed a crippling fine of £2,000 'if my said son or any other for him or
in his name or by his abetment, assent, or procurement shall directly or
indirectly interrupt at any time during the life of my said wife or trouble,
molest or disturb my said loving wife'. Furthermore, any hostile action
by his son would mean a substantial portion of these lands passing permanently to his widow's children by a previous marriage. The appointed
overseers of the will were no lesser figures than the Earl of Leicester and
Burghley himself.

It was in a frantic effort to undermine the old countess's rights that the
heir bombarded Lord Burghley with repeated denunciations of those
cunning and wicked women, his wife and stepmother, who he claimed
were not only trying to swindle him but slandering him as 'a vyllanous
devle' to the queen. These wild charges reached a new pitch as his father
lay on his deathbed with the sweating sickness. With his legal efforts to
overturn the will quickly dismissed, the new earl's reputation at court
sank even lower. His Irish stepmother was Elizabeth Fitzgerald, a long-
standing friend and confidante of the queen, who had been immortalised
in her youth as 'the Fair Geraldine' of the poet Earl of Surrey, and she

was destined to live comfortably on the inheritance from her husband until her death in 1590. It was she, not the heir, who paid for the first earl's magnificent tomb in St George's Chapel at Windsor.[30]

Only in his insatiable lust for land and property and aversion to paying bills did the second earl outshine his sire. After coming into the title he enclosed or converted to pasture at least 4,000 acres on his Lincolnshire estates alone, destroying many villages and livelihoods in the process. Nor did he hesitate to depopulate Tattershall itself, pulling down twenty farmhouses and turning over arable smallholdings to pasture. In those days people tended to stay where God had put them and the earl's dispossessed tenants had little choice but to become labourers or wanderers on the road.

However, Lincoln did seize one opportunity he must have believed would ingratiate him with his sovereign. When Mary Queen of Scots was tried for treason at Fotheringay Castle in 1587, he was one of the commissioner peers who sat in judgement and recommended the sentence of death. Wiser souls contrived some excuse to be absent. Elizabeth may have been keenly aware of the threat posed by Mary alive, but she also trembled at the precedent of killing an anointed queen. Once the deed was done, Elizabeth was frantic to distance herself from blame and turned savagely on everyone involved in the execution, from Lord Burghley to the hapless messenger who carried the warrant to Fotheringay.

But Earl Henry's brazenness knew no bounds. Months after the execution, when the conscience-stricken Elizabeth finally ordered Mary's burial at Peterborough Cathedral with regal honours, Lincoln turned up as one of the chief mourners. He was not alone in fulfilling this strange double role, however, as his neighbour the Earl of Rutland also figured both as Mary's judge and mourner. There was a sequel to this curious episode less than two years later, in September 1589, when Lincoln was chosen to represent Elizabeth at the forthcoming wedding of King James of Scotland, Mary's son. How news of his selection was received at Holyrood is not recorded, but Lincoln himself was unabashed and indeed in coming years would make repeated efforts to curry favour with this likely successor to the English throne.

Queen Elizabeth's personal stand-in at the funeral of Mary Stuart, adorned in the borrowed regalia, was none other than Lincoln's mother-in-law, the widowed countess of Bedford. This was yet another of the earl's relations who was soon to feel the blast of his fury, this time for encouraging 'treachery and perjury' against him. Inevitably, the pair fell out over his seizure of a property belonging to someone else, but again it was the lady who bested the earl. Another trusted friend of the queen, Lady Bedford refused to be browbeaten and the peer ended up, to his great astonishment and anguish, in a prison cell.

Not long after Mary Stuart's funeral, the earl began to cast covetous eyes on the valuable manor of Weston-on-the-Green, near Bicester in Oxfordshire. Originally part of the inheritance of the statesman Lord Williams of Thame, who died in 1559, it had been willed to his widow for life and was then to pass to Lord Williams's son-in-law, Lord Norreys of Rycote, a respected veteran soldier and close friend of the queen.[31] Lady Williams remarried twice before her death thirty years later, at which time Lord Norreys generously agreed that her last husband, an elderly and infirm gentleman named James Crofts, might remain at Weston for life.

It was at this point the Earl of Lincoln laid claim to the manor on the basis that he had married as his second wife the widow of Norreys's eldest son, who had expired of a fever while serving in the Irish wars. What made the earl's claim so preposterous was that the owner Lord Norreys was still alive, as were his five younger sons. Failing to win Weston by law, Lincoln's natural recourse was naked violence, and the outrages which followed were reported in fascinating detail to Star Chamber, the all-powerful body composed of key privy councillors.

Star Chamber had not yet turned into the infamous instrument of royal tyranny it would become under the Stuarts. On the contrary, under Elizabeth it was seen to offer some level of protection to commoners oppressed by those whose rank placed them beyond the reach of ordinary courts. A complaint laid before the Chamber in June 1588 stated that Henry, Earl of Lincoln, contrary to her majesty's laws and in contempt of the same, descended on Weston Manor with nearly forty 'lewd and evell dysposed persons … armed and appointed in warlike sort with swords daggers pikestaffs billes longstaves rapiers and divers other weapons'. This miniature army broke down the doors of the manor barn and administered fierce beatings to the manor workers 'to their great feare terror and amazement'[32] before carting off goods belonging to Mr Crofts.

Whether by luck or design, Lincoln chose his time well. Elizabeth's ministers were facing more pressing concerns than his private war, for this was the date of one of the greatest challenges to England in her history. The first sighting of the long-expected Spanish Armada had just been reported off the Scillies, and the ill-used Lord Norreys had bigger things on his mind than the looting of Weston. After busying himself with coastal defences against the awaited invasion, the old warrior hurried to escort the queen to Tilbury, scene of her famous speech of defiance to the powers of Europe.

A second and more serious assault on Weston came in September the following year, on the eve of Lincoln's departure to Scotland for King James's nuptials. A new complaint to Star Chamber centred on testimony from Crofts's servants describing how, at dusk, a party of about forty of the earl's armed retainers invaded the manor again with 'pistolles ready, charged bowes and arrowes, swordes and daggers, longe pyked staves, and Billes, and such like forcible and outragious weapons'. At their head was Lord Lincoln himself, brandishing a rapier and dagger. Finding the great gate 'fast locked, boulted and barred' against him, he flew into a towering rage and falsely claimed to have a warrant from Queen Elizabeth which entitled him to hang all at Weston as traitors and rebels. At length, when the attackers procured ladders to scale the walls and break into the courtyard, the manor servants retreated into the house and bolted the door. The earl, 'horriblie swearing', called for 'strawe or hedgewood to sett fire to the house' but was eventually persuaded the property would be useless to him if reduced to ashes.

Only when the raiders began to batter down the front door did the defenders give up the fight, though not before Lincoln had struck down the bailiff of the manor with his sword. In possession at last, the triumphant peer called for supper in the great hall before retiring to the best bedchamber. Crofts himself had been absent during the invasion, but returned during the night with followers of his own. There was now a prospect of serious bloodshed. Roused from his sleep, the earl appeared at the window and 'being in great heate, choler and furye, said with alli voice, swearing grete and terrible othes, "Where be the Villaynes, Traytors, Rebells and Rascalls? Set open the dores! I will beate them awaye, or leave my Carcasse amongst them!"' Faced with the threat that he and his servants would all be hanged, Mr Crofts decided discretion was the better part of valour and left the maddened nobleman in charge.

It was not for long. Soon afterwards, either remembering his royal errand or belatedly grasping that retaliation was inevitable, Lincoln galloped off towards Scotland leaving Weston in the hands of a number of his retainers. These henchmen were charged with holding the house by force, but had the sense to realise the game was up once Crofts reappeared with a posse of armed followers and justices of the peace.

In the event Lincoln never completed his journey to the Scottish court. At some point after leaving Weston he learned that James's bride Anne of Denmark was stormbound in Norway and the impatient bridegroom had decided to sail across and marry her there.

The lawsuits which ensued over Weston, involving claim and counterclaim of riotous assembly, perjury and slander, were to rumble on for no fewer than seven years. In the meantime new complaints against the earl piled up thick and fast at court, among them the pathetic suit of an old family retainer who had been stripped of a modest pension willed to him by the first earl. The Privy Council tried to shame Lincoln into behaving decently towards the poor man's family out of consideration of his long and faithful service, begging the earl to reflect 'how much it would touch your lordship in honour and otherwise, if through your lordship's hard dealing they should perish'. But to beg charity of Lincoln was like asking water to flow uphill.

At last, in June 1592, Star Chamber decided enough was enough. When the earl ignored a further stern rebuke for his misdeeds, he was suddenly arrested, forced to pay a huge fine and committed to

Fleet prison. The matter which seems finally to have tipped the scales was a new torrent of venom directed against Lady Bedford. Once recovered from his amazement at being incarcerated, the earl bombarded Lord Burghley with letters protesting his innocence and blaming everybody else for his misfortune.

'I assure your lordship of my honour,' he wrote, 'and I take the living God to witness, that I know myself clean in conscience … and would think myself happy, yea, and thrice happy, to die sooner with honour, rather than suffer this scar or blot of disgrace, laid upon me by malice and false witness.' He signed off 'from my unsavoury and disquiet lodging in the Fleet, this 15th of June 1592'.[33]

The pleas to the lord high treasurer evidently bore fruit as within a fortnight Lincoln was back at his London house in Canon Row, Westminster, taking up quill and paper to thank Burghley for delivering him out of 'that filthy and unwholesome lodging' but also to fulminate about the size of the fine imposed on him – £1,000 – and to thunder against the 'so base people' whose lies had brought him low, 'not having the fear of God before their eyes'. In his crazed imagination the chief conspirators in the affair were his mother-in-law, Crofts and Lord Norreys, who had all procured perjured witnesses against him.

As the year wore on the earl's behaviour became ever more bizarre and Burghley was repeatedly pestered to overturn unfavourable judicial rulings. In one letter Lincoln bemoans his 'lamentable state, overpressed with enemies, with griefs and sickness; without comfort, council or friends'.[34] Surely it should be crystal clear that anyone who stood against him was a liar and traitor and almost certainly a papist or atheist? In November, in the futile hope that Burghley would take his part once again, he wrote self-pityingly of being forced 'to toil out my sickly carcase at this time of year to be a humble suitor'.

But the Privy Council now seemed to have Lincoln's measure. He was again summoned before them the following May and 'dealt soundly withal by the Lords upon complaints made against him of wrongs offered'. Yet in 1595 his great adversary Sir Edward Dymoke wrote to Burghley's son, Sir Robert Cecil, to complain that he had been obliged to break up his household and disperse all his servants from Scrivelsby Court – the Dymoke seat near Horncastle since the fourteenth century – 'being forced by his Lordship's unkind molestation'.[35] Lincoln appeared to be facing another spell in the Fleet, the usual destination of prisoners committed at the royal pleasure or by order of Star Chamber.

Given the earl's track record, it seems astonishing that early in 1596 Queen Elizabeth again nominated him as her ambassador, this time to an influential German state. Possibly she was bowing to pleas to get him out of England on any pretext. And Lincoln was probably thankful to leave the country at this time as the Privy Council had just given notice of an action brought against him by the minister of Folkingham. Also to be answered was a suit by the earl's page, Roger Fullshaw, who had inherited his father's manor a few months before only to see Lincoln appropriate the deeds, pretending the property was forfeit because of a debt owed by the dead man. Fullshaw utterly refuted the claim and prayed for the Privy Council's protection in view of 'the most horrible outrages committed against him'[36] by his master, including false imprisonment.

Worse still, the earl was now facing a charge of slander brought against him by Sir John Norreys, son of the Lord Norreys of Rycote from whom he had attempted to wrest Weston Manor. Sir John, a much admired soldier, was now lord general of the queen's army in Ireland, having already distinguished himself in command of Anglo-Dutch forces in the Netherlands. The vitriol of the slander, coming soon after the earl's release from prison, showed how his hatred of Lord Norreys now extended to the entire Norreys clan, rousing him to wild accusations of murder, cowardice and corruption against various members of this distinguished family. Witnesses recorded hearing his fervent wish to see the extinction of Lord Norreys's title by 'the dissolucion of him and all the rest of his sonnes'.

Lincoln's rage was doubtless heightened by the fact that Sir John, one of his numerous creditors, had recently forced him to hand over a fine horse from the Tattershall stables in settlement of a debt of twenty marks. Yet the earl's curse was to be very nearly fulfilled, for he would live to gloat over the death of Lord Norreys and no fewer than five of his six soldier sons while on active service. But we are getting ahead of our story.

The embassy to Germany was another sorry chapter in Lincoln's career. As personal representative of Elizabeth, he set off in great state on 5 July for the court of Philip the Magnanimous, Landgrave of Hesse, to attend the christening of his son and heir, Prince Otto. Attended by one of his younger sons, Edward, and with a large personal retinue and six musketeers to guard the cart which bore the royal gift of plate to the Landgrave Philip, the earl sailed from Yarmouth to Flushing, travelling on into Germany in a stately procession of carriages.

As records of Theodore Paleologus from this period are scant, it is tempting to look for him in every shadow, and a first encounter with Lincoln during this embassy of 1596 is a possibility. The strategic importance of Flushing made it a honeypot for spies. However, there is no mention of the Italian in reports on the earl's movements which sped back to England from the agent Anthony Bacon, brother of the great Sir Francis. At this time both Bacons were key figures in the intelligence network of the Earl of Essex, Elizabeth's favourite. But by October Lincoln was home again with a European reputation to match that in his own country. 'The erle of Lincoln was return'd from the landgrave of Hesse,' wrote Anthony Bacon, 'no less charg'd with most princely honours and liberalities than he had left behind dishonours, clamours and curses for his base miserliness and insupportable fancies or rather furies.'[37]

Once again an ignominious performance by Lincoln coincided with one of the defining moments of the Elizabethan age, Essex's Cadiz expedition. Having captured and burned the town and forced the Spaniards to scuttle their anchored fleet, Essex had set sail for home on 4 July. It was as Bacon was anxiously awaiting news of his master's daring enterprise that he filed his report on the Earl of Lincoln's antics.

As was usual practice, an official tract recording the ambassadorial mission was published later in the year – *The Landgrave of Hessen his princelie receiuing of her Maiesties Embassador. Imprinted at London by Robert Robinson, 1596* – but it is remarkable among such documents because no mention is made of the name or title of the ambassador, though the accompanying son, 'Master Edward Clynton', is mentioned more than once. It is a sign of the unprecedented level of disgust and embarrassment caused by the nobleman's ill-natured deeds.

Complaints against the earl resumed in rapid-fire succession after his return from Germany. On 30 June 1597, the Privy Council wrote demanding satisfaction in 'honour and good conscience' on behalf of two poor suitors at Tattershall and followed up with an unusually heated letter on 17 August urging action on yet more outstanding petitions against him, in one case a 'very grevious complaint against your Lordship' which was causing 'pittyfull moane' among his victims. It went on: 'Wee cann doe no lesse then require your Lordship, beinge as you are a noble man, to regard your honour and calling and to forbeare to give these occacions of complaint against you, whereof even of late wee have received divers.' And so it went on. From Oxfordshire one Robert Blower protested that 'certaine disordered persons'[38] belonging to Lincoln had dispossessed him of his house and land.

The earl's mounting paranoia is palpable in his reply dated ten days later from Tattershall Castle and addressed to Sir Robert Cecil, in which he continues to blame the malice and false slanders put about by 'ancient adversaries' headed by Sir Edward Dymoke. In his crazed brain it was once again poor Earl Henry *contra mundum*.

Next in the firing line was Lincoln's own son and heir, the newly married Thomas, Lord Clinton. The earl not only appropriated the rich dowry of Thomas's heiress bride but refused to make any provision for the young couple, even when his young daughter-in-law was laid low by a dangerous illness. This time Queen Elizabeth herself was stirred to intervene.

In a letter dated August 1597, the Privy Council informed the earl:

The Queen, having heard of the recovery of your daughter-in-law the Lady Clynton, commands us that seeing God Almighty is so gracious as by this restitution to give you hope of comfort in your son and heir, so should it be a provocation of His displeasure if by a second cause any impediment should arise which might work a new alteration. Consider then what it is for young folks to want, and how far in honour you are bound to do what her father expected, though out of trust he dealt more loosely than he needed. Consider what a portion he parted with and besides all these matters the Queen's earnest request.

The earl was ordered immediately to provide a suitable home for the couple and restore the value of the lands gifted by the bride's father, the eminent courtier Sir Henry Knyvett. The letter ended:

> The Queen means not to dispute upon point of law or bonds; for she knows in such a case as this where it concerns a gentlewoman descended from a father of noble blood, and where she interposeth herself as well for regard of the young Lord as for his wife, that you will regard the obligations of honour and compassion. And we do assure you that it would be very acceptable to the Queen to find that you yielded so nobly and kindly to so princely and gracious a motion.

The earl had proved impervious to all previous appeals to the finer instincts, and words like honour and compassion doubtless continued to fall on deaf ears. Elizabeth read his character right enough with her phrase about points of law. But the royal strictures must have given Lincoln pause, coming on top of unmistakable signs of loss of patience by the indispensable Cecils. Even a man as unbalanced as Lincoln knew better than openly defy a Tudor monarch: however gracelessly, he was forced to open his purse to the young Clintons.

By now the earl was heavily in debt. Despite the great inheritance from his father, now augmented by the recovery of the Sempringham estate on the death of the dowager countess, he had been brought low by years of high living – chiefly down to expensive tastes in horseflesh and jewels – and extravagant building schemes in London, Sempringham and elsewhere. Incapable of curbing his mad spending, he had recently bought a grand house in Chelsea from Sir Robert Cecil. This new expense combined with years of ill-judged business affairs, bad investments and a passion for litigation, resulting in enormous lawyers' fees and disastrous fines. Then, late in 1599, as his new gentleman rider was settling in at Tattershall Castle, the long-smouldering feud with the Dymokes reignited, and in a later chapter we shall see how this brought new scandal upon the earl and financial catastrophe upon his enemies.

This was a time in Paleologus's life when critical events occurred in bewildering succession. The discovery of Mary Balls's pregnancy led to the overdue wedding on 1 May 1600. Their son, baptised Theodore at Tattershall on 12 June, died on 1 September. Just two days after the baptism, Sir Robert Cecil opened a hair-raising letter claiming that the Earl of Lincoln had given a notorious Italian murderer control over the countess, a prisoner at Tattershall Castle. The following day the Privy Council issued a warrant for the earl's arrest.

The irony is that the charge against Lincoln was not of plotting his wife's murder, but of non-payment of debts.

# 7

The fifteenth day of July,
with glist'ning speare and shield
A famous fight in Flanders
was foughten in the field
The most courageous officers
were the English captains three
But the bravest in the Battel
was brave Lord Willoughby.

Bishop Percy, Reliques of Ancient English Poetry.

Before we examine Theodore Paleologus's time at Tattershall in closer detail, and his role as the countess's gaoler, we must return to the question which vexes everyone who ponders on his chequered career: what or who induced him to settle in England? As for what, we have the evidence that the Low Countries were getting too hot for him following further murderous adventures there. As for who, I believe there is a strong case for naming one of Elizabeth's outstanding generals in preference to all other candidates previously put forward.

Peregrine Bertie, thirteenth Baron Willoughby de Eresby, was a leading figure in England's war in the Netherlands, where he became the key ally of Theodore's commander, Prince Maurice of Nassau. In Lincolnshire he was a neighbouring landowner of the Earl of Lincoln, and one of the very few county grandees who always managed to avoid a quarrel with the irascible peer. Indeed, the pair served together on commissions to root out Catholic sympathisers. Lord Willoughby was also the patron of the future Virginia colonist John Smith, whose friendship with Paleologus we shall see described in his autobiographical *True Travels* – a friendship which inspired some of Smith's most extraordinary exploits. Smith was brought up on the extensive Willoughby estates centred on Grimsthorpe Castle, not far from Tattershall.

A hero celebrated in song and verse, Lord Willoughby had soldiered in the Netherlands from the early days of the war, serving under the Earl of Leicester before replacing him as head of the English army. Willoughby not only cooperated closely with Prince Maurice but became a personal friend. This suggests he may have become acquainted with Paleologus as early as the 1580s. Here are credible grounds to explain the Italian's employment at Tattershall, presuming an urgent need for him to quit the Netherlands and a personal recommendation from Willoughby. Maurice and Willoughby may very well have used him as a go-between. With his *savoir vivre*, skill in languages and expert horsemanship, the resourceful Italian would have made an ideal carrier of sensitive diplomatic correspondence and secret messages between the two commanders.

This is also a time Paleologus's abilities as a spy, honed when employed by clients such as the republic of Lucca, would have proved most useful to his masters. Almost any travelling gentleman of the period was duty-bound to dabble in surveillance – reporting back to his home country was frequently the price paid for authorisation to travel – but few offered the talents of the Italian. It is not difficult to picture Paleologus in this murky world of ciphers, secret writing and forgery, his value as an intelligencer enhanced by the practical skills of a hardened mercenary.

In 1586 Willoughby was one of the heroes of Zutphen, the battle in which Sir Philip Sidney received a deadly Spanish musket-ball in the leg. Several of the characters in this story were on the battlefield under the gaze of Leicester with Prince Maurice not far away, so Paleologus may well have been present. The immediate English commander during the action was the Sir John Norreys whose family were soon to be embroiled with the Earl of Lincoln over the Weston Manor invasion. According to one contemporary source it was when Willoughby found himself in difficulties that Sidney rode fatally to the rescue.

Queen Elizabeth was to send an English contingent under Willoughby to support the Huguenot leader Henri of Navarre in his unsuccessful siege of Paris in 1590. In a later chapter we shall see evidence in Paleologus's own hand that he fought in France, and though this does not specifically link him to Willoughby there are a number of accounts of him serving in Elizabeth's army as well as Prince Maurice's.

✣

The Willoughby de Eresby title is one of the English peerages which may descend in the female line in the absence of a male heir. Peregrine's mother Katherine Willoughby, one of the great heiresses of Henry VIII's time, had been the intended child bride of the son and heir of the king's brother-in-law, Charles Brandon, Duke of Suffolk, the then owner of Tattershall Castle. In the event, the claim of this sickly youth – the last person to bear the title Earl of Lincoln before the Clintons – was set aside when the newly widowed duke decided to marry her himself. Suffolk was about fifty years old and Katherine thirteen.

Widowed in 1545, the duchess took as a second husband her gentleman usher at Grimsthorpe, an otherwise obscure figure called Richard Bertie. According to an early memoirist of the family, 'it is said he was Master of the Horse to Charles Brandon; but as it was usual for the great men of those times to retain great officers, in a sort of imitation of their prince, I doubt whether he was in so high a station'.[39] Katherine herself admitted Bertie was 'meanly born' and genealogists have since identified him as the son of a stonemason. Whatever his origins, he and his wife became fervent reformers and they fled abroad soon after the accession of Mary Tudor. By family tradition the penniless exile Katherine gave birth to her son Peregrine in a church porch in Germany and he was given the unusual name to commemorate his parents' dangerous wanderings.[40]

The Clintons' acquisition of Tattershall, where his mother had reigned as duchess, must have touched a nerve with Lord Willoughby, even more so as an earlier Lady Willoughby de Eresby was a co-heiress of

Ralph Cromwell and wrongly dispossessed of her share in his fortune. One may be confident that had matters been the other way round, the Earl of Lincoln would have launched an unrelenting campaign to reclaim a property he thought rightfully his.

As we shall see, Theodore's sinister reputation preceded him to England. Lord Willoughby may well have been aware of it through his dealings with Prince Maurice, and certainly knew of the Italian's martial talents; that he should put in a quiet word with Lincoln – a man then frantic to recruit suitable followers for his private war – seems to me a more probable scenario than any previously mooted. Indeed, Paleologus may well have been spying in the English interest around this time, with or without the Dutch leader's knowledge, and it is under one or other of the aliases in the surviving payment records of the competing English intelligence networks operating in the Low Countries that we may brush against Theodore Paleologus without knowing it.

Prince Maurice exerted himself to stay on best terms with his Protestant allies and tipped off the English about at least one foreign plot against Elizabeth's life. Having lost his father, William the Silent, at the hands of a spy-assassin, Maurice was protected by a well-oiled intelligence service of his own. As we have seen, Theodore in Maurice's service had all the credentials to make a formidable agent, along with special gifts which would commend him as a messenger between the generals. Besides being a superb horseman and expert linguist, he was intelligent, educated, resourceful and one may surmise entirely unhindered by scruples. He had the courage for desperate work and the skill to extricate himself from dangerous situations. How else had he lived so long? And just as his familiarity with court life at Urbino gave him the airs and graces to move in the highest circles, he also possessed the common touch, as we can observe in his dealings with farmer's lad John Smith and miller's granddaughter Mary Balls. The long association with the Earl of Lincoln, a singularly quarrelsome man, tells us something not only of Theodore's character but of his social skills.

In England the secret services established by Sir Francis Walsingham and the Cecils, along with the lesser known network inherited by Essex from his stepfather the Earl of Leicester, achieved a degree of sophistication unequalled elsewhere, though many of their guiding ideas had their origin in the Italian city states. It is striking how frequently the correspondence of spymasters of the time refers to the employment of Italian agents, many of them unnamed or under obvious aliases. One of Leicester's best spies was an Italian whose aliases included Rocco Bonetti and Mr Rocke, and among Walsingham's finest was Horatio Palavicino, a rich Italian merchant with a spy-ring of his own. But the great coup of Walsingham's career was to place a spy operating under the memorable alias of Henry Fagot inside the French embassy in London, a move which led to the exposure of the Throckmorton plot to depose Elizabeth in the wake of a foreign invasion. Fagot's true identity has been revealed in modern times as the Italian thinker and renegade priest Giordano Bruno, who was to be burnt at the stake in Rome in 1600.

However, Walsingham's key papers vanished immediately after his death, probably into the hands of the Cecils; Essex burnt many of his in a few fateful hours of 8 February 1601, when he grasped his rebellion had failed. With them may have gone any documentary proof that Paleologus spied for England.

Lord Willoughby returned to England from his lengthy service abroad in 1598.[41] We can not only place Paleologus in Lincoln's household the following year, but thanks to the Smith connection we have clear evidence of friendly relations with the Willoughby family circle in 1600.

Willoughby himself had received his last royal appointment in 1599. This was the governorship of the border town of Berwick-on-Tweed and the wardenship of the East Marches. Though a popular idol, the peer seems to have been under something of a cloud at this time. The new office may appear insignificant compared with his previous high commands in the Netherlands and France, but he had to lobby hard to secure it. Earlier, in response to a letter from Queen Elizabeth hinting that he should stay around the court, Willoughby had retorted stiffly that 'he was uncapable of serving her Majesty as a courtier; but as a soldier, every drop of blood in his veins was at her service against all her enemies'. To friends he was plainer, declaring he was 'none of the reptilia that could crawl and cringe upon the ground'. So off he went to Berwick-on-Tweed, where he soon attracted the ire of the King of Scots and sparked an international incident.

In early summer 1599 an English Catholic intriguer named Edmund Ashfield obtained a border pass from Willoughby under false pretences. Once in Scotland he met up with King James on two occasions, advising him on how to press his claim to Elizabeth's crown. Discovering he had been duped, the incensed governor ordered the seizure of Ashfield on Scottish soil. This sensational kidnap was carried out by Willoughby's deputy and cousin, Sir John Guevara, and three unnamed assistants armed with rapiers and daggers. With the collusion of the English ambassador they contrived a meeting with Ashfield on the sands at Leith where they plied him with drugged wine – 'which so bedulled his senses as he wist not what he did' – and rushed him back to Berwick in the ambassador's coach. It would be gratifying to identify Theodore as one of the 'craftie gentilmen' involved, perhaps on loan from Tattershall as a returned favour to Willoughby, but there is no evidence of his participation in an escapade for which Paleologo the Bravo was ideally suited.

Furious that Ashfield could be snatched 'violentlie out of the hart of our country', James subjected the ambassador to house arrest and demanded the Englishman's return, which Willoughby peremptorily refused. The controversy was still bubbling away in June 1601 – and Ashfield still a prisoner – when Lord Willoughby suddenly 'took a great cold' which proved fatal. He had suffered ill health for many years.

Willoughby and Guevara were also suspected of complicity in the mystery-shrouded Gowrie Conspiracy which rocked Scotland in August 1600. On the surface this was a wild plot against King James, but many believed it to be a plot by James against the Earl of Gowrie, a long-time enemy to whom the king owed a huge sum of money. The handsome young Gowrie was also the rumoured lover of James's queen, Anne of Denmark. According to the king's adherents, James was lured to the earl's house in Perth and exposed to a chaotic attempted murder or kidnapping to avenge the execution of Gowrie's father on trumped-up charges, while

others claimed James had fabricated the attack to justify the bloody elimination of Gowrie which promptly followed.

Relations between England and Scotland were at a new low in the wake
of the Ashfield incident, and one widely held contemporary theory had it
that Gowrie had come to an understanding with Guevara that the abducted
king would be taken off by sea on a ship owned by Lord Willoughby.
The peer and Gowrie were known to be personal friends. The ever-sus-
picious James himself muttered darkly about a mysterious English ship
which had been hovering off the coast at this time, refusing all communica-
tion. Much was made by the royal faction of Gowrie's education at Padua,
where he was said to have brooded on revenge for the wrongs done to his
family while studying 'the subtleties of Italian crime'.

It is at least true that Willoughby had a ship built at Berwick, a 140-tonner
armed with sixteen cannon, insisting to Sir Robert Cecil that the coast
needed protection from Dunkirk pirates; indeed, the peer was on board
the vessel when he died, worn out by his long years in Elizabeth's service.
He was perhaps fortunate not to live to face James's wrath on his elevation
to the English throne, or see the royal favours heaped on Edmund Ashfield.

❖

There is another Willoughby link which invites a tantalising question:
did Paleologus know Emilia Bassano, the woman most frequently identified as Shakespeare's Dark Lady? The orphan of an Italian court
musician, probably of Jewish blood, Emilia was accepted at the age of
seven into the household of Lord Willoughby's sister Susan, Dowager
Countess of Kent, a generous patroness who ensured the child was
given a humanist education and taught Latin. Emilia has been called
England's first feminist poet; her collected works entitled *Salve Deus Rex
Judaeorum* – Hail God, King of the Jews – was dedicated to Susan Bertie
as 'the Mistris of my youth, the noble guide of my ungovern'd dayes'.
Susan was also her entrée to court where her sultry good looks left many
nobles smitten and her playing of the virginals was greatly admired by
Queen Elizabeth, herself an accomplished performer.

At eighteen Emilia became the mistress of the queen's cousin Lord Hunsdon, forty-five years her senior and the patron of Shakespeare's company of actors. She was married off to an elderly cousin when she fell pregnant. Emilia is generally recognised as the most convincing contender to be the Dark Lady of the sonnets. Palcologus would have had opportunities to meet her through his friendship with the Berties and might very well have encountered her in London during his early days in the Earl of Lincoln's employ. From around 1597 Emilia regularly consulted the notorious astrologer and court intriguer Dr Simon Forman, seeking magical help to become 'a lady of title'. A compulsive womaniser, Forman kept a coded diary, deciphered only recently, which chronicles his efforts to seduce the teasing beauty, who constantly led him on only to refuse him at the last moment. Their on-off liaison continued until at least 1600 when the astrologer was still failing to have his way with her. During these years Emilia was living at Longditch, Westminster, which Stow describes in his *Survey of London* as leading directly into Canon Row. Here was the 'fair house built by Henry Clinton, earl of Lincoln'.[42]

This begs the question: did Theodore know Shakespeare? The earl was regularly in London entangled in his legal and business affairs and attempting, however unsuccessfully, to curry favour at court. His gentleman rider would have escorted him on many occasions at places frequented by Shakespeare and the likes of Webster and Jonson; Paleologus may well have frequented the theatre. London at this time had a population of 200,000, hardly more than half the size of present-day Barnsley. Inside their select milieu within this city, it is difficult to believe the assassin and the dramatist did not come across one another. And it seems more likely Theodore caught the eye of Shakespeare than the other way round: the exotic, gigantic Paleologus, henchman of the infamous Earl of Lincoln, source of endless rumour and speculation.

# 8

Above all else, be armed.

Niccolo Machiavelli, *The Prince.*

Paleologus's curious dalliance with the young John Smith must have come as a welcome respite from the domestic dramas – his own and his patron's – that engulfed Tattershall in 1600. The future Virginia pioneer was born in 1580, the son of a tenant farmer called George Smith, in the Lincolnshire village of Willoughby-by-Alford. The Willoughbys took their name from the manor house there. In his will of 1596 George Smith left 'the best of my two yeare old colts' to Peregrine, Lord Willoughby, 'under whome I have many years lived as his poore tenant'. The dying man exhorted his son and heir 'to honoure and love my foresaid good Lord Willoughbie during his lyfe'.

There was another Willoughby connection. A Nicholas Smith, George's cousin, was the owner of a small estate near Louth who considerably enhanced his status by marrying his daughter to Francis Guevara, a member of the family with close associations with Lord Willoughby. We have seen that the peer's deputy warden at Berwick was the intrigue-loving Sir John Guevara, while his private secretary was one Antonio Guevara. The pair descended from a Spanish mercenary who had converted to Anglicanism and settled locally. Nicholas Smith's brother was headmaster of the grammar school at Louth attended by John Smith, and his education there – an unusual privilege for a yeoman's son – was surely down to this link. Smith had the good fortune to be brought up with the peer's two sons and indeed at one time accompanied them on a visit to France.

In *The True Travels*, one of the earliest autobiographical works in the English language, Smith claims to have served during his late teens with the English forces in the Low Countries, returning home to Lincolnshire in 1600. Writing of himself in the third person, Smith admits he soon tired of the company of the locals and took himself off to live as a recluse in 'a little woody pasture a good way from any towne, environed with many hundred acres of other woods: Here by a faire brook he built a Pavilion of boughs'. There was much wonder at his hermit-like ways, and he goes on to describe how he was then befriended by 'Seignior Thaedora Polalaga, Rider to Henry Earle of Lincolne, an excellent Horse-man and a noble Italian gentleman'. Friends of Smith, surely the Willoughbys, had persuaded Theodore to 'insinuate into his woodish acquaintances, whose Languages and good discourse, and exercise of riding, drew him to stay with him at Tattershall'. There is a possibility that the pair first met in the Netherlands, but if so Smith fails to mention the fact.

*The True Travels* tells us that among the books studied in Smith's rustic retreat were 'Machiavill's Art of War and Marcus Aurelius'. No English edition of *The Meditations of Marcus Aurelius* had appeared at this time and Smith almost certainly means a work called *The Dial of Princes*, which includes a selection of the Roman emperor's thoughts. Originally published in Spanish in 1529 by the Hapsburg courtier Don Antonio Guevera, this had recently been translated into English by the author's kinsman and namesake, Lord Willoughby's secretary. So it is more than likely that Smith's copy came from the well-stocked library at Grimsthorpe Castle.

Biographers of Smith have always been beguiled by the connection with the imperial scion. In *John Smith, Gentleman Adventurer*, C.H. Forbes-Lindsay vividly imagines the odd couple in their 'woodish acquaintances', with Paleologus partaking heartily of Smith's offering of a venison pasty, 'the contents of which he strongly suspected to have been poached from the Earl's preserves'. The hermit is enticed to Tattershall Castle by 'the reputation of the extensive stable of fine horses, the assortment of various arms and the tilt-yard'. Having heard the earl was eccentric and hard to please, Smith is surprised to find him 'a very pleasant gentleman who bade him make himself as much at home in the castle as though he owned it'.

This hardly sounds like the Lord Lincoln we know, and I have found no contemporary evidence of this genial and hospitable side of the man apart from his friendship with the Willoughbys and a possible fondness for William Balls and his daughter. However, all authorities on John Smith agree it was during this stay at Tattershall that Paleologus honed Smith into a formidable warrior – 'entering zealously into the instruction of the young man, declaring that he had never before had so apt a pupil', as one writer puts it. But Smith himself records that 'long these pleasures could not content him', and Forbes-Lindsay describes him bidding adieu to 'his patron the Earl, and his friend the master of horse', anxious to test his new skills on the battlefield.[43]

One of the most respected American biographers, Philip L. Barbour, says that it was during the Tattershall interlude when his new mentor 'filled John Smith's fancies with further adventurous notions', inspiring him to fight those legendary monsters, the Ottomans:

> A hundred and fifty years of history were swept away by the voice of one of the Emperor's own family. And the maturing farmer-boy from Lincolnshire both lamented and repented, as he put it, having seen so many Christians slaughter one another in Europe [meaning the Netherlands] while the heathen Turks roamed at will in the East.[44]

In another American biography, Paleologus is credited with 'igniting the spirit of the Crusaders'[45] in Smith. The colonist himself, in his later work the *General Historie of Virginia*, writes of his youthful brooding on 'the miserable ruine of Constantinople' and of his desire to 'trie his fortune against the Turkes'.

Smith's quest took him to Rome where he joined the regiment of a Protestant noble in the service of Emperor Rudolf II. Since the fall of Constantinople the Turks had come close to mastery in the Mediterranean and conquered ever greater tracts of Eastern Europe and the Balkans. In response successive Hapsburg emperors had sought to stitch together a coalition of Christian powers to repel new incursions and reclaim former imperial lands. Smith's regiment was destined for Transylvania, which with much of Hungary had been under the Ottoman flag for generations. Transylvania was then the focus of the Turks' relentless drive towards Vienna.

The horrors of war pictured by Breughel and Bosch were no fantasy in war-torn Western Europe, from the Low Countries where English troops fought alongside Dutch rebels against the Spanish occupiers, to repeated scenes of slaughter in Ireland.

But Hungary was worse. English travellers of the time recorded the regular sight by the roadside of rows of impaled corpses, a favourite atrocity in the region since the days of Vlad the Impaler. Christian victories over the Turks were celebrated by soldiers playing bowls with severed Turkish heads, while Turkish victors would make merry by skinning their captives alive.

But the Hungarians standing against them were hopelessly divided into factions – Catholic against Protestant, Lutheran against Calvinist – any of which might temporarily side with the Muslims to spite a rival Christian interest. The country's woes were compounded by a constant jockeying for supremacy among warlords notorious for their violence, treachery and wanton cruelty. With the land still in the grip of feudalism, the nobility had the power of life and death over common folk who were also at the mercy of Turkish invaders, undisciplined imperial troops and rapacious private armies. Into this almighty chaos rode young John Smith, farmer's son from Lincolnshire.

There were wars aplenty closer to home for the glory-seeking Englishman. Smith could have taken his pick of Holland, France or Ireland, or signed up for daring adventures by land and sea with the likes of Walter Raleigh and Essex. The compelling reason behind his choice was Theodore Paleologus's tales of the unending struggle between Christendom and Islam. Smith was not alone in venturing so far, however, as a number of members of Raleigh's West Country circle also fought there.

Smith first saw action when his regiment helped break a Turkish siege of the city of Lower Limbach. According to his autobiography, the young Englishman distinguished himself from the outset. He happened to have met the city's governor earlier in his travels and the pair had discussed Machiavelli's reflections on warfare as studied by Smith and Paleologus in their rustic retreat. Realising that a method of signalling with torches described by Machiavelli would be recognised by the besieged governor, Smith followed up with a night attack which, reinforced by an armed sally out of the city, forced a Turkish withdrawal. The success of the stratagem led to the elevation to the rank of captain by which John Smith has since been known to history.

By 1603 Smith's regiment was attached to the army of the richest and most powerful warlord of Transylvania. Prince Sigismund Bathory, temporarily acknowledged as the Christian leader in the war, headed a family as dysfunctional, cruel and devious as the Paleologi or Borgias. Described by a contemporary writer as unpredictable as April weather, Sigismund was forced to abdicate four times but three times fought his way back to power. Rumoured to be homosexual or impotent, his inability to consummate his marriage to a Hapsburg princess was officially attributed by the Vatican to witchcraft. Other Bathory princes were notorious for mass murder, deviant lust, torture and cannibalism.

The women of the family were a spectacularly depraved lot. Sigismund's niece was the infamous Countess Elisabeth Bathory who enjoys new celebrity in our time as queen of the cinema's lesbian vampire genre. At the time of John Smith's arrival in the country the countess had recently embarked on the murderous career in which she allegedly bathed in the blood of 600 virgins in an effort to preserve her beauty. If we trace Smith's perambulations between 1601 and 1603, it seems certain that on at least two occasions he would have cantered below the brooding towers of Cachtice, Countess Elisabeth's fortress in the White Carpathians. It was here she would be incarcerated for life in 1611 when convicted of murder, sorcery and high treason. Nor was Elisabeth the only Bathory female to bring new scandal on the princely name. Her aunt Klara entered the history books as a witch, husband-killer and insatiable bisexual adventuress; her niece Anna narrowly escaped the stake when tried for necromancy, infanticide and incest.

The most sensational exploit described in *The True Travels* came in the spring of 1603 when Smith's regiment joined imperial troops laying siege to an Ottoman stronghold. On three occasions in a single day Smith accepted challenges to mortal combat by a Turkish champion from the city. Duels of this kind were known as *monomachies*, as mentioned by Robert Burton on the opening page of this book. In each clash the young Englishman emerged the unlikely victor, beheading his fallen adversary to the joyful acclaim of the watching Christian army.

Smith's biographers agree that the superlative martial skills displayed that day were taught by Theodore Paleologus. In the first contest Smith killed the Turk with a well-aimed lance; in the second he unhorsed his opponent with a pistol shot and finished him off with the sword; in the third Smith was having the worst of the encounter when he managed to slip the tip of his falchion into a chink in the Turk's armour. The three fights are vividly illustrated by engravings in the 1630 edition of *The True Travels*, with each pair of steel-clad combatants identified by cross and crescent.

Delighted by the Englishman's heroics, Prince Sigismund showered him with rewards. To the son of the 'poore tenant' of Willoughby-by-Alford the most prized of these was the grant of a coat of arms, the sign of a gentleman. The principal charges on the Smith shield are three severed Turks' heads, and while his companions-in-arms recognised these as marking his great feat, Smith himself must have revelled in the knowledge that a Saracen's head was the ancient crest of Willoughby de Eresby. Letters patent later issued by Sigismund were submitted to the College of Arms in London and accepted as authentic by Sir William Segar, Garter King of Arms.

Smith's fortunes turned with his next battle. Wounded and taken prisoner, he was sold as a slave to an Ottoman pasha, taken in chains to Constantinople and there presented to the pasha's Greek mistress. It was not the entry into the golden city he had pictured in pipe-dreams with Theodore Paleologus. Smith being Smith, however, he soon managed to stage a daring escape from the domain of the Turk. The Greek mistress fell in love with the English stranger and helped him make his way home to England via Russia.

How large a pinch of salt should be taken with this colourful narrative has long enlivened scholarly debate. Within twenty years of the colonist's death, Thomas Fuller's brief life of Smith in his *History of the Worthies of England* suggested that the 'perils, preservations, dangers, deliverancies' described in his books 'seem to most men above belief, to some beyond truth'. Generations of historians tended to view the captain as a braggart and liar, yet recent research has uncovered evidence which tends to support even the more outlandish tales in *The True Travels*, helping to reinstate the colonist as an American hero. Barbour, perhaps his most distinguished biographer, points out that despite every effort of the detractors nothing John Smith wrote has ever been proved a lie. Shall we be able to say as much of Theodore Paleologus?

# 9

A wretched soul, bruised with adversity.

Shakespeare, *The Rape of Lucrece*.

No character in this story is more pitiable that Lincoln's long-suffering second countess, the former Mistress Norreys. High rank had brought her nothing but misery, and any pretence of affection or common courtesy from her husband had ceased with the collapse of his specious claims to the Weston-on-the-Green estate. Now, in 1600, confined to Tattershall Castle with Paleologus as her keeper, she stood in fear of her life.

Sir Robert Cecil was now the power behind the throne, and desperate friends and relations of the lady bombarded him with letters begging him to intervene. Writing on 14 May, Francis Norreys, the countess's twenty-one-year-old son by her previous marriage, reminds Mr Secretary of an earlier promise to protect Lady Lincoln, either by petitioning the queen or confronting the earl himself. The countess 'exceedingly fears to exasperate the rancour of his malice towards her,' says Norreys, 'because she has resolved, how vilely so ever he uses her, to live with him for ever, in respect of the tenderness she bears to the children she has by him whom he threatens to abandon if she makes any means to depart his house'.[46]

The young man's deepest fear is laid bare in the following passage of the letter:

He keeps her now docked up like a prisoner, without suffering her either to write or hear from any of her friends, having appointed to guard her an Italian, a man that hath done divers murders in Italy and in the Low Countries, from which he fled to England, from whom, I protest, she has just cause hourly to fear the cutting of her throat.

This was a fortnight after Theodore's wedding to Mary Balls. If there was a honeymoon, it was well and truly over.

Another who warned Cecil about the earl's new man was Thomas, Lord Grey de Wilton. Related to both the Clinton and Norreys families, Grey had had ample opportunity to gain insight into Paleologus's character while both were serving with the Dutch forces. Grey was welcome in Prince Maurice's circle; indeed, in the same month the suspicions over the countess's safety came to a head, he returned to the Low Countries and in July that year was to be wounded fighting under Maurice's command at the Battle of Nieuport, a decisive victory over the Spanish.

Clearly Cecil was moved to action. A fortnight after Francis Norreys's plea came a letter from Lady Bridget, widow of one of Lord Norreys's soldier sons, offering 'many thanks for your favours showed lately to my Lady Lincoln, by whose good means I did well hope that she should have been released of her long bondage'. But Lady Bridget goes on to say the earl is still refusing to allow the countess to see her son, 'wherefore my earnest suit to you is that you would once again entreat this unkind lord that he would, in regard of her health and the necessity she hath to take physic, give her leave to come and lie at Chelsey for a time, for where she is no physician may come to her'.

But the threat of her murder at Paleologus's hands had been lifted. The countess may have remained a virtual prisoner at Tattershall, but even a man as deranged as Lincoln realised that her elimination was out of the question once the alarm had been raised with the all-powerful Robert Cecil.

Time and again in this story the threads lead to Cecil. Nearly all our chief players write to him, or are the subject of others' letters, or both. Many are related to him in one way or another; all depend on his good will. His correspondents seek favours, lay accusations, make excuses; they request a loan, licence or preferment; they beg his intercession with the queen; more often than not they relate a juicy item of tittle-tattle, for nothing is beneath Mr Secretary's attention. He is the supreme fixer of the age and his good offices are sought as an intermediary, apologist, financier or matchmaker. Rarely does a correspondent fail to offer some gift, a horse or falcon, venison or game birds.

Every petition reinforces the popular image of this deformed little man as a black spider in the middle of a twitching web. Those dark hooded eyes take in all but give little away. His influence reaches into every matter of state, domestic and foreign, and creeps into every corner of English society. All the business of the realm passes over his desk. And from around this period there are Scotland's affairs too, for Cecil, intent on being king-maker when his mistress dies, is in secret correspondence with James Stuart. At the same time he controls the spy network founded by Burghley, which after refinement at his hands is the most formidable in Europe: there are Cecil agents as far away as Moscow and Constantinople. No one is ever entirely trusted by *Robertus Diabolus*, as the Spanish call him: even as his father lay dying, Cecil slipped a spy into his household.

The puzzling forbearance which marks many of Cecil's dealings with Lincoln up to this time, and the blind eye turned to innumerable misdeeds of the peer, may have a simple explanation, and Lady Bridget's reference to Chelsea is the clue. Cecil and Lincoln had been engaged in long-drawn-out negotiations over the sale of Cecil's house in Chelsea left to him by Lord Burghley. Embarrassed by the financial strain of his other properties, especially the ruinously expensive Theobalds in Hertfordshire, Cecil needed to dispose of the Chelsea estate at the highest price possible, while Lincoln, himself hugely in debt, was predictably resolved to drive a hard bargain.

The handsome riverside Chelsea mansion had once belonged to Sir Thomas More, Henry VIII's lord chancellor, and following More's execution in 1535 went to a succession of royal favourites, ending up in Burghley's hands in 1594. Robert Cecil, having finally sold the house to Lincoln in 1599 for £6,000 with £500 down, was now experiencing great difficulty in extracting further payments from the earl.

Lincoln had proved a dogged haggler, making a last-minute threat to withdraw from the sale unless Cecil threw in various furnishings including a table, carpet, curtains and the tapestries in the great chamber. He even quibbled about a particular cushion. Under the terms of the sale, the property was acquired jointly with his son-in-law, Sir Arthur Gorges, as the major part of the dowry of Lincoln's only daughter Elizabeth, with the earl reserving a life interest. The ink was hardly dry on the agreement before the old crook reneged on the bargain, first trying to claim the property rightfully belonged to his younger son Edward and then declaring it had to be sold to pay off his own debts.

The son-in-law's frustration and indignation bubbles over in a letter to Sir Robert in September 1600 in which he brands the earl a compulsive liar:

> None can testify my careful zeal towards this ungrateful miser than you, whom I have so often solicited with excusing his vices. The love I bore his daughter made me do so, and his cankered disposition requites me accordingly … He has already brought my poor wife to her grave, as I fear, with his late most odious and unnatural despites that he has used towards her, the most obedient child in the world … I disclaim from all his favours, since he had wrought the destruction of my wife.[47]

Arthur Gorges was a much admired poet, and the poet expresses himself here with poetic licence. Lady Gorges may well have been in great distress over her father's behaviour but she was not in fact dead or dying. Indeed Elizabeth Gorges would outlive father and husband, dying in 1643 after bearing Sir Arthur twelve children.

The Chelsea house is interesting in providing a glimpse into other interiors Theodore Paleologus would have known well. The famous Holbein drawing of Sir Thomas More and his extended family was made here, and though the property was remodelled by later owners the painted versions of the portrait give us an impression of its size and sober distinction. Holbein himself called it dignified without being ostentatious. Contemporary accounts describe a rose-brick frontage of some 164 feet; a fine entrance porch opened to a screens passage and beyond it to a great hall more than seventy feet in length, rising to a beamed and timbered roof. The best-known version of the More portrait shows an interior canopied porch and diamond-latticed window. A covered gallery with oriel windows looked down into the hall, and among other admired rooms were Sir Thomas's library and private chapel.

In this setting, the creation of one of English history's great names, the Earl of Lincoln continued to plot his squalid exploits, and his occupancy of the house turns into yet another unedifying chapter in the story. Falling out with one of his new neighbours, he had a stinking load of night-soil dumped on a wharf close by to cause the maximum annoyance. With this as with other schemes, one wonders whether his gentleman rider was called on to play an active role or was allowed to be a nose-holding bystander. But as we shall see in the next chapter, Lincoln's most notorious deed at Chelsea was yet to come, and it would have confronted Paleologus with the inescapable truth that the earl's patronage wrecked any chance of ingratiating himself in courtly circles.

But at least the countess was no longer at risk once Robert Cecil was alert to the danger. Cecil had finally rounded on the earl in earnest because of the strengthening fears over Lady Lincoln's plight, and this almost certainly saved the poor woman's life.

One benefit was that this now left Paleologus free to concentrate on his official role with close control over the countess passing to lesser retainers. Lady Lincoln was to survive a further unhappy eleven years, though never escaping her husband's merciless grip. There are no apparent grounds for attributing her death to unnatural causes but as soon as she was buried the earl would bring a suit against his stepson Francis, who had since succeeded to his grandfather's title of Baron Norreys of Rycote. Lincoln alleged his dead wife had misappropriated his property for the benefit of her first husband's son. This, however, like so many of his lawsuits, was to end in cripplingly expensive failure.

Chancery archives concerning the earl's lawsuit against Norreys record the testimony of witness after witness describing the treatment meted out to Lady Lincoln. A typical deposition is that of William Hatt, yeoman, aged fifty, who stated that 'he being at a house or castle of the earl of Lincoln in Lincolnshire with the late countess did perceive that the bailiffs, officers and servants of the earl had more command in and over the house and goods of the earl than the countess had, and did take her up short as that she had been a mean and single woman'.[48]

William Smith, yeoman, aged thirty-two, similarly deposed that Lady Lincoln 'was oftentimes in want and necessity' and that the earl refused her 'such allowance and livelihood, or such command, or authority over his house and estate as did beseem the estate, degree and calling of an earl's wife'. Smith saw the castle bailiffs, servants and officers treat the countess 'as saucily and boldly as if she had been their fellow, or rather some simple servant'.

A gentleman in Lady Bedford's service, Edmund Stanton, swore that the late countess never used the earl's wealth to help her first husband's children or anyone else. On the contrary, Lord Lincoln had taken from the countess 'her rents and the fines of jointure left to her by William Norreys, esquire, her former husband', depriving her for the rest of her life.

None of the earl's retainers is named in these depositions, but it is difficult not to implicate Theodore Paleologus in the campaign of humiliation waged against the countess. Only Francis Norreys deliberately points his finger at the gentleman rider: though he does not accuse Theodore by name, there is no record of any other Italian in the earl's employ at this or any other any time, let alone one of a murderous reputation. But it is only fair to Paleologus to note that the second Lord Norreys led a troubled life and it is conceivable that his mental state steered him towards an exaggerated view of the dangers facing his mother during her incarceration.

Described by contemporaries as 'of a melancholy humour', Francis Norreys was married in 1599 to Lady Bridget de Vere, daughter of the seventeenth earl of Oxford – the poet-peer who has been claimed as the true author of the works of Shakespeare – and a granddaughter of Lord Burghley. Coincidentally, Lord Willoughy de Eresby was himself unhappily married to Lady Mary de Vere, sister of the earl of Oxford. The couple separated four years later with Norreys disclaiming paternity of her only child, a daughter called Elizabeth. It is also of note that he was a sworn enemy of the earl's allies, the Willoughbys. He quarrelled repeatedly with Peregrine Bertie, younger son of Lord Willoughby, wounding him badly in a duel in 1610, and the two had to be parted when about to fight again in 1613. In 1615 an affray in a churchyard resulted in a verdict of manslaughter against Norreys for slaying a Willoughby servant.

However, killing an inferior was not regarded as gravely as an incident in 1621 when Norreys was sent to the Fleet for jostling a fellow peer in the presence of the Prince of Wales, the future Charles I. This occurred shortly after Norreys had been raised to the earldom of Berkshire, one of the prodigal scattering of titles by King James, who during his reign more than doubled the number of English earls. This, however, paled beside his reckless creation of knights, beginning with forty-six gentlemen being dubbed before breakfast during James's halt at Belvoir Castle in 1603, when he travelled down from Scotland to claim the crown. Francis Norreys enjoyed his new dignity as earl for just a year and a day before committing suicide by the eccentric method of shooting himself with a crossbow.

There is a curious postscript to this story. Norreys failed in his efforts to have his daughter declared a bastard, largely because well-placed figures like Robert Cecil, the wife's uncle, were determined to avert a major scandal. So Elizabeth Norreys went on to inherit the barony of Norreys and passed the title down to her only daughter. This Lady Norreys married Montagu Bertie, fifteenth Lord Willoughby de Eresby, thus carrying Francis Norreys's barony to his sworn enemy's descendants, along with the bitterly contested manor of Weston-on-the-Green.[49]

# *10*

For greatest scandal waits on greatest state.

Shakespeare, *The Comedy of Errors*.

We now come to an affair which, in the eyes of Elizabethan society, would have dwarfed every other outrage committed by the Earl of Lincoln.

To entertain the queen at home was one of the greatest honours a subject might aspire to, though a hugely expensive one. Arriving with a large retinue of hungry and thirsty courtiers, Elizabeth would expect lavish gifts served up with elegant play-acting and a round of pretty, flattering speeches. Rich men had ruined themselves hosting the queen on her many progresses. On a visit to Lord and Lady Norreys in 1592, for instance, she had been treated to an elaborate play in the course of which actors presented her with weapons of gold set with diamonds and rubies, for allegorical use against her enemies in Ireland, France and Spain, and a jewel-studded key to the gates of Ostend. In approved manner, these extravagant gifts were offered apologetically as 'trifles'.

No one should seriously have expected the miserly Lincoln to live up to such standards, but what happened in April 1601 shocked Elizabethans to the core. Faced with a home visit from the queen, Earl Henry did a bunk, leaving the dumbfounded monarch to knock in vain outside his new Chelsea mansion as he galloped off north to Tattershall Castle. It is most likely his gentleman of horse rode beside him; since Cecil's intervention over the countess, it was impossible to ask Paleologus to exercise his deadly talents.

We can picture the scene at Chelsea from the graphic account contained in a letter of admonishment sent to Lord Lincoln on 30 April in the joint names of Robert Cecil and the Earl of Nottingham, horrified witnesses of the fiasco. Though ostensibly from both, the letter was undoubtedly dictated by Mr Secretary:

> Such has been the mischance and great folly of your servants at Chelsey, as when her Majesty did lately ride abroad and was accompanied by the Scottish Ambassador, she was desirous to have gone into your house and gardens, from where she was kept out in so rude a fashion as we protest unto you your enemies wanted no colour to say it was by your direction.[50]

Despite 'a great knocking at both gates', the earl's servants not only failed to open up but were glimpsed by the royal party furtively peering out from windows of the house. 'These things did not a little trouble the Queen,' Cecil continues, 'though she would make no speech of it then, but we have found it since so suspiciously to move in her as she did almost seem to take it to be done of purpose.' Cecil and Nottingham tried to persuade the queen there had been some unfortunate mistake or misunderstanding on the earl's part, 'out of our care that she did not in any public place speak disgracefully of you'. They fibbed that Lincoln had actually been eagerly looking forward to entertaining the royal party and would be mortified at accidentally missing her.

Seeing Elizabeth disinclined to believe this story, Cecil upped the ante:

> Rather than fail, we durst undertake that you (in token of how much you despised the matter of charge) would be contented to make us your stewards for a dinner and anything that belongs to it. Of this your offer, her Majesty hath spoken since with very great contentment and honour of you (whereof although you will say, you are not like to taste benefit) yet we are sure that your good judgment serves you, that it cannot be good for you (who have so many enemies) that the world should conceive that her Majesty had an ill conceit of you.

The queen was indeed incandescent at the loss of face witnessed by King James's ambassador, and insisted the promised dinner should be enjoyed before his departure for Scotland, or as Mr Secretary put it, 'that he (for these were her words) that saw her kept out, may see her also let in ... and so on Saturday next her Majesty will dine there'.

The earl may have been impervious to Cecil's sarcasm – 'how much you despised the matter of charge' – but the next passage of the letter must have caused such a groan of anguish as rarely ever heard at Tattershall: 'We will moderate expenses as if it were for ourselves, and we will also find out some present, such as we presume you will not think too much.' As Lincoln knew well, Cecil and Nottingham never stinted on their banquets and gifts for the sovereign. In other words, by trying to evade a fairly hefty bill for entertaining the queen, the hapless earl had landed himself with a colossal one.

That Lincoln's letter in response is dated 2 May, only two days later, indicates the paramount importance Cecil attached to the scandal. The horseback journey usually took a full three days, so his messenger must have ridden hell for leather all the way from Whitehall to Tattershall and back.

Predictably, the earl's confused, rambling reply seeks to blame anyone but himself. He laments the fact that the behaviour of his foolish, rude and base servants has gladdened the hearts of his enemies and protests that he has ever been willing to lose his life to serve her majesty, 'notwithstanding my old and sickly years'. He pleads 'what care I took to prepare for her Majesty's coming' while admitting he had left before her arrival as he was late for the assizes, 'to my great loss and hindrance' – presumably a reference to another of his unsuccessful legal actions. He ends with a dig at never receiving 'great favours and graces' from the queen which so many other nobles enjoyed, and signs off pathetically with the line: 'Always ready to honour and obey you as far as my pressed down estate will suffer, as knows the living Lord.'

For Robert Cecil, any lingering sense of obligation to Lincoln had disappeared by this time, and he may well have felt some kind of vicarious responsibility as the former owner of the house from which the queen had been so humiliatingly excluded. This was a particularly sensitive time for Elizabeth, just weeks after the trial and execution of her former favourite

Essex. He was also exasperated by the earl's repeated failure to keep up payments on the property. Evidently he wrote another stinging letter in response to the earl's excuses, for before the month was out Lincoln was writing again to complain of 'bitter threats' made against him by Cecil.

His letter said: 'Since I have always carried to dutiful heart to her [the queen] and testified it many ways, and that you have had proof of my love to you more than to others; the wrongs now offered by you are greater than my tongue or pen can or dare express.' He moans of the many thousands he is in debt to the queen, Cecil and others, 'besides the money which I lay in prison for'. The charges against him, he claims, 'by general report amounteth to as much as seven noblemen's subsidies, with disgraceful terms unworthily applied'.

The paper was endorsed by Cecil's private secretary: 'The Earl of Lincoln to my master. A desperate letter.'

Desperate indeed, but that did not stop Cecil writing back in withering terms. He was prepared to make a kingly present, he declared, to 'whosoever will bring me the man that had ever power to persuade you to do anything but for your own lucre'.

It was now, when the earl had forfeited the friendship of the most powerful man in the kingdom, that closer to home the long-standing feud with the Dymokes was approaching its climax. At the same time the bishop of Lincoln was joining in the chorus of complaint against Earl Henry. As lay impropriator of Sempringham and four other neighbouring parishes, the earl received their great tithes and was therefore responsible for repairs to the church chancels, but the bishop's commissaries reported a depressingly familiar story: all five churches were ruinous or in great decay 'through the default of the earl of Lincoln'.[51]

# 11

Rustically solemn or in rustic laughter
Lifting heavy feet in clumsy shoes,
Earth feet, loam feet, lifting in country mirth …

T.S. Eliot, *Four Quartets*: 'East Coker'.

County elites were used to maintaining the queen's peace through-out the realm by exploiting family ties and by a collective control of magistracy, militia and parliamentary seats. This order was seriously threatened in Lincolnshire for around twenty years because of the strife between Lincoln and the Dymoke affinity, for few of the aristocracy or gentry could avoid being embroiled in the feud at some point or other. Lord Willoughby's success in staying relatively aloof was no doubt helped by his long absences abroad.

Sir Edward Dymoke headed a distinguished family with extensive estates throughout Lincolnshire. His mother was a daughter of the first Earl of Lincoln, making Earl Henry his uncle. The Dymokes held the hereditary dignity of king's champion whose function was to ride in full armour into Westminster Hall during a coronation banquet and chal-lenge all comers to dispute the king's title. The head of the family had performed this duty since the fourteenth century. Edward's grandfather had issued the challenge at the crowning of Henry VIII, and he himself would fling down the gauntlet at the coronation of James I.

As a long-serving knight of the shire, Dymoke was a stalwart of Protestantism in parliament, all the more anxious to stress his anti-Catholic credentials as his father had died in Lincoln Gaol as an alleged recusant. The Earl of Lincoln frequently sought to exploit this background, accusing his enemy of 'the secret practices of these cun-ning papists'. Parliamentary records show Sir Edward Dymoke as a conscientious and hard-working member, noted particularly for his attention to resident aliens who engaged in business against the interests of English traders. He was counted among the wealthiest men in the county until the last phase of the desperate clash with Lincoln brought him to the brink of ruin.

The origin of the feud is uncertain, though considering the earl's insatiable lust for property it may well have started with a sense of grievance over the Dymokes' ownership of the manors of North and South Kyme, a short distance from Tattershall Castle. These had come to Sir Edward through his grandfather's marriage to Anne Talboys, sister and heiress of Gilbert, Lord Talboys of Kyme. Lord Talboys was the first husband of Bessie Blount, the cast-off royal mistress who went on to marry the first Earl of Lincoln. Given the second earl's unconventional theories on inheritance, it is more than likely he convinced himself these manors were rightfully his. As we shall see, Lincoln's particular bête noire was Sir Edward's younger brother Talboys Dymoke, named in honour of the family's benefactor.

The notion of Morris dancers as dangerous libertines sounds charmingly preposterous to the modern ear, but to the Puritan faction of Elizabethan and Jacobean times the traditional rustic pleasures of the Morris, maypole-dancing, football, hobby-horses and the like were clear incitements to drunkenness and lust or else harked back to popish superstition. Bitter divisions rose throughout England over incessant moves by the evangelical clergy and their sympathisers to abolish celebrations such as May Day and Midsummer Day. In the 1580s Sir Francis Walsingham and the bishop of Lincoln had eagerly backed the city mayor's ban on May games, maypoles and Sunday trading, only to see all restored by the mayor's successor.

Typical of Lincolnshire Puritans was John Vicars, minister at Stamford St Mary in Jacobean times, who regularly harangued those depraved members of his congregation known to frequent inns and flock to stage plays 'accompanied with painted Jezabels and whorish Delilahs'. On the opposite side locally were the likes of Robert Sanderson, rector of Boothby Pagnell and a celebrated sermoniser, who could have had this same John Vicars in mind when he wrote: 'We know not how far a sanctified believer may fall into the snares of sin, nor how far a graceless hypocrite may go in the show of godliness.' And the rift went right to the top. A Privy Council vote of 1589 to make maypole-dancing unlawful was over-ruled by Elizabeth herself, an example of her instinctive support for tradition. Her Archbishop of Canterbury, the Lincolnshire man John Whitgift, was another stout defender of the old ways.

One might expect an out-and-out Puritan like Walsingham, generally characterised as a humourless figure of morbid religiosity, to be an enemy of the country delights symbolised by the maypole, yet great courtiers like the Dudleys and Sidneys – notable for conspicuous extravagance and self-indulgence – were leading patrons of the Puritan clergy. They found no difficulty in drawing a line between their own entertainments and the merrymaking of lesser folk. With the social, religious and political changes wrought by the Reformation, the new English establishment was constantly discovering reasons to outlaw boisterous seasonal pastimes, especially those which encouraged a degree of disorder or disrespect of their betters, as exemplified by mock kings and queens, boy bishops, Robin Hood plays and lords of misrule.

The Elizabethan historian John Stow wrote wistfully of times not long gone when a lord of misrule was to be found 'in the house of every nobleman of honour or good worship, be he spiritual or temporal', a tradition encouraged at the royal court. But to the zealot these figures were dangerous agents of Catholic worship and sedition and the Morris was 'the Devil's Dance'. In his *Dialogue against Light, Lewd and Lascivious Dauncing*, published in 1582, the ardent reformer Christopher Fetherston railed against Morris men, football on Sunday and May games, and reported breathlessly on 'ten maidens which went to set May, and nine of them came home with child'. Anyone seeking salacious details of Elizabethan times should start with the books of the godly.

Theodore Paleologus, observing the bucolic customs of his adopted country for the first time, would have found little strange about the English maypole dance in which participants interweave coloured ribbons, as its origin was in Mediterranean lands. But the notorious events of the May Day games of 1601, in a group of towns and villages dotted around Tattershall, must have opened his eyes to a midsummer madness of a distinctly English kind, and – if he still harboured the slightest doubt in the matter – to the almost universal hatred felt for his noble patron. As an Italian he knew all about the dynamics of the blood feud, and it is certain that the earl would have called upon Paleologus's talents during the course of a vendetta which reached its climax soon after his arrival at the castle. As we shall see, this was a critical time for his employer, with the sudden calamity of the queen's visit to Chelsea overshadowing his trials in rural Lincolnshire.

This was a particularly bad spell for the Earl of Lincoln. We have seen how he had been committed to gaol for the second time in June 1600. This was after Star Chamber heard a new litany of complaints against him from a Lincolnshire gentleman called Henry Ayscough, a cousin of the Dymoke brothers. Lincoln had refused to obey an order to pay Ayscough damages of £760, plus awards to other litigants, and went into hiding. Apprehended the following month, he refused to pay the fees owing to the arresting officer. While still at large he had picked another almighty quarrel with his son-in-law Sir Arthur Gorges, with each denouncing the other as a damnable liar. The earl claimed Gorges had advised him to commit suicide, an accusation furiously denied.

More family trouble surfaced in November 1600 when the earl was denounced by his younger brother. Thomas Clinton complained to Cecil about 'the extreme dealings of his unnatural brother' who had cheated him out of his inheritance from their father.

The South Kyme troubles of 1601 centred on what was known as the Summer Lord Game. This was a comic play or pageant featuring a local incarnation of the Lord of Misrule. Performed in that part of Lincolnshire from time immemorial as the climax of summer revels, it was staged between 1 May and the end of summer and was teasingly anarchic or subversive in tone. A similar entertainment is the theme of Thomas Nashe's play *Summer's Last Will and Testament*, first performed in the early 1590s in the household of Archbishop Whitgift, and Shakespeare draws on the same tradition in comedies like *Twelfth Night*.

Lord Lincoln was a deep-dyed Puritan, at least in the popular sense of being a hypocrite and killjoy, and no one was less likely to turn a blind eye to merrymakers of the lower orders poking fun at their superior 'with scoffs, jests, wanton gestures, or ribald talk', as he saw it. To the earl's mind, a playful challenge to his power might easily turn into an insurrection in earnest, and this was what made a play performed by 'the vulgar people' that summer at South Kyme, a village a few miles from his castle, an intolerable insult. Worse, a satire upon him on the stage was orchestrated by his sworn enemies the Dymokes. In his own bill of complaint to Star Chamber, the earl would accuse the brothers of 'disgraceful, false, and intolerable slanders, reproaches, scandalous words, libels, and irreligious profanations'.

The renewed conflict with the Dymokes can be traced back to the August of 1599 when a mounted company of Sir Edward's retainers stopped outside a 'tipplinge house' in Tattershall and called out for drink. Their leader was Sir Edward's unmarried brother, a minor poet, would-be author and general mischief-maker named Talboys Dymoke – 'being a man of verie disordered and a most dysolute behaviour and condicion,' according to later testimony of the earl. But though undeniably a hothead, Talboys was no stripling, being well over forty at the time.

Flirting with the landlord's wife Anne, Talboys called out in a loud voice: 'Commend me, sweetharte, to my Lorde of Lincoln, and tell him that he is an Asse and a fool.'[52] Further merriment followed at the earl's expense, there in the very shadow of the castle. Anne's husband, William Hollingshead, scurried off to report the offence.

This Hollingshead had his own axe to grind. Before taking on the ale-house he had been a gaoler at Lincoln – infamous for starving inmates to death during the earl's watch – and chief constable at Horncastle, a town where the earl and the Dymokes vied for mastery. In 1593 Sir Edward had accused Hollingshead of taking bribes, falsifying tax accounts and maliciously charging an innocent man with theft.

The Clinton ascendency in these parts dated from the first earl's marriage to Bessie Blount, when part of the Talboys inheritance fell into his lap. Nothing had happened since to endear the dynasty to the locals, and with the Dymoke faction enjoying greater public sympathy, Earl Henry had by this time bolstered his fighting force of tenants by recruiting outsiders at the rate of a shilling a day – over £50 in today's money. This is why it must have been a heaven-sent opportunity to the earl, smarting from the Dymokes' merriment at his expense, to acquire the services of Theodore Paleologus.

The South Kyme games of 1601 began as customary on 1 May, the first anniversary of Paleologus's marriage to Mary Balls. The date is noteworthy because of what was to occur in distant Chelsea shortly after this time, causing the earl to flee to Tattershall. Hostilities flared again between supporters of the two parties at Coningsby, the neighbouring village to Tattershall, on a Sunday in late July. The flashpoint came when about a dozen men led by Talboys Dymoke rode into Coningsby 'to be merry' at an alehouse with villagers who had joined in games at South Kyme a fortnight before.

These Dymoke men brought with them a number of theatrical props used in the games including a drum, flag and toy spears and 'did march on horseback two and two together through the streets' while their Coningsby friends added to the racket with a drum of their own. According to their later sworn evidence, 'there were not above two swords amongst them' or, in the words of one of the accused, they had 'no warlike weapons but only some daggers'. While denying 'they had drunk the town of Coningsby dry', the visiting party accepted they had patronised three or four alehouses.

Just as the revellers were leaving the last alehouse for home, the retinue of the Earl of Lincoln happened to ride through Coningsby and was obliged to pass this merry company in a narrow lane. The visitors then 'behaved themselves very rudely, with shoutings, noises … that some accompted them to be madmen,' according to the testimony of Thomas Pigott, gentleman, a companion of the peer. Pigott was sent to entreat them not to scare the earl's horse, whereupon Talboys Dymoke gleefully called for the drummers to strike up. As gentleman rider, Paleologus would have been at the earl's side, alert to any threat to his master.

A reluctant witness, the innkeeper Edward Miles, said he saw Mr Pigott cast down from his horse, 'but by what means he knoweth not, neither what hurt he had'.[53] Pigott himself declared that when he delivered the earl's message, Talboys and others of his party 'answered with great oaths that they had a Lord as good as he, and called the company and drums to them back again, and cried aloud, "Strike up drums! Strike up drums!"' Drummers and flag bearers then ran at the earl's man, 'and the whole company after and amongst them in such violent sort, that his horse did fling and plunge, and the more he entreated them to be quiet, the more fierce and angry they were ... insomuch as his horse cast him to the ground to his great bruising, hurt, and damage, being a heavy, corpulent man'.

Pigott heard cries of 'Strike him down! Knock him down!' as an acquaintance helped him to his feet. In the meantime the earl 'did make haste away from the company homewards, and the disorderly company followed and pursued him a good pace'. No other member of the earl's retinue is named in the record, but Paleologus would have been responsible for hustling Lincoln away from the scene of danger. Pigott informed the Star Chamber the incident 'had like to cost him his life; and he was forced to keep to his bed a good space after, and to take physic for the same'.

According to another witness, the earl did not ride off to his castle but returned to the scene with a constable, ordering him to arrest Talboys Dymoke and his henchmen. A scuffle with brandished swords ensued in the churchyard, though seemingly without bloodshed. Dymoke forbad his followers to go to the castle and appear before the earl as demanded by the constable. From the confused evidence presented later in Star Chamber it appears that this hapless constable, caught between the warring bigwigs, allowed the affair to fizzle out without conclusion beyond the confiscation of the drum. But as so often with records dating back four centuries or more, incomplete documents leave questions hanging in the air. It is unclear whether the earl was still excluded as a justice of the peace at this date, but if so Talboys was certainly within his rights to ignore a summons issued without lawful foundation.

Even as these scenes were played out at Coningsby, a new cause of conflict arose between followers of the earl and Sir Edward Dymoke at the market town of Horncastle, nine miles from Tattershall. Famous for its horse fair, it had been a centre of Dymoke influence for 200 years or more. At Horncastle, alleged Lord Lincoln, 'Sir Edward had unlaw-fully and riotously, by such as he had thereunto appointed ... made entry into the parsonage house there', claiming various rights the earl declared belonged to him. There is something ironic about these expressions of outrage from a serial invader of other people's property, but this did not prevent the earl adding the Horncastle incident to his suit against the Dymokes for riot and unlawful assembly. However, lawsuits over Horncastle were to end with a court order confirming Sir Edward as in lawful possession of the manor.

Horncastle had already been the scene of two unseemly episodes in this epic feud. The first was when the earl called a petty sessions meeting which culminated in the arrest of Sir Edward and seven of his men for disturbing the peace. Lincoln then sat on the bench with his younger son, who remained loyal despite many indignities heaped upon him, the pair of them 'outfacing and appalling the jury'. The earl 'gave Sir Edward the lie thrice and told him he was in a mad fit, with other most foul and opprobrious words not befitting that place'. When the jury retired to consider their verdict, the two parties clashed at an inn with Lincoln pulling one adversary by the beard and his son wounding another with his rapier while attempting to kill Sir Edward.

In a later scene, two Lincoln supporters summoned a private ses-sions under a pretext, then indicted Dymoke servants for riotous assault. The earl packed the jury with his own men, selecting as foreman an indi-vidual who was locked in a lawsuit against Sir Edward. The knight foiled the plot by arriving with two friendly justices who insisted on joining the bench and the sessions ended in a bloody riot with the rival Justices of the Peace at each other's throats.

The troubles came to a head five weeks later, on the last Sunday in August, when a dramatised 'death of the Lord of Kyme' − a thinly dis-guised Earl of Lincoln − was performed on a makeshift stage at South Kyme, 'hard by the maypole standing upon the green'. Sir Edward had moved to the manor house there six years previously after the earl's pri-vate army forced him out of Scrivelsby Court, the Dymoke ancestral pile near Horncastle. Neighbours were invited to feast on venison at the home of a servant of Sir Edward, one John Cradock the elder, yeoman, whose son John the younger was that year's summer lord. On offer was a surprise entertainment to mark the end of the revels. According to the earl's suit, Talboys Dymoke was the author and principal actor of this play, aided and abetted by South Kyme villagers who had been involved in the earlier fracas at Coningsby. According to one witness, about 100 men, women and children assembled on the green immediately after evening prayers at the parish church, though another witness spoke of 300–400. Stools and cushions were set for the guests of honour, Sir Edward Dymoke and his lady, though witnesses later denied they were present.

What happened next showed how the amateur playwright Talboys had appropriated the Summer Lord Game to strike at Lincoln. He began by 'counterfeiting the person' of the peer and mimicking 'his speeches and gesture', then 'termed and named the earl of Lincoln, his good uncle, in scornful manner' until he was dragged offstage by a villager acting the part of the Devil. In a later scene, which was largely in verse, the same man reappeared in the role of the Fool and read out his last will and testament, bequeathing his wooden dagger to the earl and 'his coxcomb and bauble' to any who refused to follow Sir Edward Dymoke to Horncastle to confront his foe. In the interval there was 'a dirge sung by Talboys Dymoke and others' in which they referred by name to 'most of the known lewd and licentious women in the cities of London and Lincoln and town of Boston, concluding in their songs after every one of the names, *ora pro nobis*'.[54]

As this book devotes much space to the sins of Earl Henry, it is fair to draw attention to what might be a rare virtue. This was an age when the great openly acknowledged mistresses and bastards, but during my researches I have found no hint of sexual laxity on Lord Lincoln's part, unless – and this is by no means clear – the roll-call of loose women in Talboys's script is a personal dig at his uncle. The one exception is the mention of a bastard daughter born prior to his first marriage, though only one source refers to her in passing and gives no further detail. This matter apart, the earl's interest in women appears to be exclusively focused on their ownership of property, real or supposed, and familiarity with local ladies of easy virtue fits more easily with what we deduce of Talboys Dymoke. A later libellous document allegedly published by Dymoke refers to the earl's heir Lord Clinton as a 'cuckold and brat, bastard, son of a whore'[55] along with other choice insults, but it is notable that no aspersions of this kind are cast at the earl himself.

If Talboys counted on popular hatred preventing the play from coming to the earl's attention, he was badly mistaken, and this was to have dire consequences for the Dymoke clan. Retainers of Lincoln got wind of the promised performance and a few infiltrated the crowd on the village green. When the play was over, the party hurried back to Tattershall to report to their master. According to some witnesses, Sir Edward only heard about the satire on the earl some time afterwards and then 'did with grief bitterly reprove and check Talboys for the doing thereof'.

In the complaint to Star Chamber dated 23 November 1601, Lincoln predictably concentrates on the outrage to his dignity by the lower orders. The queen and her ancestors, he says, 'have ever had a gracious regard of the honour and estate of the nobility and peers of this your highness's realm, and men of more inferior condition to them have carried such respective and due observance to the nobles of this kingdom, as they have not once presumed to scandalise or deprave there persons and place by public frowns and reproaches'. How was it then that 'one Talboys Dymoke, a common contriver and publisher of infamous pamphlets and libels … by the direction, consent or allowance of Sir Edward Dymoke of Kyme, knight', had committed these intolerable offences?

Yet when the case came before Star Chamber, what sealed the Dymokes' fate was not so much the lese-majesty suffered by a noble as the disrespect shown to the great shibboleth of the age, the Protestant religion. For after the make-believe earl had been carried off by the Devil, a mock funeral service was conducted by John Cradock senior in the role of a tipsy clergyman. As told by one of the informers, 'In frown of religion, and the profession thereof, being attired in a minister's gown and having a corner cap on his head, and a book in his hand opened', the Dymokes' bailiff mounted a pulpit next to the maypole and delivered 'a profane and irreligious prayer'. A pot of ale hung beside him in place of an hourglass, 'whereof he did drink at the concluding of any point or part of his speech'.

The sermon began with a burlesque prayer for the departed earl:

*Now blessed be his body and his bones;*
*I hope his legs are hotter than gravestones,*
*And to that hope let's all conclude it then,*
*Both men and women pray, and say, 'Amen'.*

All that survives of the manuscript is a few remembered scraps like this given in evidence, mostly by hostile witnesses. There is nothing here to suggest that a successful future beckoned for Talboys in the professional theatre. Much of the sermon was in cod Latin which must have mystified the rustic audience, and the most striking lines quoted in court was another spoof prayer – 'The mercy of Mustard-seed and the blessing of Bull-beef and the peace of Pot-luck be with you all. Amen' – and a passing reference to 'the story of Mab'.

Students of Shakespeare may sit up at the mention of Mustard-seed and Mab. *A Midsummer Night's Dream*, in which Titania orders her fairy Mustard-seed to attend on Bottom, was written about 1595 and first printed in quarto in 1600, a year before these events at South Kyme; the first recorded mention of Queen Mab, 'the fairies' midwife', occurs in *Romeo and Juliet*, also written around 1595 and printed two years later. This suggests that Talboys Dymoke enjoyed early performances of these great plays during visits to London, whether at The Theatre,where the troupe then called the Lord Chamberlain's Men took to the public stage for the first time, or at The Globe itself, which had opened as recently as 1599. Or did the aspiring playwright carry home to South Kyme some of Shakespeare's earliest published works? Either possibility might account for an admirer of the most successful dramatist of the day borrowing these names for his own composition.

Shakespeare himself was not above taking revenge of the kind aimed at the earl. Though cruder and more malevolent, Talboys Dymoke's piece compares with the lampoon of Sir Thomas Lucy, the Warwickshire landowner who by tradition prosecuted the young bard for poaching, as the absurd Justice Shallow in *Henry IV Part Two* and *The Merry Wives of Windsor*.

The mischief did not end at South Kyme. Talboys penned a scurrilous rhyme mocking the earl and his son Lord Clinton which he subsequently nailed up in the towns of Sleaford and Louth, and scandalised the congregation at Billingborough, another village close to Tattershall, where he interrupted the preacher in the pulpit by calling out: 'Why dost thou not pray for the good earl of Lincoln? He hath as much need to be prayed for as any other.'

The earl was to enjoy a last triumph. The Star Chamber suit against the Dymokes was to drag on till 1610, when Lincoln obtained a rare legal verdict in his favour, though the wording of the judgement indicates that the severe sentences handed down owed more to the 'frown of religion' than to the libel against the earl. Talboys Dymoke, principal cause of all the trouble, was by this time beyond the judges' reach – in what circumstances he died we do not know, but he was buried at Horncastle only a year after the notorious South Kyme games – and retribution fell on his brother Sir Edward and the lesser fry. Their defence that everything had been done 'in the merriment at the time of the May game' was dismissed out of hand.

The bailiff John Cradock and two other chief actors in the play were hauled off to London and committed to Fleet prison, paraded through Westminster Hall 'with papers' – that is, having signs around their necks naming their crimes – before being pilloried and whipped. They were then dispatched to the assizes in Lincoln where they were again set in the pillory, whipped and required to acknowledge their offences and to beg forgiveness of 'God and the earl'. They were also fined £300 apiece, a ruinous sum for common men, and bound to good behaviour before release. As a gentleman Sir Edward escaped the degradation of physical punishment but was committed to the Fleet during the pleasure of the monarch, by this time King James. His fine of £1,000 began a permanent decline in the Dymoke fortunes, a course confirmed during the Civil War by hardships suffered for loyalty to the royal cause.

The judgement signalled a growing intolerance of festive licence as the Tudor era ended. Star Chamber's role under the Stuarts was as an instrument of tyranny. The increasingly assertive demands for religious conformity sounded the knell for a tradition which had remained virtually unchanged for centuries but would be entirely erased during the Commonwealth. The South Kyme game might be seen as a last hurrah for Merry England.

✤

The early years of the new century witnessed repeated reverses for the earl. As a high-ranking peer, however, he was still called upon to perform official duties, and in February 1601 he was summoned to Westminster Hall for the indictment of the Earl of Essex. A witness of the trial, the French ambassador de Boissie, reported home to his master Henri IV with a biting description of the jury comprised of Lincoln and his fellow senior peers: while Essex and the counsel were pleading, he wrote, 'my lords guzzled as if they had not eaten for a fortnight, smoking also plenty of tobacco'[56] before speedily pronouncing the unanimous verdict of guilty of high treason.

Lincoln was also a juryman at the perfunctory trials of co-conspirators in the revolt, and once again displayed his true colours. During the trial of Essex's chief lieutenant in Wales, Sir Gelli Meyrick – whose knighthood failed to exempt him from being hanged, drawn and quartered – Lincoln discovered that during the Cadiz raid the Welshman had looted a magnificent set of marble columns, intending them for use on his own tomb. Lincoln wrote to the Privy Council submitting that such pillars were too fine to mark a traitor's grave, and sought to appropriate them for the grand monument he planned for himself in the church at Tattershall. Cecil was still being pestered on the matter on 18 April. 'I pray you will not forget your promise to help me to the stones for my tomb,'[57] wrote the earl. It was a shameless performance, though nothing less than what one would expect of the man.

But the trial of Essex would come back to bite him.

1. Archbishop Gregorios, head of the Orthodox Church in Britain, officiates at a service in remembrance of Theodore Paleologus at his grave in Cornwall. The Paleologus brass on the wall is draped in the Greek colours of blue and white for the ceremony.

2. Preamble to the 1578 legal judgement given against Leonidas Paleologus and his gang after they barricaded themselves inside a church to thwart pursuers. Leonidas, Theodore's uncle, was later executed for attempted murder but the youthful nephew escaped with a sentence of exile.

3. Cleric turned detective Canon John Adams was the first researcher to expose the murderous proclivities of Paleologus. The long-serving rector wrote of his regret over the secret life of Landulph's famous parishioner.

4. Maurice of Nassau succeeded as commander of the armed forces in the Low Countries when a double agent assassinated his father William the Silent, the first head of state to be murdered with a handgun. Paleologus wrote of shedding his blood under Prince Maurice's banner. A contemporary engraving of the Dutch hero.

5. Henry Clinton, second Earl of Lincoln, seen here as a mourner on his father's tomb at Windsor. Lincoln was feared and loathed by family, tenants and neighbours alike; his son-in-law claimed his wickedness was 'not amongst the heathens to be matched'. The earl employed Paleologus at the height of his marathon vendetta against the Dymoke family.

6. The great tower of Tattershall Castle, the Earl of Lincoln's seat in Lincolnshire, was home to Theodore Paleologus for more than sixteen years. Here he acted as gaoler to the countess who had 'just cause hourly to fear the cutting of her throat'.

7. Viewed from the castle battlements, the Church of the Holy Trinity at Tattershall and the churchyard desecrated by the earl to enlarge his moat. On the right is the site of the tilting ground where Paleologus instructed the young John Smith in the military arts.

8. The armorial achievement of the second Earl of Lincoln impaling the Hastings arms of his first wife and supported by the heraldic greyhounds of the Clintons. Stained-glass windows depicting the arms of Tattershall's owners were commissioned when the castle was saved from demolition in 1911.

9. Praised as 'brass without, but gold within', the colonist John Smith pictured on an early map of New England. An eager pupil of Theodore Paleologus in his youth, Smith rode off from Tattershall Castle to fight the Turks. He later wrote of his sorrow that Christians continued to fight among themselves as Islam spread deeper into Europe.

10. 'The Fair Geraldine', widow of the first Earl of Lincoln and hated stepmother of the second earl. The pair fought ferociously over a will which had been carefully worded to shield the dowager countess's inheritance from her rapacious stepson.

11. Captain John Smith in one of the three epic fights against Muslim champions from which he emerged victorious. The heavily armoured combatants are identified by cross and crescent in this engraving from the earliest illustrated edition of Smith's autobiographical *True Travels*.

12. The humiliating end of Smith's crusading adventures in another engraving from the *True Travels*. Taken prisoner by the Ottomans, he is delivered up to a military commander who sends him on to Constantinople as a gift to his mistress. Note the contemporary rendering of the Turkish titles *dragoman* and *pasha*.

13. Peregrine, Lord Willoughby de Eresby, commander-in-chief of Queen Elizabeth's army in the Low Countries. A personal friend of Prince Maurice of Nassau, Willoughby would have been aware of Paleologus's potential usefulness to his embattled neighbour the Earl of Lincoln. This allegorical portrait at Grimsthorpe Castle is heavy with references to the rigours of a warrior's life.

14. The most powerful man in England after the downfall of Essex, Sir Robert Cecil was horrified when the Earl of Lincoln's retainers insulted Queen Elizabeth. Paleologus had earlier been reported to Cecil as 'a man that hath done divers murders' abroad before fleeing to England.

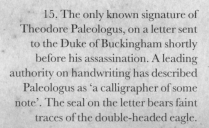

15. The only known signature of Theodore Paleologus, on a letter sent to the Duke of Buckingham shortly before his assassination. A leading authority on handwriting has described Paleologus as 'a calligrapher of some note'. The seal on the letter bears faint traces of the double-headed eagle.

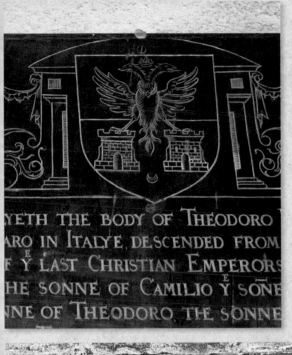

16. The memorial brass in Landulph Church is at the heart of the legend of Theodore Paleologus. The twin towers on this unique version of the imperial eagle are believed to represent Rome and Constantinople, but the crescent on the shield remains an enigma.

17. The simple gravestone of Theodore II at Westminster. He was one of only a handful of parliamentarians buried in the abbey who were not dug up by vengeful royalists at the Restoration.

THEODORUS PALÆOLOGUS
1644

18. The author at the tomb of Ferdinand Paleologus in Barbados. A previous visitor to the churchyard, the Cuban author Alejo Carpentier, pioneered the Magic Realism genre after reflecting that if the heir to the Byzantine emperors could end up as a Church of England vestryman on a Caribbean island, life was much queerer than people realised.

19. St John's church, admired by Evelyn Waugh on his visit to the Paleologus tomb, is surrounded by the vaults of planters who made Barbados the richest colony of the early British Empire. Ferdinand's plantation was less than a mile from the church.

20. A detail of Philip Lea's map of Barbados showing sugar plantations along the east coast. The Paleologus property is below the word 'Topp', and has a pineapple plant drawn immediately above it and symbols for a windmill and cattle mill to the right. First published in the 1670s, the map was still being printed in Georgian times with the same title 'A New Map of the Island of Barbadoes' and the owners' names unchanged.

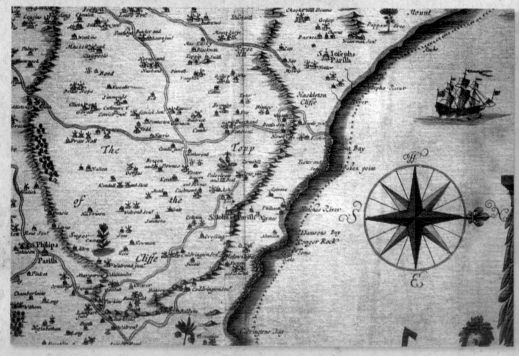

# 12

OLIVIA:    What is thy parentage?
VIOLA:    Above my fortunes, yet my state
             is well. I am a gentleman.

Shakespeare, *Twelfth Night*.

We have seen that the first child of Theodore and Mary Paleologus was born in June 1600, only to die in September that year. There is now a gap of six years before the Tattershall baptismal records of the next three children, displaying the common vagaries of spelling of the time: *Dorathie*, daughter of *Theodore Palaloga*, on 18 August 1606; then *Theodore Palalogo*, son of *Theodore Palalogo gent*, on 30 April 1609; then *John Theodore*, son of *Paleologo Theodore gent*, on 11 July 1611. In August 1614 there is a partially legible entry for *Elizabeth, daughter of Theo …* which is very likely to be another Paleologus child, but as no other record can be found of an Elizabeth Paleologus – crucially, she is not named on the Landulph monument – it seems certain she died in infancy. Of the births of Mary and Ferdinand we find no record in the Tattershall register, though we might reasonably infer that Ferdinand was the youngest son from the sequence of their names on the brass, and indeed we shall later find evidence of his later birth in Devon.

Here is something of a mystery. Mary Balls first became pregnant soon after Theodore's arrival at the castle, giving birth in June 1600; between 1606 and 1614 she had children at regular intervals, there being at least four and possibly six live births. Why, then, no children for this fertile woman between 1601 and 1606? Once again Paleologus has melted into the shadows. Canon Adams deduced that like many other mercenaries he was shut up in Ostend during the notorious bloody siege – one of the longest in history – which due to its heroic defence and appalling slaughter excited the admiration and horror of all Europe between July 1601 and September 1604.

This theory fits in with Theodore's handwritten claim of service in the Anglo-Dutch cause, which we will examine later, and the lack of any evidence of involvement in his patron's doings in England over this period. After our multiple sightings of him in Lincolnshire and Yorkshire in 1600 – with his marriage, the birth and death of his first son, his 'woodish acquaintances' with John Smith and his role as the countess of Lincoln's gaoler – the local record suddenly falls silent. With Paleologus under the spotlight of suspicion for planning Lady Lincoln's murder, the earl must have been persuaded of the wisdom of his temporary absence, though Mary continued to maintain the family home at the castle.

Commanding the defence of Ostend was Elizabeth's famous general Sir Francis Vere, who led an English force of 3,000 regulars and mercenaries in support of a Dutch army totalling perhaps 5,000. These were vastly outnumbered by the surrounding Spanish troops. The siege was called 'a long carnival of death' but for officers on both sides it was valued as a university of war, witnessing the appearance of novel weaponry and siege techniques. A Cornishman called William Lower was a captain in Vere's army and encouraged other Cornish gentlemen to join his 'war school' there. Lower is a name we will meet at a later stage of Theodore's life.

Though the Spanish grip on the landward sides of Ostend could not be broken, the secure harbour allowed Allied ships to land reinforcements and provisions. This meant it was possible for the wounded or those of rank and influence to take home leave, though if our supposition that Theodore was there is correct we have no idea if he was among those officers granted this privilege. Nor do we know if he was there for the beginning of the siege on 5 July 1601 – which would mean he left Lincolnshire before the infamous Kyme play – or was among the reinforcements who arrived at a later date.

The Spanish finally broke into the fortress's outer defences and forced Ostend to surrender on 20 September 1604. But the cost of victory was shattering with 35,000 men killed or wounded. The astonishing bravery

of the defenders prompted the Spanish to allow the surviving soldiers
full military honours and they marched out of the gates with drums
beating and flags flying. The Spanish general treated the enemy officers
to a magnificent banquet.[58] The scale of the defeat at Ostend persuaded
King James to begin peace negotiations with Spain that same year,
and the Dutch later signed the Twelve Year Truce.

⁌

After hugely damaging losses during Elizabeth's final years, the Earl of
Lincoln now enters a relatively quiescent period. Perhaps the enormity
of the break with Cecil has finally sunk in; perhaps the mountainous
debts have left him too embarrassed to plot new offensives; perhaps in
his sixties he is simply too exhausted. And if our theory about Paleologus
at Ostend is correct, the peer has, for the time being, lost his most formidable henchman.

Hated more heartily than ever by the townsfolk of Tattershall, the earl
had taken to spending more time at his second seat at Sempringham,
though we have already seen how he was at loggerheads with the local
parson, John Hoskin of Folkingham, and had brought the wrath of the
bishop of Lincoln down on his head for allowing his parish churches
thereabouts to fall into ruin. Sempringham Hall, erected on the site of a
priory granted to the first earl at the Dissolution, was in fact far grander
than Tattershall Castle, comparable with Renaissance prodigy houses
of the likes of Burghley and Longleat. Earl Henry's increasingly chaotic financial state meant there was nothing to spare for its maintenance,
however, and one pictures the peer's residence there as falling far short
of the standards expected of a senior peer. Indeed, continuing neglect of
the property by future earls would mean that virtually every trace of the
mansion had gone within 100 years.

But then in July 1602 a former servant in Lincoln's London household, a man called William Wright, informed on Earl Henry for
slandering the queen and entering into a conspiracy to ensure the succession of James of Scotland. Accusations by a discharged servant with

a grudge would normally carry little weight with the Privy Council, but matters threatened to take on a more serious character when the name of the lieutenant of the Tower of London, Sir John Peyton, was dragged into the affair.

According to Wright's statement, Lincoln had said in his hearing two or three days after Essex's arraignment: 'I cannot be persuaded that the queen will be drawn to consent unto the death of one with whom she has been so familiar as with the earl of Essex … by God I myself have seen her kiss him twenty times and methinks in reason that she should not then cut off his head.'

Regarding his allegation that the earl had plotted in the Scottish king's interest, William Wright offered a reason why he had not spoken out during his four years of employment at Canon Row and Chelsea. 'I was then his lordship's servant and stood in fear to deal against one so mighty,' said Wright, adding that he was 'a very poor man, having a wife and three children whose lives depend upon my industry'. The ex-servant also invited a sinister interpretation of a meeting held many years earlier at Tattershall between Lincoln and the Duke of Norfolk, later executed for high treason, and of a letter signed James R, discovered and copied by Wright in April 1601, which was 'shut in a box hid very secretly under a boarded floor in a little chamber within the earl of Lincoln's bedchamber'.

If the earl corresponded with the Scottish king, he was doing nothing more than a host of eminent Englishmen who were now acutely conscious of Elizabeth's mortality. That list, of course, began with Robert Cecil. However, admitting as much was a different matter in 1602 when the ailing queen might still dash James's hopes. But Lincoln appears to have had no difficulty convincing Cecil that this accusation was false, the concealed letter being only the king's thanks 'for a loving offer of some horses of your own breed' from the Tattershall stables. Reading this, one easily conjures a picture of the earl and Paleologus deliberating over the most suitable mounts to present to the hunting-mad king, and of Lincoln's inner struggle between a need to curry favour and his innate meanness.

Exonerated by the Privy Council, the relieved Lincoln wrote to Sir Robert Cecil on 30 July. As ever, he was moved to eloquence by self-pity:

> All false slanders being cleared and discovered, I shall by your means the better retain her majesty's good opinion, without which I were better out of this wicked world than in it. For I am so oppressed and beaten down by the practices of my adversaries here and in the country, and brought to so low an ebb with continual vexatious charges and impositions, that I am weary of my life.[59]

Denying again he had ever spoken against the queen's 'sacred person', he said that his adversaries 'daily oppress me with intolerable wrongs … to answer every malicious surmise either in controversy for the title of my lands, lease, or other question or difference in law whatsoever, whereby I am so impoverished and tired with continual charges and losses and hindrances that I receive thereby'.

James was proclaimed King of England on the green at Whitehall on 4 March 1603. Lincoln failed in repeated efforts to ingratiate himself with the new sovereign, however, and in July his claimed hereditary right to a major role at James's coronation, bearing the orb and cross and serving as carver, was firmly rejected. How galling was it, then, to witness Sir Edward Dymoke's dramatic appearance at the ceremony as king's champion? Soon afterwards the earl made another bungled attempt to get in the royal good books by informing on a courtier who, as Lincoln alleged, had indicated his opinion that the Spanish Infanta possessed a superior title to Elizabeth's crown, and that in any case the great powers of Europe would depose James if he did not favour the Catholic religion. According to Lincoln's account, four days before the queen's death he was approached by the Earl of Oxford – the premier earl as well as the alternative Shakespeare – who tried to persuade him that the peers of England should band together to decide the succession. Lincoln entangled Peyton in the intrigue by claiming he had gone to the Tower to urge the lieutenant to inform the Scottish king of opposition to his title.

Furious at Lincoln's charge that he failed to alert James to a serious plot, Peyton told the Privy Council that in the tense period of Elizabeth's last days, when he provisioned the stronghold in case of strife over the succession, the earl 'determined to send his money, plate and jewels unto me in the Tower, and to come thither himself with his servants and attendants, which afterward he performed'.

Once again the earl's maladroit scheming did him no good, though a shadow was cast over the career of a respected public servant. Not long after the coronation, Peyton was relieved of the lieutenancy of the Tower. Though soon compensated with the post of governor of Jersey, his removal from the more prestigious office clearly still rankled in October when he submitted his evidence against Lincoln to the Privy Council.

'Touching the earl of Lincoln's imputations laid upon me,' Peyton declared, 'his fashion is to condemn the world, if thereby he might excuse himself.'

The great triumphs of these latter years, to the earl's mind, were the ruin of his great enemy Sir Edward Dymoke in 1610, and the near extinction of the Norreys family on whom he had pronounced his curse. Of the surviving sons, Lord Norreys's youngest, Maximilian, was killed in Brittany; John died on official business in Ireland; Thomas and Henry were both mortally wounded the same day fighting the Irish. It is easy to imagine Lincoln exulting at the news. Only the earl's hated stepson, Francis Norreys, survived into James's reign, but what wretched fate awaited him we have already seen.

The earl's lust for land remained unappeased, and encouraged by reports of John Smith's explorations he began to cast covetous eyes towards the New World. On 23 May 1609, the charter incorporating the first Company of Adventurers and Planters for Virginia listed 'Henry Earle of Lincolne' as one of the grantees and named him among 'our Counsell for the Companie'.

We have a late glimpse of Lincoln in June 1611, when the heir of the landgrave of Hesse arrived at the court of King James in the hope of winning a Stuart bride. This was Prince Otto, now aged seventeen, at whose christening the earl had disgraced himself in 1596. A contemporary manuscript in the library at Cassel records the young prince's lengthy visit to England in great detail, describing the learned conversations between James and his guest, their exchange of costly gifts, the feasting and hunting they enjoyed together, and their church attendance on 5 November to give thanks on the anniversary of the Gunpowder Plot. There is a passing reference to Lincoln being present when James honoured two of Otto's attendants by dubbing them knights, but one senses that the earl was invited for form's sake. As representative of the previous monarch at Otto's christening, he could not have been entirely excluded from the visit without occasioning further unwelcome gossip.

But he was still in the grip of the same obsessions at the age of seventy. In a letter of 6 May 1612 to the courtier Sir George More, father-in-law of the poet John Donne, the earl was still complaining of 'horrible plots to overthrow me' and destroy his reputation with the king. One wonders what reputation he dreamt he had.

# 13

England is a paradise for women, and hell for horses:
Italy is a paradise for horses, hell for women.

Robert Burton, *The Anatomy of Melancholy*.

In the grand parish church of the Holy Trinity, to the east of Tattershall
Castle, is the font at which Theodore and Mary stood on at least four
occasions between 1600 and 1614 for the christenings of their children.
In 1614, when her second daughter was baptised at Tattershall, Mary
was nearly forty, a late age for child-bearing at the time.

If Theodore walked through the door today, the first thing to strike
him would be how the interior is flooded with daylight from thirty-two
enormous windows of plain glass. In his time the entire church glowed
with stained and painted glass, every panel vivid with saints or angels,
biblical scenes, fabulous beasts or royal heraldry, the work of fifteenth-
century glaziers whose names have come down to us from workshops in
places like Peterborough and Stoke-on-Trent. Somehow the glass passed
unscathed through the iconoclastic vandalism of the Reformation,
so Theodore saw the windows in their perfect state. It must have been
like standing inside a great jewel box, all the more captivating for the
contrast with the dreary fen landscape outside.

Even more remarkably, the church glass was to escape the attentions
of zealots during the Civil War, probably because the Earl of Lincoln of
the time was a leading Puritan. But to the townspeople's never-ending
regret, an eighteenth-century vicar objected that the deep colours made
it hard for him to read his sermons and despite furious protests nearly all
the glass was removed and sold off.

Today only a few original panels survive in the east window, but by a
strange coincidence one of these shows Constantine the Great receiving

the True Cross and Holy Nails from his mother St Helena. It is a subject rarely depicted in English churches, and one must wonder how many times Theodore gazed up at this image of his most exalted forebear and pointed out details to his wife and offspring, the imperial triple-crown, the ermine-lined purple robe, the Holy Nails that Constantine fixed to his helmet to make him invincible in battle. Did it strike him as odd that the fourth-century Roman emperor and all the figures crowding the scene are dressed in the high fashion of the English fifteenth century?[60]

In the rows of pews reserved for the castle people the family would have sat through lengthy homilies. Before the King James Bible of 1611 swept all others away, the church might have possessed any of a number of versions, perhaps the Great Bible commissioned by Henry VIII or the revised Bishops' Bible of 1568. In the Paleologus household the most likely version was the Geneva Bible, a volume which was lighter and easier to handle. Given his personal history, Theodore very likely owned a Greek Testament, probably one of the Stephanus editions published half a century before.

In an Elizabethan household the father's word was law. Children were expected to be dutiful and obedient and at the start of each day would kneel for a paternal blessing. The Paleologus sons would have been brought up to admire their father's accomplishments, marvelling at his horsemanship and listening to tales of wars and tournaments and Italian courts; there were stories spun too of his early life, whatever version of it he chose to tell them. Like John Smith, they would listen entranced to the romance of Byzantium's emperors and conquering generals; unlike John Smith, they were told they were of the imperial blood.

Yet from childhood they must have wondered where they belonged, for the only family they could have known was their mother's, the millers, clothiers and brewers of Hadleigh. What standing did they derive from a father who, whatever his ancestry, was without fortune, land or title, and subject to the whim of an erratic patron? How far did an English identity assert itself? Was it the bond with modest English forebears which would one day see them take up arms in the Civil War, or the martial instincts of the paternal line? The homilies endured at Tattershall

Church must have played a part in moulding their characters, though with different endings: for at some point young Theodore embarked on a path which would place him in the psalm-singing Roundhead army, a rebel against his king and an enemy to brothers upholding the royal cause. Yet it was Theodore who would end up buried in the temple of English worthies, Westminster Abbey.

What did these children make of their father's fabulous past and present circumstances? That past was another country, indeed a succession of countries, impossibly remote from their daily experience. Were they stirred by dreams of lost Constantinople or more concerned with the tangible benefits of the Hadleigh connection? Perhaps the brothers were divided even in these early days; perhaps Dorothy was already beginning to fret about her matrimonial prospects as the daughter of a landless man.

A Tattershall character that the growing brood would have known well was the town's most famous commoner resident, the dwarf known as Tom Thumb. Just eighteen inches high, Tom was reputedly eighty years old when Paleologus and Mary set up home together; on his death in 1620, supposedly aged 101, he was buried near the font in which their children were baptised. One imagines Tom being regularly summoned to the castle when his lordship demanded entertainment. As Theodore was exceptionally tall, he and the dwarf provided the kind of spectacle that would amuse the earl's guests hugely, with Tom's head bobbing around the horse master's knee.

It is likely the family had quarters in one of the buildings reserved for the higher class of retainer, rather than in the castle itself, though during the time of Paleologus's shadowy employment as the countess's gaoler he may have required a place within the tower. Mary was close enough to the common people and no doubt capable of performing menial tasks, though Theodore's position protected her from the indignity of physical labour. Surviving Elizabethan accounts at Grimsthorpe Castle give an indication of wages paid to staff in noble households, with senior officials receiving up to £5 a quarter. The steward, gentleman usher, comptroller and master of the horse are all recorded as having their own servants. It is probable that staff at Tattershall enjoyed similar conditions of employment, despite the notorious stinginess of the second earl. Both he and his father prided themselves on their stables, so Theodore would have had at least the equivalent of the four grooms who assisted the Willoughbys' master of horse.

As Paleologus was known as a scholar we can see him owning a book chest and book rest, and take a guess at a handful of volumes he might have cherished: Italian authors almost certainly including Dante, Castiglione and Machiavelli, perhaps Petrarch, Boccaccio and Aristo; among classical authors might be Aristotle, Pliny, Homer and Horace. He would surely have owned a number of works on the art of warfare, perhaps including that of the earlier Theodore Paleologus; contemporary books on the martial arts – almost all by Italians – would have included the first book printed in English on duelling, Vincentio Saviolo's 1595 treatise on the use of the rapier and dagger which taught how to 'kill any man, bee it with a thrust *punta*, a *stocada*, with an *imbrocadda* or a changing blow', or a weapon concealed under the cloak. As he prided himself on his penmanship, as will be seen when we consider the surviving letter in his hand, we can add to his possessions a box in which he kept his writing materials, the quills of goose-feather, a penknife and inkwell. There would have been sealing-wax also, for a prized possession was a seal of the Paleologus arms with the double-headed eagle, probably in the form of a signet ring. It seems certain this was made for Theodore rather than an heirloom as it bore the initials TP.

How did Mary cope with his absences? According to Robert Burton, a close contemporary of Paleologus, every Italian was a jealous husband, horrified by the freedoms enjoyed by wives in countries like England and France: 'Upon small acquaintance,' writes Burton, 'it is usual to court other men's wives, to come to their houses, and accompany them arm-in-arm in the streets … The Italian could never endure this, or a Spaniard, the very conceit of it would make him mad: and for that cause they lock up their women.'

Having shown frailty in the early days of their courtship, one imagines Mary avoiding further cause for gossip, and if Theodore conformed to Burton's stereotype of the Italian husband all who knew the man would steer well clear of the wife. But so far as we can judge for the next eight years or so Theodore was at her side, or absent for relatively short periods. Perhaps it was the first time he was able to give proper attention to his wife and children as well as the earl's business. Yet there is the question of what was happening to the countess. That poor woman survived until 1611, and we have no way of knowing whether Theodore resumed his earlier rule over her on his return from abroad.

It is very likely the boys had their first lessons at home, and Paleologus would have made sure they practised the use of weapons from the earliest age; the church would then have supervised their schooling, drumming Protestant doctrine into their heads from the age of five or six. Few teachers of the time followed the example of Roger Ascham, the queen's own tutor, who declared that 'young people are sooner allured by love than driven by beating, to attain good learning', and lessons were usually underlined by the application of the birch. The seal of Louth Grammar School, attended by John Smith, actually depicts a master vigorously applying the rod to a pupil's backside.

# 14

For what is't to have
A flattering false insculption on a tomb,
And in men's hearts reproach? The bowelled corpse
May be seared in, but (with free tongue I speak)
The faults of great men through their sear-cloths break.

Thomas Middleton, *The Revenger's Tragedy*.

The old earl had been ailing for some time at his now favoured retreat of Sempringham. He had reached the great age of seventy-three. Perhaps in these last days his mind finally dwelt on a lifetime of misdeeds and fearfully recalled sermons by the fire-and-brimstone preachers favoured by the Puritan persuasion. There was, for instance, Henry Greenwood's thunderings from the pulpit at St Paul's Cross only a year before, when his subject was the lake called Tophet which awaited sinners in hell.

'Hell is a most lamentable and woeful place of torment,' cried Greenwood, 'where there shall be screeching and screaming, weeping, wailing, and gnashing of teeth for evermore: and this is Tophet. Where torment shall be upon torment, each torment easeless, endless, remediless; where the worm shall be immortal, cold intolerable, stench unendurable, fire unquenchable, darkness palpable, scourges of devils terrible, and screeching and screaming continual: and this is hell.' There was worse. 'Nay moreover,' said the preacher, 'great men, noble men, and mighty princes, are not only liable to Tophet, but the greatest part of them shall to the devil.'[61]

Or was Earl Henry comforted by a belief in preordination? During his lifetime most English clergy taught the curious Calvinist view that the world was divided into the elect and reprobate whom God had arbitrarily predestined, the one to heaven and the other to hell. He had committed more than his fair share of the enormous villainies listed in Robert Burton's great obloquy on his age, his life made up of now tragical, then comical matters. Yet to one of Lincoln's cast of mind it must have been unthinkable that God would disoblige a belted earl.

We have no idea whether the gentleman rider was at his master's bedside when, as recorded in the parish register, 'Henry layt Earle of Lincolne departed out of this lyf at his manor howse of Semperingham, the xxjx day of September, anno domine 1616.' He died the same year as Shakespeare. After bringing so much suffering down on so many heads throughout his long reign, perhaps his passing was mourned by no one but Theodore Paleologus, a confidante of the old tyrant in later years and his accomplice in delinquencies known and nameless. With his master gone, Theodore's prospects were in freefall.

Lincoln was buried at Táttershall three days later. Despite long and careful preparations for a tomb befitting his exalted station in life – one meant to incorporate the grand marble statuary appropriated from the goods of the executed rebel Mayrick – there is no sign or record that it was ever erected. Given Earl Henry's atrocious relations with his heir Thomas, it is no surprise that the new earl declined to be confronted by a monument to his father's glory every time he set foot in church. With more foresight, he might have followed the example of many a Jacobean grandee who erected his tomb when alive, doubting the reliability of his heirs. Lincoln left a will which almost certainly included instructions for his tomb, but the will is no longer extant and it was in any case nullified by the Prerogative Court of Canterbury, a decision which may well indicate an attempt to spite his kin from beyond the grave. This was the same court which had thrown out his legal application to overturn the will of his own father.

I remarked earlier on my frustration at having no portrait of Theodore Paleologus to offer the reader. Far more remarkable is the absence of a likeness of the second Earl of Lincoln, one of the great nobles of the realm. All we have is a kneeling 'weeper' flanking the tomb of the first earl, the centrepiece of the Lincoln Chapel at St George's, Windsor, and some doubt may be cast even on this identification. For behind this tomb is a curious story.

The alabaster effigies of the earl and his third wife and widow lie on a tomb chest with figures of mourners ranged around its sides. An eighteenth-century engraving of the tomb shows the figure of Henry as the first of three sons on the earl's side of the tomb chest. By convention, sons are on the same side as the male, placed in order of seniority, while daughters kneel beside the female. The tomb is in excellent condition, yet for a reason unknown two of the mourning sons disappeared at some point after this engraving was made for Joseph Pote's *History and Antiquities of Windsor Castle*, published in 1749. The three sons are almost indistinguishable, so a tentative identification of the survivor as Henry rests on the presumption that the all-important heir was spared when the others were removed. If this is indeed Henry, the portrayal of him as a mourner has a certain irony, given his undisguised eagerness to take his father's place. But then we have seen how he mourned Mary Queen of Scots.[62]

The lack of a portrait of Earl Henry is intriguing. Portraits of anyone but a king, queen or archbishop were uncommon at the beginning of the Tudor age, but by Henry VIII's time the peerage and higher gentry routinely commissioned portraits – several survive of the first Earl of Lincoln, for instance, including a magnificent drawing by Holbein – and by the end of Elizabeth's reign many a squire, alderman or merchant was leaving his likeness to posterity, whether as a portrait or effigy. Around 5,000 sculptural tombs were erected in English churches between the dissolution of the monasteries and the Civil War, and most of these remain alongside large numbers of monumental brasses. The absolute peak in production came in the last years of Elizabeth and the reign of James. By 1631, when John Weever published the first book on funeral monuments, the author complained that upstart tradesmen were building tombs as grand as those of the highest nobles.

It is difficult to believe that a man of such high rank as Lincoln failed to have his portrait painted. To take an obvious example among his neighbours, Lord Willoughby was painted at various ages, both in armour and civilian costume, often in a fashionably melancholy pose;

in one equestrian portrait an African page trots behind his lordship's horse in what may be the earliest English painting to include a black servant. We can also see Willoughby's life-sized effigy in Spilsby Church, the family's ancestral burial place. Considering countless such examples I conclude that a portrait of Earl Henry certainly did exist, and can only suppose that such was the loathing he inspired even among close relations that no one cared to preserve it after his death.

✛

There is no record of Paleologus at Tattershall after 1616. We can take it that the third earl lost no time evicting the master of horse and his brood. The eldest boy, Theodore II as we should now call him, was only seven at the time, and we shall have no sight of him for the next fifteen years. Evidence of how Mary later moved to the West Country with Theodore will be presented in a later chapter. Meanwhile the loss of his patron the earl led Theodore himself into one of those enigmatic disappearances into the twilight zone which inspire many of the later fantasies about him.

What became of them all in the years immediately afterwards is unknown, but it was common practice for adolescents to be placed in service for a few years, typically in a household of a higher class. So the yeoman class served the gentry and the gentry served the nobility. Where exactly the young Paleologi fitted into this is a moot point; their father could justly boast of his social connections, however, and the long association of Theodore with the Berties of Grimsthorpe suggests one possible destination when the sons reached a suitable age. One or more of them may have gained a place as a page here or in some other noble household, making himself useful while learning how the best people behaved. Certainly the Paleologus boys in adult life would have no difficulty mixing with the higher classes. But in 1616 the family was effectively out on its ear, and the children may well have found temporary asylum with their humble Balls relations. Perhaps they ended up as guests of the illegal brewer who was troubling the respectable folk of Hadleigh around this time.

Or did Theodore have a relative then living in London? There are scattered documentary references to an Andrew Paleologus who was resident in the East End in the reign of Charles I, though possibly much earlier. When he arrived and exactly what relation he was – if any – is unclear. In the Calendar of Domestic State Papers for January 1634 is an intriguing note that a 'Grecian minister' had come to England the previous September bringing letters from the Patriarch of Constantinople to 'Andreas Paleologus, a Grecian' and another document shows him still resident in 1641. Andrew lived at St Katherine Dock near the Tower of London, and in a later chapter we will find the only grandson of Theodore at addresses in neighbouring Wapping and Stepney. The Elizabethan historian John Stow called Wapping 'a continual street, or a filthy strait passage, with alleys of small tenements or cottages, built, inhabited by sailors' victuallers'. But any family link between Theodore and Andrew remains conjectural without new evidence.

Though now in his mid-fifties, Theodore himself may have returned to the Continent in search of a war. Following the suppression of the Irish revolt in 1603 and the peace treaty with Spain the following year, King James strenuously avoided further armed confrontation, resisting efforts to embroil his subjects in wars in Europe. Theodore's old stamping ground of the Netherlands offered a mercenary few prospects until the expiry of the Truce with Spain in 1621. The best opportunity may have come in 1618 when the Thirty Years War was sparked by the offer of the Bohemian crown to the Elector Palatine Frederick, husband of James's daughter Elizabeth. Oddly enough, in the twenty-first century this romantic figure known as the Winter Queen would become a character in one of the more phantasmagorical works of fiction based on the Paleologus legend, in which she and Theodore are the ancestors of the true queen of England.

However, the Thirty Years War may have come too late as we next have news of Theodore in 1619 when he is again in England. The plain truth is we do not know where he was for three years. Once again he has slipped away into the shadows.

❖

Thomas Clinton, third Earl of Lincoln, did not rule the roost at Tattershall for long, dying at the castle in January 1618. His son, the sturdily Puritan fourth earl, Theophilus, was a more formidable character, and in his time Tattershall provided America with some of its earliest settlers. His wife fitted out a ship named *The Lady Arbella* after their daughter, which sailed to the New World from Southampton in 1629. Among the passengers was Thomas Dudley, formerly the earl's steward at the castle, Dudley's daughter Anne and her husband Simon Broadstreet, another of the peer's retainers. Broadstreet was to become the governor of the Massachusetts Bay Colony and overseer of Harvard College. Arbella herself married a Puritan worthy, a Rutland squire called Isaac Johnson, who migrated to America with John Winthrop, while her younger sister Lady Susan married John Humphrey, another prominent New England figure.

An early critic of Charles I, Earl Theophilus was imprisoned in the Tower in 1626 for organising opposition to the king's forced loan. In 1647, a year that saw him made speaker of the House of Lords, he was impeached for levying war against the king. He inherited something of the political acumen of his great-grandfather the first earl, however, and cannily lent money to the exiled Charles II. At the Restoration he was granted the privilege his grandfather had schemed for in vain, serving as carver at the coronation banquet.

There is a different story to tell of Earl Henry's son by his second countess. Another of the family who preferred the name Fiennes to Clinton, this son was also called Henry, and certainly took after his sire rather than his mild, self-sacrificing mother. Although hated by the earl and cheated out of his mother's legacy, he seemed to be making up for a bad start in life when King James took a fancy to him, making him a knight and a gentleman of the Privy Council. Things went downhill from there, and he proved himself a true chip off the old block.

Sir Henry seduced a woman of good family by a promise of marriage, claiming his existing wife Eleanor was on the point of death. Lady Fiennes declined to die, however, and the mistress was then kept for two years in a secret apartment of Henry's London house, after which time he attempted to poison his wife. In June 1620 Lady Fiennes appeared to be dying in earnest, whereupon the mistress rushed out invitations to her wedding. When Lady Fiennes rallied once again, the mistress ran off with another man. Mad with jealousy, Sir Henry and two retainers chased after the pair armed with 'swords, daggers, stilettos, pistols, petronels and guns', the kind of armoury familiar to us from his father's exploits.

A witness who was due to give evidence against Sir Henry was murdered on the eve of the trial, apparently by ruffians hired by the knight. Even so, he appeared before Star Chamber on 19 February 1622, and was found guilty of the attempted murder of his wife, of robbery and 'other grave charges'. He was fined £2,000 and gaoled, only to be let out at the instigation of a king with a life-long partiality for dangerous young men.

The later story of the Clintons is an illustration of the vicissitudes which have faced noble families with striking regularity. In the eighteenth century the ninth earl of Lincoln was made duke of Newcastle, but this title became extinct in 1989 on the death of the tenth duke, a bachelor lepidopterist. However, the Lincoln earldom survived with the discovery in Australia of a direct descendant of none other than wife-poisoning Sir Henry Clinton alias Fiennes, son of our Earl Henry by his long-suffering second wife. The heir was a seventy-five-year-old retired miner and butcher, Ted Clinton, who inherited as eighteenth earl. Though disappointed to find no castles or rolling acres came with the title, the new Lord Lincoln travelled to London with his countess, a former waitress named Linda, to claim his seat in the House of Lords. 'I thought of going into politics in Australia,' he told a reporter, 'but decided I was too honest.'

# 15

POOH-BAH:   I accept refreshments at any hands,
however lowly. I also retail state
secrets at a very low figure.

W.S. Gilbert, *The Mikado*.

Among miscellaneous papers in the Adams archive I found a brief note
that a friend of a friend had mentioned spotting an entry for the baptism of a Ferdinando Paleologus in the parish register of St Andrew's,
Plymouth. Canon Adams appears not to have followed up this lead with
his usual zeal, for in his Royal Institution of Cornwall lecture he stated
that no baptismal record had been discovered for Ferdinand or his sister
Mary, repeating this in its later publication in the Institution's journal.
'The records may turn up some day but I doubt it,' he noted. 'I fear the
entries are likely to have been among the many registers which have
succumbed to neglect or the ravages of time.' The friend's information
was good, however, and the proof was right on Adams's doorstep. With
the help of staff at the Plymouth and West Devon Record Office I had
no difficulty finding the record of the youngest boy's christening on
15 June 1619:

*Ffardinando son of Theodore Paleologus an Ittalian.*

How the entry was missed by Adams may be explained by the mistake of
an early archivist who transcribed the surname as Paledayne, an error
now corrected. The gratuitous information about Theodore's nationality is unusual in register entries of this kind and suggests he was a relative
newcomer to the town; it also appears to confirm that despite a twenty-
year residency in England and an Anglican marriage he never sought

naturalisation. He was still the outsider, the other. At this time Theodore was nearly sixty and Mary Paleologus in her mid-forties, a notably late age for bearing children.

The search was now on for further Paleologus records at St Andrew's and an entry was quickly found for the burial of Theodore's wife Mary, *née* Balls, on 24 November 1631. She would have been fifty-six at the time of death. These missing pieces of the jigsaw are important in narrowing down the couple's 'lost years' after leaving Tattershall from twelve to three. So Theodore settled in the West Country long before 1628, the date previously fixed on by researchers as the first to show him living there. That his kin moved with him to Devon at the earlier time is shown by a legal paper which describes the eldest boy, Theodore II, as resident in the county at least as early as 1623. But this is a document to be considered later.

Proof that Paleologus lived in Plymouth at the earlier date means he was very likely a witness to perhaps the most famous event in the town's history. The *Mayflower*, crammed with 102 members of the Plymouth Company, set out on its perilous journey to the New World on Wednesday, 6 September 1620. It had been delayed in the port for over a month due to appalling weather, and it is easy to picture Theodore chatting to the party as they kicked their heels on the quayside.

A steady trickle of non-conformists left England during James I's reign, prominent among them the Lincolnshire pioneers. Many were inspired by the colonising exploits of Captain John Smith, but none would capture the popular imagination so much as the Pilgrim Fathers, though only a third of the ship's passengers were actually Puritans. Blown far from the intended destination of Virginia, the *Mayflower* finally sighted land on 9 November. A child delivered on board to a woman called Susanna White, as the ship rode at anchor in Cape Cod Bay, is recognised as the first European to be born in New England; he was christened Peregrine. Though half the band died in the first winter, Plymouth in Massachusetts became the earliest permanent settlement in New England. However, John Smith himself castigated the Pilgrims as full of 'pride, singularity, and contempt of authority', though his view may have been coloured by their refusal of his offer to guide their expedition.

❖

'Of mankind,' wrote Machiavelli, 'we may say in general they are fickle, hypocritical, and greedy of gain' and this was clearly something of a guiding principle in Theodore's life. For we now find his name associated with Sir James Bagge of Saltram, the notoriously corrupt West Country agent of the royal favourite George Villiers, Duke of Buckingham. The connection with Bagge is revealed in a letter – the only one known in Theodore's handwriting – sent to the duke from Plymouth on 6 March 1628, and endorsed at Dover on 19 March.

Implausibly handsome, George Villiers had become a major player in the land since his introduction at court in 1614. A younger son from the minor gentry, he quickly displaced all other young favourites in James's affections and shamelessly exploited the king's infatuation. Promotion through the peerage came at an unprecedented speed: viscount in 1616 at the age of twenty-four, earl in 1617, marquis in 1618 and the dizzy height of duke in 1623. After the methodical elimination of great peers under the Tudors, Buckingham found himself the highest ranking personage in the realm outside the royal family.

Showered with confiscated estates and lucrative posts including monopolies and customs farms, he had become England's second richest man, endlessly interfering in politics at home and abroad. On James's death he maintained his ascendancy over Charles I, but his arrogance, incompetence and corruption – above all, his promotion of disastrous wars against Spain and France – made Buckingham the most hated man in the kingdom. Two attempts by the House of Commons to impeach him were foiled by Charles dissolving parliament on each occasion.

As the duke's key agent, James Bagge had already survived numerous attempts to bring him down on charges of corruption, fraud and extortion. Foul-mouthed and haughty, yet grotesquely servile to those he courted – to Buckingham especially – here was a prospective patron for Paleologus in the mould of the Earl of Lincoln. Bagge's most outrageous swindle had come in 1625, when Buckingham persuaded Charles to sanction an ill-fated attack on the Spanish at Cadiz. Charged with victualing the expedition and organising the press gang, the newly knighted Bagge not only embezzled the £55,000 for provisioning the fleet, cheating soldiers out of their pay, substituting rotten food which was said to have killed 4,000 of the king's subjects, but ran up further debts in Charles's name and plundered a friendly foreign vessel in Plymouth Sound. King Charles doggedly absolved his favourite's agent from blame.

In the aftermath of Cadiz, Buckingham sought to retrieve his reputation by relieving Huguenots besieged at La Rochelle, and Bagge was again directed to provision the expedition. But this action too was a humiliating failure, with half of the ill-equipped English soldiers killed; on the fleet's return angry householders in Plymouth were forced to house the sick and unruly survivors. These two naval disasters, followed by nationwide indignation over Ship Money, a tax the king attempted to impose without the consent of parliament, were important milestones on the road to civil war.

This was a testing time for James Bagge. He was in severe financial difficulties, not least because of his recently acquired mansion of Saltram overlooking Plymouth Harbour. In 1628, the year of Paleologus's letter to Buckingham, he was dubbed 'that bottomless bag' by Archbishop Laud who with other former allies turned against him; he was also facing further accusations of extortion and embezzlement in a new parliament. Hemmed in by enemies, Bagge needed what support he could muster, and it was at this moment of crisis that Theodore appeared on the scene to offer his services to the king. Paleologus was now in his late sixties, yet one imagines he could still render practical service as a spy. Buckingham had many adversaries in Plymouth, a town with marked anti-royalist sympathies.

Theodore was now a householder in Plymouth, for in the monthly assessments for poor relief in Old Town Ward that year *Theodore Palliologus* is rated at a halfpenny a week.[63] Of seventy-three households in the ward, twenty-seven were assessed for higher sums – between one penny and eightpence – so Paleologus was by no means among the better off residents in the city. Though his wife Mary was presumably with him in the Old Town, not all the children were still at home. The locally born Ferdinand would have been only nine at this time and daughters Dorothy and Mary were unmarried; however, nineteen-year-old Theodore II was making his own life elsewhere and John, aged seventeen, was probably still in service.

The Buckingham letter is the only evidence of Theodore's history in his own words. It is also a strikingly flamboyant example of calligraphy of the time. Written in courtly French and addressed to *Monseigneur*, the letter followed up a meeting with Buckingham at Plymouth at which Theodore appears to have extracted a fairly firm promise of employment. He thanks the duke for the honour and courtesy shown to him and pledges he will be faithful and capable, adding: 'I say, sir, capable, as one who has lived and shed his blood in war since his youth, at the pleasure of the late Prince of Orange, and other diverse English and French lords who have seen and known me and can bear witness.'

The reference to French nobles is the only clue that Theodore may have fought in France as well as in the Netherlands, and this presents another opportunity for him to have served alongside Lord Willoughby. The English lords mentioned as ready to vouch for his character are very likely to have included Willoughby's son and heir Robert, the newly created Earl of Lindsey. His name would have come up at Paleologus's meeting with the duke, for the two had known each other since the time of the Italian's friendship with Captain John Smith. Robert Bertie was one of Charles I's most active supporters and indeed would be fatally wounded at the first battle of the Civil War.

Theodore describes himself as born a gentleman of good house and in possession of accomplishments worthy of the name he bears, 'but unlucky in the misfortune experienced by my ancestors and myself'. He writes of his desire to serve the king in his diverse endeavours and offers 'all manner of benefits and contentment'. The letter goes on: 'If it should please your greatness (*Vostre grandeur*) to employ me in the service of the King, and instruct Sir James Back' – Theodore's rendering of Bagge – 'that he should be kind enough to give me, on your behalf, something to help me pass the remainder of my life, there would be no more grateful employee.'

There is something of a shift of emphasis in the course of the letter, from the confident assertion of a promise made by the duke with tangible benefits to be delivered in exchange, to something like a plea for a pension. He signs off praying to God for the duke's health and prosperity, 'your very humble and very obedient servant'. (The full text in French appears at Appendix B.)

Two of Britain's leading authorities on early handwriting, co-authors of a standard work on the subject, scrutinised the letter at my request to evaluate Theodore's skill as a penman and, since handwriting can offer clues to personality, perhaps cast some light on the writer himself. Each expert gave an opinion before being informed of Paleologus's story, other than what could be gleaned from the letter, though both cautioned that with correspondence of this date there is always the possibility that a letter was written by a skilled professional scribe or secretary rather than the man himself.

According to David Iredale, the language is formal textbook italic French of the early seventeenth century. Such a script would typically be written by a well-educated man during the period 1590–1630. It might be Paleologus's 'best' handwriting, carefully crafted with painstaking attention to the rules and not necessarily indicative of character, other than showing a healthy and sensible willingness to please for the sake of obtaining a patron.

The writing is large and smoothly composed, probably slowly. 'Large handwriting is sometimes stated as being a sign of a big ego, a larger-than-life character who thinks a lot of himself,' says Iredale:

> Our writer's relaxed smooth handwriting suggests a balanced man, one who will not sacrifice quality for speed … The line of writing is more or less level, perhaps aided by pencilled lines, perhaps from much practice. Level lines denote a stable character. There is a distinct slant to right, normal in italic writing of this date. This is usually stated by graphologists to be the characteristic of an outgoing confident man, an enthusiast, a person who gets on with other people.
>
> Our man has joined-up lower-case letters which can be a sign of a logical thinker. I see his letter-forms generally as bold and rounded, clearly written … these characteristics suggest a man with dreams and ambitions, though well aware of the importance of worldly possessions, a forceful man, a man capable of forming lasting friendships.

Mr Iredale adds that the careful dotting of each *i* and crossing of each *t* suggests a tidy, organised person, a good manager, a protective leader. 'I notice that the lower-case *o* is generally closed, which is a good sign, because an *o* open at the top implies a person who does not keep confidences. Fortunately he closes the lower-case *a*, so the man can be trusted.'

My second authority, John R. Barrett, describes Theodore as a calligrapher of some note. He adds: 'Although the script is of its time, it is a pretty modern script for the period – even allowing for the fact that continental writers were ahead of British in the use of this kind of fluent italic. The final page is a rather fine piece of calligraphic design.'

Of special note was the large size of the paper chosen, as paper was expensive: 'Perhaps this was a deliberate ploy to catch the duke's eye, and to give the impression that the writer was a man of some consequence ... but the large sheet may tell us something about the larger-than-life personality of Paleologus.' Mr Barrett draws attention to the care with which the letter is set out with notably neat justification of the left-hand margin: 'Similarly the evenness of the text-block and the large lower margin on the two principal pages suggest extreme care. It is almost a printer's lay-out ... It is tempting to regard this as indicative of a personality trait.'

The almost universal hatred of Buckingham at this time verged on the mass hysteria which characterised contemporary witch persecutions. This was shown by the murder of the duke's adviser, Dr John Lambe, two months after Paleologus despatched his letter. An astrologer and fortune-teller, Lambe was both feared and courted for his supposed magical powers, earning a remarkable £40 to £50 for a consultation at the time he won Buckingham's patronage. He rapidly became 'the Duke's Devil' in the popular imagination and blamed for a diabolic influence on the king. The previous year Lambe had been found guilty of raping an eleven-year-old girl and sentenced to death. Political connections allowed him out on the streets, however, and on 13 June he was surprised by a mob as he left a theatre and stoned to death. A pamphlet which immediately made the rounds ran:

*Let Charles and George do what they can*
*The duke shall die like Doctor Lambe.*

On 29 July Buckingham was in the audience at the Globe Theatre for a performance of Shakespeare's *Henry VIII* and reportedly left in a hurry after watching the play's Duke of Buckingham executed. Less than a month later the duke himself was assassinated, stabbed to death by a disgruntled army officer at a public house in Portsmouth. We have no means of knowing whether James Bagge had gratified Theodore in the meantime with funds sanctioned by the duke, but it seems unlikely any arrangements were made for the regular income he craved.

With his high hopes of the great Buckingham dashed, the Italian was immediately on the look-out for another patron. The man we once heard termed Teodoro Paleologo the Bravo and Very Magnificent Signor was on his uppers: we might now call him the Halfpenny Emperor. But as Machiavelli said, 'One change always leaves a dovetail into which another will fit', and his attention quickly fixed on a rich Cornish squire named Sir Nicholas Lower. Throughout his life Paleologus had always seemed to gravitate towards wicked men, but from what we can deduce of Lower's character for once he attached himself to a good man, if a vain and gullible one. Not long afterwards he was invited to Sir Nicholas's comfortable home at Landulph across the Tamar, and he was to stay there till the day he died.

# 16

But who knows the fate of his bones,
or how often he is to be buried?

Sir Thomas Browne, *Hydriotaphia, or Urn Burial.*

The parish of Landulph stands on the banks of the Tamar, the river which separates Cornwall from the rest of England. Despite an entirely rural identity, it is remarkably close to teeming Plymouth on the Devonshire side. Today the village is probably smaller that it was in the seventeenth century when its principal dwelling was the manor house of Clifton. According to the county's first historian, Richard Carew, whose *Survey of Cornwall* was published in 1602, Clifton was 'a neat seat house, appertaining to one of the Arundels'. This cadet line of the famous family descended from the branch seated at Trerice near Newquay. Clifton passed into the hands of Sir Nicholas Lower in 1627, and he and his wife Dame Elizabeth immediately set about branding the parish church of St Leonard and St Dilph with the heraldic insignia of their two families, like so many stamps of ownership. Elizabeth was born a Killigrew, another name of renown in Cornwall.

In the church windows you can still see the Lower arms in painted glass, a chevron between three white roses on a black shield, with the Lower crest of a unicorn's head; against the west wall are ranged elaborately carved panels with twenty-eight ancestral shields of arms, originally the family box pews installed by Nicholas and Elizabeth in 1631. Indeed, this childless pair left the simple granite church with more visible reminders of their occupancy of the big house than most churches show after many generations in the same family. The couple even have two funerary monuments apiece, but more of this later.

Interestingly to students of heraldry, the double-headed eagle appears with far greater frequency in the armoury of Cornwall than elsewhere in England, a notable instance being the arms of Killigrew. Also of note is the coincidence that the simple historic arms of the duchy are, in heraldic language, *Sable bezantee* – a black shield charged with discs called bezants, a name derived from the gold coinage of Byzantium. Still displayed today in the heraldic achievement of the heir to the throne as Duke of Cornwall, these arms have been associated with the county from early times. The Killigrew shield of Sir Nicholas Lower's wife is seen in profusion inside Landulph Church and combines the double-headed eagle and a border studded with bezants, a double dose of Byzantine allusions.

A curious coincidence must have struck Theodore when the villagers spoke of earlier incumbents of Landulph. Among recent rectors was a colourful character named William Alabaster, born in Mary Balls's home town of Hadleigh. He had been installed at Landulph in 1596 thanks to the influence of the Earl of Essex. The Alabasters were the most influential family in Hadleigh and evidently connected with the Balls clan. Thomas Alabaster, uncle of this William, had witnessed the 1568 will of the miller Roger Ball, Mary's grandfather.

A cleric, mystic, intriguer, soldier, playwright and poet, William Alabaster had been speedily deprived of the £100-a-year living when he announced his conversion to Catholicism. He was also implicated in Essex's rebellion. Clapped in Clink Prison in Southwark, he contrived an escape but on recapture was incarcerated in the Tower of London. He was pardoned on King James's accession. An almost exact contemporary of Theodore Paleologus, Alabaster was castigated as 'the wickedest creature on two legs' by the English ambassador to the Netherlands when he turned up there, only to be gaoled for plotting against Prince Maurice.

Alabaster was the nephew of John Still, Hadleigh's most distinguished rector, the incumbent from 1571 to 1592. This means Still was in all probability the priest who christened Mary Balls. He later became master of both St John's and Trinity colleges at Cambridge and bishop of Bath and Wells. Bishop Still made vain attempts to reclaim his nephew for the English Church but did not live to see his recantation of Catholicism in 1614. William Alabaster then preached before King James and was rewarded with a fat living in Hertfordshire, to the horror of parishioners who accused him of frequenting a bawdy house and uttering 'frivolous and salacious jests and ribaldries'.

Alabaster married a wealthy widow called Kathryn Fludd, thereby becoming stepfather of the occultist and alchemist Robert Fludd who anticipated Harvey in correctly describing the circulation of the blood. According to the bloodline-of-Christ conspiracy theory expounded in *The Holy Blood and the Holy Grail* – the claimed inspiration of Dan Brown's novel *The Da Vinci Code* – Robert Fludd was the grand master of the sinister secret order The Priory of the Sion.[64]

❖

Royalist and conservative to his core, Sir Nicholas Lower appears to have been a somewhat credulous man. There is a document of 1626 which indicates that 'by cunning' he was duped by a neighbour over the terms of a lease of a property. Certainly he was obsessed by heraldry and genealogy and consumed by a love for ancient and grand names. Canon Adams recorded seeing in a private collection a nine-foot-long genealogical roll compiled for Sir Nicholas by the College of Arms in 1620, and a pedigree still to be seen in the church traces the Lowers' claimed descent from dukes of Normandy and kings of England and Scotland besides showing Arundel ancestors from the important branches of Lanherne and Tolverne. 'Not entirely trustworthy,' remarks Adams mildly, and goes on to spot 'an amusing example of faking in the case of Lady Lower's ancestors'.

The Elizabethan and Jacobean period was indeed the golden age of fraud in pedigree-making, with many of the characters in this book, most notably the Berties and Cecils, paying the heralds to draw up fabulous family trees to disguise their standing as new men. Sir Nicholas Lower was relatively unambitious in tracing his ancestry to royalty; around this time the Heskeths of Lancashire ordered themselves an illuminated pedigree scroll detailing their descent from Adam and Eve.

Canon Adams's researches established the curious fact that Lady Lower was not only a first cousin of Sir Nicholas but a niece of his great-grand-mother. Her family was far more important than his, her father being the Sir Henry Killigrew who served as Queen Elizabeth's ambassador to Venice and Genoa, and whose name occurred in an earlier chapter as one of the Cornishmen wrongly credited with enticing Paleologus to England. Lady Lower's mother was one of the four celebrated daughters of the humanist sage Sir Anthony Coke, and the girls' marriages connected the relatively obscure Lowers with some of the great names of the time. Lady Lower's sister Mildred married Lord Burghley and was the mother of Sir Robert Cecil; sister Anne married Sir Nicholas Bacon, becoming the mother of Sir Francis and the spy Anthony; a third sister Elizabeth mar-ried John Lord Russell, heir to the Earl of Bedford.

The Coke girls were reputedly the best educated females in England, and if Lady Lower inherited anything of her mother's love of scholar-ship she must have welcomed the company of Theodore Paleologus for his erudition and knowledge of Greek, as Sir Nicholas cherished him for his exalted lineage. And indeed, on an epitaph in the church composed by her husband, Lady Lower is praised as the equal of any of her ances-tors 'for true virtue, piety and learning'.

Sir Nicholas would probably have been disappointed to know that the name Lower is remembered four centuries later only because of his brother William, and that its fame has nothing to do with the glories of lineage. The elder brother of Sir Nicholas, William Lower was a pio-neer astronomer and close friend of Thomas Harriot. The owner of one the first telescopes in Britain, William described what was later known as Halley's Comet long before Edmund Halley was born, sending Harriot a meticulous account of his observations in 1607. This was the same year it was seen by Johannes Kepler, astronomer to Emperor Rudolf II at Prague. It was not until 1705 that Halley recognised the periodicity of the comet that is known by his name. William Lower was also among the ear-liest observers of solar spots and the craters of the moon. Another famous scientist in the family was Richard Lower of Bodmin who carried out the first experimental blood transfusions on a human subject in 1666.

Both Jago Arundell and Adams imagined Paleologus in contented old age, a respected, white-bearded scholar enjoying the generous hospitality of a barren, well-to-do couple. That Paleologus's two daughters were soon invited to settle in with him burnishes this image of a comfortable retirement. Jago Arundell recorded that the old manor house of Clifton was still partly standing in his day, and showed clear signs of having been divided to accommodate two families.

How did Paleologus see out his days? After our long investigation, our subject remains almost as elusive as ever and our knowledge of the inner man almost non-existent. To Sir Nicholas and Dame Elizabeth the live-in guest was not the multiple-murderer and apostate we have tracked over many years, but a scholar, paterfamilias and no doubt an earnestly practising Anglican: above all, this was a man who had brought the enchantment of royalty into their little corner of Cornwall.

Perhaps as his life drew to a close Theodore took to brooding on his sins, like Calyphas in Marlowe's *Tamburlaine*:

> I know, sir, what it is to kill a man;
> It works remorse of conscience in me.

On the other hand, he may have had no conscience at all. Yet it is tempting to go along with the rosy image of Theodore in these final years at Landulph, a reformed character spinning airy glories of Constantinople for old Sir Nicholas, as he had done thirty years earlier for young John Smith. He had lived an extraordinary life, though one imagines the greater part of it was concealed from his hosts. Worldly success may have eluded him; he might be, in Sir Bernard Burke's words, 'unnoticed and altogether undistinguished' to the outside world. But he had evaded countless perils since his youthful banishment and there were three healthy sons to carry on the bloodline. In this picture of his last years we may easily see him as resigned to the whims of fate and grateful for the modest comforts he has. And who could guess when another turn of Fortune's wheel might allow his descendants to claim their birthright? That is, if we assume that Theodore himself actually believed in the imperial pedigree.

Carew's *Survey of Cornwall* laments the lack of resident noblemen in the county but finds solace in the abundant gentry – 'and I make question whether any shire in England, of but equal quality, can muster a like number of fair coat-armours,' the historian adds, quoting the old proverb that all Cornish gentlemen are cousins and praising the sociability of the class: 'They converse familiarly together, and often visit one another. A gentleman and his wife will ride to make merry with his next neighbour, and after a day or twain these two couples go to a third, in which progress they increase like snowballs.' Sir Nicholas served as sheriff of Cornwall in 1633, a post which further extended the circle of friends and relations he would visit or entertain at Clifton, eagerly showing off his imperial guest.

We have seen that a Master William Lower served at Ostend but it is also worth noting that Richard Carew's son John was one of a number of Cornish adventurers who had fought there from 1601, distinguishing himself by extraordinary fortitude when a cannonball took off his right hand. If, as we surmise, Theodore was present during the siege, John Carew may well have met up with him again in Cornwall, and indeed was possibly instrumental in introducing his old comrade-in-arms to the Lowers.

Yet Landulph was far from being the idyllic spot which charms the visitor today. In the words of Carew, who was the squire of Antony House not many miles from Landulph, few counties were as plagued by the poor as Cornwall where 'those vermin swarm in every corner', though the historian is insistent that the majority are not native Cornish but Irish migrants, arriving daily by the shipload. 'To the high offence of God and good order,' rumbles Carew, 'they maintain idleness, drunkenness, theft, lechery, blasphemy, atheism, and, in a word, all impiety'. The proximity of a magnet like Plymouth ensured that Landulph was not free of the attentions of these marauding beggars and thieves.

The plague remained an ever-present threat. Plymouth had seen one of its worst outbreaks in 1626 when 2,000 died. Theodore was still living in town with Mary at this time, and an invitation to a village like

Landulph must have been welcome. No other major epidemic struck the area during the next few years, though the plague raged in London almost continuously throughout 1636, Theodore's last year of life, with well over 10,000 recorded victims.

Landulph felt unsafe during these years for another reason, for Muslim raiders from North Africa had made themselves a dreadful menace to Devon and Cornwall. Admiralty records of Jacobean times list many hundreds of English ships captured by Barbary pirates with no fewer than twenty-seven vessels being taken off Plymouth alone in 1625, the first year of Charles's reign. Crews and passengers were sold into slavery at Algiers, Tripoli or Tunis. Not content with preying on shipping, pirates would land at coastal villages in the hours of darkness and round up terrified men, women and children to sell in the slave markets.

To Theodore it must have seemed as if the heathen who chased his ancestors from Constantinople would dog him to the ends of the earth. His life had been punctuated by the remorseless advances of the Ottomans through the outposts of Greek civilisation: Chios had been conquered in 1566; Malta had come within a hair's breadth of falling in the Great Siege of 1565; Cyprus, evangelised in AD 45 by Paul and Barnabas, fell in 1571. That same year Crete, last bastion of Hellenism, was temporarily saved by the great Christian sea victory of Lepanto, but though the Ottoman fleet was annihilated the Christian allies failed to follow up with an attack on undefended Constantinople.

Even easier than England for the pirates were targets in lands close to their lairs, especially Italy and Spain; in all, an estimated 85,000 European Christians were sold into white slavery during the hundred years beginning 1580. However, English captives had slim hopes of being ransomed, lacking the go-between services long offered by Catholic clergy. Yet there are numerous records of West Country authorities helping efforts to ransom prisoners, supporting their dependants, or giving alms to escapees. In 1607, for instance, the Cornish town of Liskeard gave a local man three shillings 'towards the ransoming of his brother being taken by the Turks' and the following year two shillings and sixpence to two sailors 'which had there tongues cutt out of there heades' when their ship was seized. Generous donations to the cause, supported by prayers, were offered by many churches.

Things were so bad by 1625 that the West Country's maritime trade virtually came to a halt. Fishermen and merchants refused to put to sea, prompting the Duke of Buckingham to dispatch a naval squadron to deal with the threat. Shamefully, the squadron took refuge in Falmouth harbour after a brief tussle with the raiders, 'the sayd Pyrats being farre better saylers then our English shipps'. In a matter of days during August the Turks took at least twenty-five ships belonging to the town of Looe, captured Lundy Island and its entire population, snatched many inhabitants of Padstow, and seized sixty men, women and children seeking sanctuary in a church in Mount's Bay. Buckingham's abject failure to protect the English seas, not only by the lack of fighting ships but by the decay of coastal fortifications, fuelled the bitter resentment burning against the duke and, increasingly, the king himself.

The level of piracy eased off for a while between 1627 and 1630, but the coast then faced danger from French men-of-war thanks to Buckingham's foreign policy. Thereafter Turkish attacks resumed with a vengeance, however, the raids peaking in 1636, the year of Theodore's death. Again, towns and churches throughout Cornwall responded generously to redeem captives, with Plymouth organising monthly collections. In the accounts of the mayor of Liskeard that year were more donations to unfortunates 'spoiled' by the Turks including another poor man minus his tongue.

Pirates were not the only threat, as young able-bodied men – the breadwinners in most families – risked being taken by the press gang. Cornwall was the navy's first target on the eve of the Cadiz expedition, and on Sir James Bagge's orders 350 Cornishmen were levied in April and May 1625 and marched into Plymouth. The quest for men continued throughout the summer; in September, shortly before the fleet sailed, the Privy Council ordered a further 500 be impressed to replace those who had died, deserted or fallen sick while billeted in Plymouth. At one time, 10,000 snatched men were crammed into the port. The Cadiz impressments were furiously resented in Devon and Cornwall and there was stout opposition two years later when Buckingham demanded yet more men for his La Rochelle adventure. Bagge was then ordered to impress all sailors on board merchant ships in the West Country.

❖

The rector of Landulph at the time of Theodore's death was the oddly named Bezaleel Burt – in the Book of Exodus, Bezaleel is the workman called by God to build the Ark of the Covenant – and it was presumably he who conducted the service. Burt had been incumbent at Landulph since 1624 when he succeeded William Hele, the replacement for the disgraced William Alabaster.

Burial inside a church had always been expensive and was officially discouraged by this time, not only due to pressure of space but because of a growing concern for hygiene. As one bishop declared, bodies were no longer to be interred below the church floor 'for that by their general burying there great infection doth ensue'. However, exception was to be made for 'those of the best sort of the parish'.

The date of death is given on Theodore's brass as 21 January 1636, though by present reckoning this would be 1637. However, the Bishop of Exeter's Transcripts record the date of burial as 20 October 1636. The discrepancy was first noted by Jago Arundell, but the Landulph register does not resolve the problem as entries between the years 1628 to 1648 are missing. Errors in bishops' transcripts are not unknown, but Canon Adams believed the monument was erected some years after Theodore's death when memories had grown hazy: Dame Elizabeth died in 1638, and Sir Nicholas may well have ordered her brass and Theodore's at the same time. However, it is just as likely that these two monuments were commissioned along with one for himself as Sir Nicholas felt death approaching. As a widower with no children, he almost certainly ordered his own memorial, a supposition strengthened by the three brass plates being indistinguishable in terms of heraldic draughtsmanship, decorative elements and style of lettering. Each sets out the pedigree of the deceased to a degree unusual even in that ancestry-conscious age, and we have seen that the elderly knight's passion was genealogy. Sir Nicholas died in 1655, and as this was nearly twenty years after Theodore's burial it would not be surprising if the recollection of his date of death was faulty.[65]

The Lower brasses are fixed side by side on the wall above the Clifton family pew and mounted so high that the inscriptions are difficult to read. Strangely, a large tomb chest also bearing the names of Sir Nicholas and Dame Elizabeth stands in the chancel below Theodore's brass. A large and magnificent monument of black marble, this is also carved with the impaled arms of Lower and Killigrew. Why the couple should be commemorated twice is a mystery.

A casual visitor might easily overlook the brass which has inspired the Paleologus legend. Measuring only twenty-one inches high by nineteen inches across, it is fixed to the vestry wall to the right of the altar and is thought to be the work of a London engraver, a good but not outstanding craftsman. The monument was first illustrated in Edwin Dunkin's *Monumental Brasses of Cornwall* in 1882. Though of great interest, the coat-of-arms above the inscription throws up a number of problems. On the shield is the crowned and double-headed eagle of Byzantium but with its talons resting on two squat towers, supposedly representing the gates of Rome and Constantinople. What is not shown on Dunkin's engraving, though clearly visible on the brass itself, is that the shield is in heraldic terms *per fess*, which means it is divided by a horizontal line to signify that the background is of two colours. There is no clue as to what these colours might be, or indeed the colour of the eagle: the imperial eagle was sometimes black and sometimes gold.

Another puzzle is the small crescent at the base of the shield. In English heraldry this is the mark of difference for a second son; the difficulty is that such a mark often becomes hereditary, so its original purpose is lost. There is the added complication that in Italian heraldry the crescent has no such significance. My guess is that the crescent was not used by Theodore himself but added by order of his pedantic if misguided friend Sir Nicholas when he commissioned the monument. Either he had been told that Theodore was a second son, though we have no evidence of this, or he was deriving the arms from the ancestor Thomas the Despot, described on the brass as second brother to the last emperor.

I can find no Italian record of the arms borne by Theodore's ancestors in Pesaro. However, by chance I have seen a plainly related coat-of-arms in one of the remarkable painted churches of Cyprus which date from the Byzantine era. This is the tiny church of St George at Xylophagou, not far from Larnaca, where a recent cleaning of smoke-blackened grime from the fifteenth-century murals has revealed a similar shield. The blazon here is *per pale gules and argent* – that is, divided vertically red and silver – with a crowned double-headed eagle *sable*, or black. Instead of resting on towers, each of the eagle's talons grasps a roundel: one is the gold disc or *bezant*, the other a roundel of red called a *torteau*, said to be a representation of the Sacred Host. The choice of red and white may be explained by the fact that the Paleologus emperors quartered the cross of St George with the family arms on their banner, so we might surmise these were the colours of Theodore's shield.

The leading authorities on Cyprus's painted churches, Andreas and Judith Stylianou, believe the Xylophagou arms are of the noble donor or benefactor of St George's, one of the Paleologus family connected with Queen Helena Paleologina, a niece of Constantine XI who married a Latin ruler of Cyprus. The last of this Cypriot line, a Demetri Paleologo, was killed during the Turkish conquest of the island in 1571.

We can catch something of the veneration of ancient families that animates people like Nicholas Lower in the awe-struck tone of the Victorian historian Hamilton Rogers, who ends his book *The Strife of the Roses and Days of the Tudors* with a chapter on the Paleologus monument. After a wordy description of how a casual visitor might stroll around Landulph Church, Rogers goes on:

> Now stay thy foot, and hearken! For we are standing not on princely, nay, nor royal, but even over Imperial dust. Give thy thoughts wing, from these leaden skies and mist-hung coasts, – nor stay them until they reach the sunny

shores of the Bosphorus and the Golden Horn, the classic precincts and immortal traditions of that superlatively beautiful city, and to the illustrious dynasty that erstwhile ruled her ... then learn that a direct descendant of this distinguished race, an exile from his native clime, and almost an outcast on the face of the earth, found his last refuge in this life, under a friendly roof nearby, and lies at rest, – not in marble sarcophagus under a vaulted dome near the home of his royal ancestors, – but, equally well, beneath the simple pavement of this rustic sanctuary.

The burial of Theodore was not his last appearance. In his lecture to the Society of Antiquaries, Jago Arundell described how about twenty years previously – that is, about 1795 – the vault below the Paleologus brass was opened: 'The coffin of Paleologus was seen, a single oak coffin; and curiosity prompting to lift the lid, the body of Paleologus was discovered, and in so perfect a state, as to ascertain him to have been in stature much above the common height, his countenance oval in form, much lengthened, and strongly marked by an aquiline nose, and a very white beard reaching low on the breast.'

Disturbing the dead may be an almost universal taboo nowadays, yet few scruples were observed in earlier and, as one supposes, more god-fearing times. Accounts of coffins being opened out of curiosity are legion, and not even the royal dead at Westminster and Windsor have been safe from inquisitive antiquaries: on occasion a souvenir would be taken from the body, a ring or a lock of hair. Nor was this morbid interest limited to men. 'The curiosity of some ladies' caused the coffin of Queen Katherine Parr to be opened in the ruined chapel of Sudeley Castle in 1782, though such was their alarm at the sight and smell of the exposed body that they ordered its immediate reburial. Readers of Pepys will remember his vivid account of lifting up the mummy-like corpse of Queen Katherine de Valois, wife of Henry V, during a tour of the abbey: 'This was my birthday, thirty-six years old, that I did kiss a Queene.' How the 'body-snatcher' dean of Westminster uncovered the coffin of a son of Theodore Paleologus is told in the next chapter, followed by the story of the opening of the coffin of yet another son over 4,000 miles away in Barbados.

Hamilton Rogers in his history ruminates on how the remains of the great have always been rummaged over by irreverent hands – 'the cunningly embalmed Egyptian potentate in his burial fortress of the great pyramid, – the Roman emperor in his grand mausoleum, – Greek hero in costly sarcophagus, – British chieftain in flint-piled barrow' – and laments that Theodore has not been spared this outrage. However, he notes with satisfaction that the remarkable preservation of the body confirms 'a physiognomy and stature eminently representative of his imperial descent'.

❖

We can be reasonably confident that Theodore was surrounded by family members and close friends on his deathbed, as was customary at the time. The two daughters and at least the youngest son would be present. Who closed his eyes and composed his limbs immediately after death cannot be known, or who came to measure the body for its extra-large coffin. Until comparatively recently every village in England had someone ready to perform these tasks.

Considering the excellent state of Theodore's body when it was exposed long afterwards, despite the damp ground on which Landulph stands, it seems very probable he was embalmed. This treatment could be pricey. From the beginning of the seventeenth century the medical profession in the guise of the barber-surgeons had petitioned against unqualified persons such as butchers and tailors trying to break their monopoly of 'opening searing and imbalmeinge of the dead corpses'. And no wonder, for it could be a very lucrative business. Embalming King James in 1625 netted one barber-surgeon £50 – say £7,000 in today's money – though attending to lesser persons would obviously command a smaller fee, especially in the provinces.

From what we know of Nicholas Lower, the old ways would have been observed as far as possible in the funeral rites. Family and friends would have been joined at Clifton Hall by the rector and parish clerk and the cortege would then set off for the church, the clerk leading the procession with a hand-bell, the priest following beside the coffin. Landulph's *leche bell wt his clapper*, first recorded in church accounts in 1559, would have been tolled seventy-six times or thereabouts, once for every year of Theodore's life. In this country area it is unlikely the coffin was shouldered because of the uneven ground, and the bearers would have carried the coffin on short poles at waist height. A line of hooded mourners led by male relatives brought up the rear of the procession; John Theodore, then aged twenty-five, would act as chief mourner if the eldest son was away at a foreign war; if John was absent also it would have been the sixteen-year-old Ferdinand. Mourners would usually carry a sprig of rosemary for remembrance to cast into the grave at end of the ceremony, an expedient custom in the case of burial in church as it helped to disguise unseemly odours.

Given Sir Nicholas's predilections, it may be that a hatchment, a diamond-shaped board painted with the Paleologus coat-of-arms, was carried before the coffin for later display in the church. Hatchments had come into vogue in the early seventeenth century following the Dutch fashion, though few examples of this early date survive.

An indispensable feature of obsequies for the best sort of parishioner was the funeral sermon, usually costing about ten shillings, preached on an appropriate text such as 'How are the mighty fallen', a theme with particular resonance for a Paleologus. Theodore was of the last generation at whose funeral the Order of the Burial of the Dead remained as it had been in Elizabeth's time, for in less than a decade the Puritans would abolish what they saw as the tainted ceremonial of popish superstition. Theodore's son and namesake would be one of the very first whose burial was shorn of all ceremony, albeit in the grand setting of Westminster Abbey.

The Paleologus tomb brings many Greek visitors to Landulph, and the 2007 ceremony led by Archbishop Gregorios[66] was not the first to be held in this Anglican church by an Orthodox priest. An earlier memorial service for Theodore was celebrated by a revered figure known as Archimandrite Barnabas, who since his death at the age of eighty in 1995 is referred to by the faithful as 'of blessed memory'.

Orthodox, in any sense except in reference to the Eastern religion, is not a word that would readily spring to mind to describe Archimandrite Barnabas. The very image of a Greek priest with his bushy white beard and traditional black garb, Barnabas was in fact a Welshman born in 1915 as Ian Burton. In his twenties he was ordained in the Church of England but later converted to Catholicism before finding his true calling in Orthodoxy. On his ordination in 1960 he became the first Welsh Orthodox priest since the Great Schism of 1054. He went on to found small monasteries in Wales and Devon and revived pilgrimages to sites associated with Welsh and Cornish saints.[67]

To discover an imperial Byzantine connection with Landulph gave great joy to the archimandrite and he was the first Orthodox priest to celebrate a memorial service for Theodore Paleologus in the church. It was the first service of any kind to be conducted in his name since his funeral in 1636.

# 17

But when the planets
In evil mixture to disorder wander,
What plagues and what portents, what mutiny …

Shakespeare, *Troilus and Cressida.*

Theodore II's next appearance in the records is in 1631, the year of
his mother's death, when he came forward as a witness in a Chancery
suit brought by the infamous turncoat Sir Richard Grenville, known as
Skellum Grenville. This was the unworthy grandson and namesake of
the great Elizabethan seaman Grenville of the *Revenge*. The court papers
describe his friend as *Theodore Palaeologus of Tavistock, gent*, aged twenty-
one, who gave evidence that he had been present on 1 April the previous
year when Sir Richard paid over money to redeem some jewels pawned
by his wife Dame Mary.

Like his father before him, Theodore II seems to have been magneti-
cally attracted to the worst of humanity. Skellum Grenville, a veteran of
the failed Cadiz and La Rochelle expeditions, had married the widowed
heiress Mary Howard two years before the court case, only to discover
that her fortune was held in trust and beyond his reach. The violent
beatings he handed out, and his repeated but frustrated efforts to get his
hands on her money, quickly led to their separation. The action involving Theodore was one of the couple's many acrimonious milestones on
the way to divorce.

Theodore deposed that he has known Grenville since 1623, and as
he would have been fourteen at the time this strongly suggests he
had been taken into service at one of the households of the Grenville
affinity. His father would almost certainly have known members of

these inter-related West Country gentry families while fighting in the Netherlands, among them Arundells, Carews and Lowers, of whom we shall hear more presently. Skellum Grenville's father had himself served in the Anglo-Dutch forces at the same time as Theodore I.

Soon after the Chancery hearing, Grenville was imprisoned following an action brought by his estranged wife, but he escaped from gaol in 1633 and fled to Germany. It was there he earned his nickname Skellum, said to derive from the German *scheim*, meaning scoundrel. He returned to England to join the army raised by King Charles against the Scots in 1640, and so met up again with his friend Theodore Paleologus, now aged thirty-one, who is found listed among the lieutenants who marched north under the command of the Earl of Northumberland.

In the footsteps of his father, Theodore II was now a professional soldier. He may have gained his first experience of warfare either as a mercenary in the renewed European wars, or like Skellum Grenville in one of the Duke of Buckingham's naval expeditions. Their first taste of active service at home was best forgotten, however, as the move against Scotland ended in a humiliating flight before the Scottish army. Theodore is next heard of in an army list of the same year 'after the Armies Retreat from Newcastle into Yorkshire'. This time his name is given as a lieutenant in the regiment of Sir Jacob Astley, who was to be an energetic royalist general in the coming Civil War. Like Theodore I, Astley was a Low Countries veteran who had served under the banner of Maurice of Nassau. This may possibly explain the son's attachment to Astley's force.

Soldiers were now deciding where their loyalty lay in the conflict between king and parliament. This was the parting of the ways between Theodore II and Grenville, as it was between Theodore and his brothers. In 1641 Skellum led royal troops against the king's foes in Ireland and reaped further notoriety for the savage treatment meted out to his prisoners. Arrested by parliament on his return to England, he changed sides and was rewarded with a commission in the rebel army. He was sent to join the parliamentary forces and immediately deserted to King Charles at Oxford, revealing the enemy's plans. He was denounced as a traitor by the Roundheads, who erected a gibbet in London on which was nailed a proclamation against Grenville: 'Traitor, Rogue, Villain, and Skellum, incapable of all acquaintance and conversation with men of honesty and honour.'

In the meantime Theodore had thrown in his lot with the rebels. By June 1642 his name was on parliament's Reformado List – a roll of officers whose merits entitled them to half pay even when unemployed – which seems a clear indication of previous experience abroad. Soon afterwards 'Theo Paholigus' was named a captain-lieutenant in a regiment of foot raised in Oxford by Oliver, Lord St John of Bletso. This regiment was based at Worcester on 23 October 1642 when the first major engagement of the war began at Edgehill, but Lord St John hurried off to take part in the battle with his troop of horse and sustained a fatal wound that same day. Whether Paleologus fought with him is unknown.

Facing the parliament's forces as the king's general-in-chief was the son and heir of Peregrine, Lord Willoughby. Robert Bertie, first encountered in these pages as the childhood friend of John Smith, was now a grizzled veteran of nearly sixty. He had been created Earl of Lindsey by Charles I, and when hostilities broke out he raised a regiment of infantry from his roll of Lincolnshire tenants. Here was yet another who had served in the Low Countries under Prince Maurice. Beside him at Edgehill fought his son Montagu, now bearing the courtesy title Lord Willoughby; this was the same Montagu Bertie who was the friend of John Smith. He had married the daughter of Francis Norreys, who accused Theodore I of being a serial murderer. Lindsey was shot in the thigh during the first stage of the battle and fell surrounded by Roundhead cavalry. Montagu surrendered to take care of his father but was unable to staunch the wound, and the earl died the following day after refusing a surgeon sent to him by the parliamentary commander.

Following Lord St John's death the colonelcy of the regiment passed to Sir Thomas Essex, a little known figure. Theodore was named among his company commanders. The next thing we hear of him is on 9 May 1643 when a warrant was made out for payment to Theodore Paleologus of £50 arrears of pay, and only a year later he was dead and buried.

It has long been believed that Theodore II was killed at the second battle of Newbury in 1644. Among the authorities who state this is Peter Young, praised by the great C.V. Wedgwood as the leading military historian of the Civil War. Then serving under Sir Philip Stapleton and promoted to the rank of lieutenant colonel – meaning his monthly pay rose to £42 – Theodore is referred to by Brigadier Young as 'of Landulph, Cornwall', though we have seen it is unlikely he ever lived there. Young's book on Edgehill names him among the slain or mortally wounded at Second Newbury.

The trouble is the dates do not fit. Second Newbury was fought on 27 October 1644 and according to the Westminster Abbey register Paleologus's burial had taken place on 3 May. This date cannot seriously be questioned as records show that on the same day the House of Lords agreed with a decision of the Commons to pay arrears to Captain Paleologus, 'lately deceased in the service of the Parliament'. A draft order was made out to pay £50 to Stapleton, presumably acting as Theodore's executor. However, no will has been found to confirm this and Stapleton may have stepped in as his superior officer.

The historian Chris Scott, an authority on the Civil War battles, examined at my request the movements and engagements of Stapleton's regiment in 1644 alongside the known facts surrounding Paleologus's death, and has concluded that he probably died of camp fever during the preliminary stage of the protracted Siege of Oxford. Camp fever, also known as epidemic or louse-borne typhus, had arrived in Europe during the fifteenth century. It became a common cause of mortality during the Civil War due to the poor sanitation and standards of hygiene attendant on military life. An early account of the epidemic arriving during a siege speaks of fever accompanying the appearance of red spots over the arms and torso, the symptoms progressing to delirium, gangrenous sores and the stench of putrefying flesh. The parliamentary record of Theodore's death shorn of comment seems to support Scott's deduction of death due to disease as officers killed in action were generally lauded for their valour and dedication to the cause. If this is the case, it was a miserable end to Theodore II at the age of thirty-five.

The Siege of Oxford was actually three sieges staged over three years, between 1644 and 1646. During the first siege, two parliamentary armies attacked the city late in May. Their general, the third Earl of Essex – son of Elizabeth's fallen favourite – was an indecisive and introverted commander who set off to war with his coffin carried before him. His assaults on Oxford proved ineffectual and by early June poor leadership and lack of cooperation between the Roundhead forces allowed the king to escape with the bulk of his army.

Sir Philip Stapleton was colonel of Essex's Lifeguard and a close personal friend. A cavalry leader at Edgehill, he commanded the right wing of horse at the first battle of Newbury in 1643 when he reportedly discharged a pistol at point-blank into Prince Rupert's face, only for the weapon to misfire. It is always possible that the story of Theodore's death at Second Newbury arose from a mix-up between the two battles. However, the first action was in September 1643 and it seems unlikely he would succumb to wounds so long afterwards; in any case there is nothing to connect him with Stapleton at this earlier date.

Westminster Abbey had always been the most prized burial place in England because of its royal associations, an exclusivity confirmed by an order of Elizabeth I limiting interment within its walls to 'those especially who shall have well and gravely served about our person, or otherwise about the business of our kingdom'. Its pre-eminence continued under the parliamentary regime and it is hard to imagine Theodore being buried in this English Valhalla at any other time.

The Puritan-inspired *Directory for the Publique Worship of God*, published by parliament in the year of Theodore II's death, introduced radical changes to funeral practices. To start with, it ruled that no minister need be present at the burial. The body was to be 'immediately interred without ceremony' though marks of respect were still to be observed 'suitable to the rank of the deceased'. It is probable that Paleologus's funeral took place by torchlight; the first nocturnal burials occurred late in Elizabeth's reign and became increasingly fashionable with the accession of James. The new king himself lent his prestige to the trend by ordering the night-time reburial of his mother, Mary Queen of Scots.

A nocturnal funeral allowed the rigid laws governing traditional funerals to be flouted, for instance by enabling a widow to act as chief mourner rather than a senior male relation. A further advantage was that the ruinous expense of the gorgeous display expected of daylight obsequies could largely be avoided. A wartime funeral dictated extra constraints on expenditure, and the fact that the family were usually unable to attend was a clinching argument for dispensing with show. Then again, a busy senior officer like Sir Philip Stapleton who felt duty-bound to be present would find it easier to spare time at night, and the cortege would largely avoid the undignified sights and sounds of a populous city street in daytime.

Much has been made of the location of Theodore's burial place in the chapel of St Andrew, off the north transept of the abbey and near the foot of the tomb of a Lady St John who died in 1615. This was Catherine, widow of John, second Baron St John of Bletso, uncle of the fifth Lord St John who was slain at Edgehill. Her alabaster effigy lies propped on its side in the so-called toothache pose, with the right hand pressed against the cheek. That Theodore's place in the abbey was secured by the influence of the St Johns, as stated by Canon Adams and indeed repeated by the Westminster authorities, is I think open to question. Confusion may have arisen between the two Lords St John, with Theodore's proximity to the lady buried nearly thirty years before being entirely coincidental. But whatever the reason he was buried at Westminster, we can be confident it was not to honour his imperial descent.

The simple gravestone we see in the abbey bears only the name Theodorus Palaeologus and the date 1644, but not all is as it seems. For the presence of the stone we need look back no further than 1864 when the distinguished churchman Arthur Stanley was appointed dean of Westminster.

Known to Queen Victoria as 'the little dean' because of his diminutive stature, Stanley was morbidly obsessed with coffins, corpses and the like. Earlier in his career he had avidly examined a supposed head of Oliver Cromwell and the bones of James III of Scotland, and the Westminster Abbey job was the answer to his dreams. Stanley's decision to install heating in the Henry VII chapel meant the excavation of the floor, which to his delight exposed the coffin of Charles II. The dean then insisted on continuing to delve amid the abbey's foundations, his many finds including the lead coffin of James I and a vault occupied by Henry Tudor and his queen, Elizabeth of York. He also exposed the coffin of Elizabeth I but refrained from prising open the anthropoid lead shell in which the body was encased. Appalled by Stanley's rummaging among her ancestors, Victoria now took to calling the little dean 'that body-snatcher'. It was Stanley who discovered Theodore's coffin in St Andrew's chapel and ordered the inscribed stone to mark its location. Given the dean's incurable inquisitiveness, one must wonder whether he yielded to the same temptation as the finders of the first Theodore's coffin.

At Westminster as at Edgehill, once again we see different strands of the Paleologus story coming together, reminding us that the world of the time was a very small one. Whether or not there was a St John connection with Theodore II's burial place, it is certainly coincidental that he was interred only a few steps from the enormous Jacobean monument of the Earl of Lincoln's bête noire, the first Lord Norreys of Rycote, whose recumbent effigy lies flanked by the kneeling figures of his six soldier sons in full armour. Among these is William, first husband of the unhappy countess of Lincoln and father of the Francis Norreys who denounced Theodore I as a murderer. Among other characters in this book who are buried a stone's-throw from Theodore II are the third Earl of Essex, his last commander-in-chief, the Earl of Oxford, claimed as the real author of Shakespeare, and Sir Francis Vere, English commander at the Siege of Ostend.

Theodore II's body was spared the fate of prominent parliamentarians buried in the abbey who bore the wrath of royalists at the Restoration, when their remains were dug up and subjected to symbolic execution and quartering as traitors, with their heads impaled on spikes at Tyburn. Charles II signed an order that the bodies of all other persons 'unwarrantably buried' in the abbey since 1641 should be exhumed and cast into a pit in the nearby churchyard of St Margaret's. According to Dean Stanley's *Historical Memorials of Westminster Abbey*, an exhaustive directory of burials within its precincts, only seven bodies interred during the Commonwealth were spared this 'mean vengeance'. But whether Theodore was left in peace because he was a simple soldier or because his grave was then unmarked is uncertain.

❖

As Theodore II was throwing in his lot with the Roundheads, his youngest brother Ferdinand backed the other side. The next surviving record of him after his baptism is at the age of nineteen, in January 1639, when his name occurs on the list of soldiers at St Michael's Fort in Plymouth Sound. Better known today as Drake's Island, this rocky six-acre outcrop was first fortified against the French in 1549, with barracks for 300 men being added at the end of the century. Ferdinand was not an officer like his brother Theodore but a common soldier paid £12 a year. The start of the Civil War found few Englishmen with experience of fighting, which made the seasoned veterans of European conflicts eagerly sought by both sides. But most troops – probably including most of the thirty then stationed at St Michael's Island – were unwilling, undisciplined and ill-equipped.

At the outbreak of hostilities Cornwall sided with the king and Devon with parliament. Plymouth itself was governed by the royalist Sir Jacob Astley, Theodore II's old commander, but King Charles blundered in summoning him to join the main army. The moment he was gone the city declared for the rebels. As the king's forces took control of the rest of Devon in the early stages of the war, Plymouth remained the only port loyal to parliament through nearly four years of siege. The final onslaught came in January 1645 when Skellum Grenville was in command of the royal forces investing the city. Now infamous for atrocities and profiteering in his home county, Grenville launched a reckless full-scale attack by 6,000 troops but failed to break the city's defences. When one of the royalist officers protested at the senseless loss of life, Skellum drew his sword and killed him on the spot.

Once the rebels seized control of Plymouth, St Michael's Island became a gaol for royalist prisoners and declared traitors. What happened to Ferdinand after 1639 is unclear, and his name is not found in the army lists compiled by both sides in 1642, though in any case these are of officers only. Canon Adams concluded he had left the army and England before war broke out; alternatively, he may have been among the many royalist sympathisers who chose shipment to Barbados rather than imprisonment at home, but this option seems not to have been available until the closing stages of the conflict.

As we shall see, Ferdinand was in Barbados by 1644, which effectively disposes of the legend that he escaped to the West Indies after fighting on the royalist side at Naseby, the battle which destroyed Charles's hopes of winning the war. Similar stories are woven around the second of the sons born at Tattershall, John Theodore. In the Adams papers from 1946 I found a copy of a letter written from Landulph Rectory to one of the rector's regular correspondents, and in this he mentions his frustrated efforts to pin down the source of the claim that John and Ferdinand served together at Naseby in the regiment of a Major William Lower, where by one account John was slain. However, another story has him falling at the battle of Lansdown Hill in Somerset in 1643, a pyrrhic victory for the royalists in which Major Lower himself was killed. Adams reproaches himself for his carelessness in losing his original reference – 'I am very cross with myself' – which might have clarified a continuing link between the young Paleologi and the Lowers during the Civil War.

John Paleologus remains the most enigmatic of the three brothers. It is certain that he was not killed at Lansdown Hill because on 26 June 1644 he was in Barbados with Ferdinand, as the pair witnessed a deed together on that day. It seems highly improbable that he returned to fight at Naseby the following June when the king's army was all but wiped out. Yet apart from witnessing the deed with his brother there is no further trace of him in the West Indies or anywhere else. Clearly we can dismiss out of hand the contention of Charles Sandoe Gilbert, author of *The Historical Survey of the County of Cornwall* published in 1817, that 'it is probable that John and Ferdinando returned to their native country', and not only because their native country was England. But we will return later to what may have befallen John in the New World.

✣

Before following Ferdinand to Barbados, where the Paleologus saga takes more of its remarkable twists, we must complete the story of his surviving sisters, Mary and Dorothy, who both appear to have remained in the manor house at Landulph after their father's death.

Of Mary or Maria very little has come to light and she is now the only one of the five children surviving into adulthood whose year of birth is unknown. Canon Adams assumed she was the youngest of the Paleologus girls, though her name comes before that of Dorothy on the Landulph brass and the order in such cases usually goes with age, as it does with their three brothers. When Sir Nicholas Lower made his will in January 1654 he left Mary ten pounds 'to be paied unto her within one quarter of a yeare after my decease'. The will refers to her as *Mrs Maria Paleologus*, leading some earlier historians to suppose this was Theodore's wife, the former Mary Balls. But the prefix is a contraction of mistress which at this time was equally applied to a spinster; that this was indeed the daughter Mary is clear from the burial record.

As will be seen, she was also bequeathed twenty shillings when her brother Ferdinand died in Barbados. The fact that she received these two legacies is practically all we know of Mary Paleologus, except that she was buried at Landulph on 15 May 1674. As an unmarried woman she would have had her coffin carried to church by young women dressed in white with a garland of flowers on the lid. This custom lingered on for centuries and mouldering examples of these 'maidens' garlands' can still be seen in a handful of English country churches.

The other daughter, Dorothy Paleologus, married William Arundel, son of the Alexander Arundel from whom Sir Nicholas purchased Clifton. The striking thing about this marriage, on 23 December 1656, is that Dorothy was then fifty years old. There is a minor mystery about where the couple wedded as the ceremony is recorded in the registers of both Landulph and St Mellion, the latter presumably being where William Arundel worshipped, though to add to the confusion the register entry there describes him as *de St Dominick*. St Mellion and St Dominic are neighbouring villages not far from Landulph. The clerk of St Mellion grandly describes the bride as *Dorothea Paleologus de stirpe Imperatorum* – of the imperial stock – while the Landulph register entry is balder: *William arundel and darythy pallealogus were mayed the twenty 3 december*. The marriage dates from the Commonwealth years, and the Revd Bezaleel Burt had been replaced in 1643 by one Edward Amerideth, the nominee of parliament. Amerideth was in turn ejected after the Restoration.

Jago Arundell claimed the couple settled soon afterwards in St Dominic parish but as he offered no evidence this may be no more than a guess based on the St Mellion entry. What undermines Jago Arundell's statement is that he also claimed the St Dominic registers were accidentally destroyed, whereas Canon Adams quickly established they were extant. Registers for the next twenty years threw no further light on the couple's later history, however, and Adams found no other Cornish record of any issue of the union. Given Dorothy's age, the chances that she bore children are virtually nil, and Adams seems to suspect Jago Arundell speculated on the couple having issue to prop up his oft-quoted suggestion that 'the imperial blood perhaps still flows in the bargemen of Cargreen',[68] the neighbouring village to Landulph. In Carew's *Survey of Cornwall*, Cargreen is called 'a fisher town', though dismissed with laborious wit as being so poor 'it can hardly muster a mean plight of dwellings or dwellers; so may their care be green, because their wealth is withered'. Dorothy was buried at Landulph in 1681 and her husband three years later.

This is the last time we need mention the researches of Francis Jago Arundell in this book, and is an appropriate place to complete our brief biography of the first historian of Theodore Paleologus.

Born in 1780 the only son of a surgeon of Launceston, Francis Jago was seized by a love for Cornish history in his youth, and the rectorship of Landulph saw his passion channelled into the study of Paleologus. He was elected a fellow of the Society of Antiquaries in 1811 though finally removed from the fellowship for being twenty-eight years behind with his subscription. Canon Adams was sniffy about his Georgian predecessor's assumption of the name Arundell. He changed his name in 1815 on the basis that a Jago ancestor had married a co-heiress of the Arundells of Trevarnoe, a branch of this great family of Cornwall; that they were the former owners of Clifton and had actually married into the Paleologus line was clearly an irresistible attraction to Jago. Adams does not disguise his view that his predecessor's claim to Arundell blood was unconvincing. But whether it was bogus or not, by assuming the renowned name the rector sprinkled himself with a little imperial stardust.

Adams also formed a low opinion of Jago Arundell's business acumen. In his files he recorded how his predecessor had 'built a great embankment at Landulph and thereby practically ruined himself', doing so with the hare-brained idea of developing the village as a popular spa. At that time the river Tamar at high tide flowed up to the churchyard wall and across the road and footpath from the rectory, so that Jago Arundell sometimes had to go to church in a boat. The inspiration for the spa project came when he was told of an ancient holy well within a quarter of a mile of the church which had been described in an eighteenth-century source as 'an excellent medicinall spring'. Water from this well was brought into church for baptisms.

Next the rector began to build a spa hotel, the unfinished edifice of which was later made into a farmhouse. It was generally presumed he had obtained a lease of the land from the Duchy of Cornwall, to which it belonged then as now. In a marginal note Adams says he was told by an old villager that Jago Arundell did not obtain a lease but 'squatted' on what he believed to be ownerless wasteland. The note adds: 'The Duchy allowed him to ruin himself and then stepped in and claimed everything under their foreshore rights.'

Jago Arundell lost so much money in the failed scheme that he was forced to leave the country. In 1822 he obtained a position as chaplain to a British factory at Smyrna, and a portrait of the rector now hanging in the church seems to have been painted there. Smyrna was the perfect bolthole for a cleric of his interests. He wrote a well-received book on a pilgrimage he undertook to the Seven Churches named in the Book of Revelation and published other scholarly works on the ruins of Antioch. He also amassed a huge number of early manuscripts and other antiquities, his prized collection of ancient coins finally ending up in the British Museum.

Francis Jago Arundell was eventually able to return to Landulph, dying there in December 1846. He was buried under the church floor close to Theodore Paleologus and is commemorated by an enamel plaque of his assumed arms of Arundell, which was set up on the wall below the Paleologus brass. Despite his pioneering studies, the antiquarian rector never came close to discovering the true nature of Theodore's early adventures, and one can only wonder what he would have made of them.

There is a terrible irony in Jago Arundell's choice of Smyrna for his self-imposed exile. Exactly 100 years after his arrival, the city was destined to be the place where the Great Idea – the old Greek dream of driving the Turks from the Byzantine lands – would finally end in ruins.

With the Ottomans defeated in the Great War, Smyrna was awarded to Greece by the victorious Allies and the restoration of a Christian empire with its capital at Constantinople – then occupied by British troops – seemed finally within grasp. But the resurgent Turkish army's entry into Smyrna in 1922 led to an orgy of ethnic cleansing that shocked the world. Estimates of the Greek and Armenian Christians murdered or expelled are still furiously contested by Turkey, but up to 100,000 were claimed to have been burnt alive when the Greek quarter was deliberately set ablaze. A year later the war between Greece and Turkey ended with each country casting out their minority populations of over a million Orthodox Greeks and half a million Muslims. It was the end of a romantic vision that had inspired Greek patriots since the death of Constantine XI.

# *18*

The coffin … was found to contain the perfect
skeleton, which impressed all present with the
idea he must have been a man of extraordinary
stature, and this, as a local octogenarian
observed, was known traditionally to have
been the Greek prince from Cornwall.

Henry Bradfield, 'The Last of the Paleologi'.

Exactly when and in what circumstances Ferdinand left for Barbados
is a matter for conjecture. His presence in the island is first recorded
in 1644, the year his brother Theodore was buried at Westminster, but
how long he had then been there we do not know. He may have been
a royalist seeking refuge, or just conceivably one of the king's soldiers
transported by Cromwell as an option to imprisonment at home. But it
is far more likely he was simply seeking to make his fortune with the aid
of kinsfolk, the Ballses of Suffolk, who figured among the very earliest
settlers in the new colony.

Ferdinand was now in his early twenties and a giant of a man like his
father. He would have embarked at Plymouth or a neighbouring port,
with the Lizard as his last sight of England. Stretching before him was
a journey of 4,000 miles in wretchedly cramped conditions on a diet of
broth, porridge, boiled biscuit and the like. Even a civilian ship would
be heavily armed as an Anglo-Spanish peace treaty signed in 1630 was
ignored by Spain in her 'backyard' of the New World, and freebooters
of all nations were an ever-present danger. If the trade winds were kind
the vessel could make good time and the passengers might be confined

on board only five weeks or so. But low-lying Barbados was notoriously difficult for a lookout to spot, and if the island was passed the crew had great trouble beating back against the wind. One settler who arrived in Barbados in 1638 wrote a harrowing account of his crossing, with 350 passengers jammed together below decks during the cold weather and so many being sick it was almost impossible to escape infection. Eighty who died on the voyage were thrown overboard.

Captain John Smith had explored the Caribbean in 1607 and encouraged its settlement. The islands were colonised over much the same period as the American mainland, the first settlers in Barbados arriving in the same kind of numbers as the founding fathers in New England. Puritans and Quakers were prominent in both waves of migration. The Earl of Lincoln's *Arbella*, crammed with its Tattershall contingent, sailed for Massachusetts three years after the permanent settlement of Barbados. Inauspiciously, the first settlers' ship had arrived on the island with an unplanned cargo of ten black slaves from a captured Spanish vessel.

When James I succeeded to Elizabeth's throne, a locust-like swarm of Scots had followed him to England. One of these was an early infatuation of the king, a handsome young man named James Hay who was rewarded with money, titles and a rich heiress as his bride. Like Buckingham, he retained the favour of Charles I who advanced him in the peerage as Earl of Carlisle. Extravagant and grasping, the Scot showed an acquisitive interest in the new colonies and in 1627 obtained a grant of all the Caribbean islands including Barbados. The quit-rent demands of this indolent absentee landlord led to constant friction with the pioneer planters, and Carlisle's death in 1636 left the island in the hands of a governor who squeezed what taxes he could from each inhabitant. A succession of governors struggled to impose rule over a burgeoning population – there were over 10,000 settlers by 1640 – and to cream off what they could from the booming economy.

The Barbados planters quickly earned a reputation as a dissolute, avaricious and hard-drinking set, short-sightedly cruel in their treatment of slaves and apprentices. One English visitor in 1655 reported: 'This island is the dunghill whereon England doth cast forth its rubbish. Rogues and whores and suchlike people are those which are generally brought here. A rogue in England will hardly make a cheater here. A bawd brought over puts on a demure comportment, a whore if handsome makes a wife for some rich planter.'[69]

Mortality was staggeringly high among the planters, with yellow fever as one of the commonest causes of death. It took the place held by bubonic plague in England. Mosquitos thrived in the enervating humid heat, and once bitten by an infected insect the victim suffered a sudden splitting headache followed by burning fever, jaundice, a failing pulse and nausea, leading to haemorrhages, black vomit and delirium. Six thousand deaths from yellow fever were reported in 1648 alone. Other dreaded maladies were dysentery, leprosy and dropsy, while yaws afflicted its sufferers with hideous ulcers which deformed or destroyed facial features, hands and feet; hookworm larvae burrowed into the foot and passed into the intestines, settling there as blood-sucking adult parasites. The enigmatic dry bellyache, now thought to have been caused by processing rum in lead containers, caused unbearable cramps in the stomach and bowels. The physicians' remedy for almost every disorder was bleeding, a disastrous treatment given the extreme anaemia characterising most tropical complaints.

But money was the spur, and the Civil War in England proved a blessing in disguise by heralding an era of free trade. In the early days of the conflict islanders firmly put their business interests first and declared Barbados neutral, but as King Charles's fortunes waned more royalist sympathisers headed out there. This new wave of immigrants seized power and declared for the king, confiscating the estates of leading supporters of the rebels.

With the execution of Charles in 1649 a familiar name reappears in the story. The exiled Charles II, continuing his struggle against parliament from Holland, appointed Francis Lord Willoughby as governor of Barbados. This was not the holder of the ancient peerage of Willoughby de Eresby but of the much younger title of Lord Willoughby of Parham, although by many he was regarded as the rightful Eresby. The reason he failed to inherit the barony dating back to 1313 is a complicated story. His forbear William, younger brother of the eleventh Baron Willoughby de Eresby, would in normal circumstances have inherited the title and estates on the death of the peer without a male heir. Controversially, it was the daughter Katherine Willoughby who was recognised as baroness in her own right, but as she was the ward and then wife of the Duke of Suffolk, the bosom friend of Henry VIII, it is little wonder that William's repeated attempts to claim his rights by law were doomed to failure. The Parham title seems to have been created for him in 1547 as a sort of consolation prize.

Francis Willoughby reached Barbados in 1650 and sought to reconcile the warring parties. One of his first acts was to overturn the act confiscating the Roundhead supporters' land. But these developments did not suit the new rulers of England and a Commonwealth fleet blockaded the island the following year and forced the Barbadians to capitulate. The Commonwealth's terms proved generous, however, and the acquisition of money became once again the main preoccupation of the island.[70]

The island's spectacular growth came with the introduction of sugar cane. Sugar made Barbados the richest English colony with bigger plantation owners making vast fortunes overnight, and its cultivation drove an insatiable demand for African slaves. A family called Balls were listed among these first owners. Three plantations appear under this name in the earliest records, the biggest of 400 acres and named simply the Balls Plantation.[71] The first map of the island, printed in 1657, is marked with the names of the principal landowners and shows all three Balls properties.

The exact relationship of this family to Ferdinand's mother is unclear. The Victorian historian Dunkin writes that Mary Balls's father William had an estate in Barbados but quotes no source for the information. This seems highly improbable as the first settlers did not arrive till 1627 and William was pursuing a successful career in Hadleigh way back in the 1570s. However, Mary Balls's family are repeatedly identified as the Barbados planters by early chroniclers, and Tregelles adds the detail that William's estate was called Ashford, a name we will come across again. The authors of the *Barbados Diocesan History* printed in 1925 state that Mary's father was a landed proprietor in the island, though they wrongly call him John Balls. The Balls of Hadleigh were numerous, however, and it is significant that the name more or less disappears from the parish registers in Suffolk by this time. The Barbados landowners were most likely nephews of William Balls and therefore cousins of Mary.

Ferdinand became a freeholder some time before 1649, a strong indication of early support from well-off relatives established in the island. His estate was named Clifton Hall. His marriage to Rebecka Pomfrett, the daughter of a landowner, was another step towards acceptance into the ruling elite and 1649 marked an important milestone when he was elected to the vestry of St John's Parish. Vestrymen were powerful establishment figures in the island in these early days. Contemporary Barbados documents show how Ferdinand gradually added to his holdings in St John's Parish over the years. A deed for a sale of land to a Captain Thomas Hotherall dated 1658 describes the property as 'bounded north by Ferdinando Paleologus'; in July 1662 Ferdinand extended his estate by five acres, the purchase grant stating that the land was made over to him by the previous owner in consideration of 'ten thousand pounds of good muscovado sugar paid to me by Ferdinando Paleologus of ye same parish planter'. Perhaps the most attractive of the early plans of Barbados, Lea's map of 1685, labels a plantation to the west of St John's Church as 'Paleologus and Beal', the latter having previously been presumed to be Ferdinand's partner in the business. However, as this date is after Ferdinand's death there is another explanation we will come to later.

Like Ligon's map before it, Lea's states that 'every Parish, Plantation, Watermill, Windmill and Cattlemill is described with the name of the Present Possessor and all things else Remarkable' and is dotted with little vignettes. Above the Paleologus-Beal estate is a drawing of a pineapple and it is an appealing idea that in addition to sugar Ferdinand cultivated what Richard Blorne, one of the earliest historians of the Caribbean, called 'this rarest fruit of the Indies'. Another commentator pronounced it 'the prince of all fruits' and King James himself swore it must be the apple with which Eve tempted Adam.

Evidence to support Tregelles's talk of a Balls estate called Ashford comes in an article on Barbados published in 1843 by the colonial officer Henry Bradfield. He records an interview with an old man, father of the then owner of Clifton Hall, who said the original estate was also known as Ashford. This is a strong indication that at least the nucleus of Ferdinand's holding was acquired from his maternal family, by gift, purchase or inheritance. The estate grew over the years to nearly 200 acres, but I have found no indication of how many slaves were bought to work on it. Some historians of the slave trade have calculated that one labourer was needed for each acre of sugar cane, though it is clear many highly profitable estates managed with a lower ratio.

The sugar industry came to depend entirely on the slave trade. After the accidental introduction of the 'tenn negroes' taken from a Spanish prize ship, African slaves quickly replaced indentured whites as the main source of labour. The first record of a large-scale sale of slaves comes in 1644, the same date as our first record of Ferdinand in Barbados, when an auction of the cargo from a vessel called the *Mary Bonadventure* saw slaves sold at an average price of £22 a head. It was immediately recognised that transportation of slaves offered excellent commercial prospects and competition to satisfy the demand grew so quickly that ten years later the average price had dropped to £14 and to £13 the year after. During Ferdinand's career on Barbados, at least 2,000 slaves were imported each year.

The St John's records show Ferdinand steadily consolidating his position in local affairs. On his election as vestryman in 1649 his name appeared in the parish vestry book as *William Fernando Paleologus*, but this is the single reference giving him the name William. In 1654 he is recorded as a sidesman and lieutenant of the militia; the mapmaker Richard Ligon, who had been a Lincolnshire landowner before setting out on his travels, wrote that despite being outnumbered the white settlers maintained control by intimidating the slaves through regular militia musters where there were impressive displays of firepower.

In 1655 Ferdinand was churchwarden. Among the churchwarden's duties was 'to search Taverns, Ale-houses, Victualling-houses, or other Houses, where they do suspect lewd and debauched Company to frequent' during the time of church services. Should they discover any people 'Drinking, Swearing, Gaming, or otherwise misdemeaning themselves',[72] the offenders were to be placed in the stocks for four hours and fined five shillings. Ferdinand was a trustee in 1656 and again in 1660, when he was also surveyor of the highways; the following year he was vestryman again. In January 1670 a recorded absence from a meeting seems to have been caused by ill health, a condition worsening over the following months.

On 26 September 1670, he made a will which begins:

> In the name of God, Amen. I Ferdinand Paleologus, of the parish of St John's,
> being sick in body, but in perfect memory, commit my soul into the hands of
> Almighty God, my most merciful Creator, and my body to be interred in a
> Christian burial, there to attend the joyful resurrection of the just to eternal
> life by Jesus Christ my most blessed Saviour and Redeemer.

Half his estate was willed to his wife for her life and the other half to his son, the name being oddly spelt as *Theodorious*. We will call him Theodore III. His inheritance was 'to be imployed for his maintenance and education, together with the increase of his Estate, until he attains the age of fourteen yeares'. Other bequests were to Ferdinand's sisters Mary and Dorothy in Cornwall, who were each to receive twenty shillings, godson Ralph Hassall, who was left 'my stone black colt', and to Edward Walrond went a grey mare. The Walronds, among the richest families in Barbados and fanatically royalist, had led the uprising against the Commonwealth in 1650. Though there is no direct evidence of Ferdinand being an active supporter of the exiled Charles II, this connection with the Walronds indicates where his sympathies lay.

On 2 October a codicil was made to the will which provided for Ferdinand's wife Rebecka to inherit the entire estate if Theodore should die before her without issue. Witnesses to the will were Tobias Bridge, George Hanmer and Thomas Kendall, all men of influence. The same witnesses signed the codicil with the addition of Abraham Pomfrett, brother of Ferdinand's wife. By the date on the codicil Ferdinand was too ill to sign his name in full and could only write his initials between Ferdinand and Paleologus in someone else's hand. Will and codicil were proved before Colonel Christopher Codrington, deputy governor and one of the biggest planters.[73] Various inaccurate dates for Ferdinand's death have been given by historians of Barbados, probably caused by misreading the crabbed handwriting on these documents, and this accounts for 1678 being chiselled on his gravestone as the year of death. Thanks to enquiries initiated by Canon Adams, this was shown to be wrong only in recent times. Ferdinand actually died on or soon after 2 October 1670, the date of the codicil. Few planters lived beyond thirty-five, which makes Ferdinand a Methuselah in Barbadian terms. Passing his fiftieth birthday was a feat as remarkable as his father reaching his mid-seventies in England.

New light was thrown on the Lea map's label of 'Paleologus and Beal' on the St John plantation in 1685 with the discovery of the will of Abraham Pomfrett, Ferdinand's brother-in-law. Dated 6 July 1672 and proved on 8 August that year, this left legacies of five shillings each to his sister Rebecka Beale and his nephew Theodore Paleologus. So Ferdinand's wife had remarried sometime between October 1670 and July 1672. Her new husband was almost certainly the Captain Alexander Beale of St John's who was recorded in the Census Papers of 1679 as the owner of 111 acres of land and seventy slaves. It is unclear whether he was established as a partner in the business in Ferdinand's lifetime or picked up a handsome estate when he married the widow. In the latter case the Paleologus named on the map would not be Ferdinand but his son Theodore III. The evidence that the second husband was indeed Captain Beale is backed up by Rebecka's own will in which she leaves to a son called Alexander a silver plate marked with the initials A and R, for herself and her second husband, and with a B above for the surname.

Beale took over Ferdinand's church role as well as his wife and plantation. I found his name in the St John's vestry minutes as sidesman in 1676 and by 1677 he was churchwarden and 'overseer of ye poore'. Control of the vestry consolidated the power of the magnate families, both economic and political, as indeed did intermarriage. Meanwhile Rebecka continued to play a very active role in the business and was evidently a tough-minded lady with an eye to the main chance. In 1685, after the failure of the Duke of Monmouth's rebellion in England, she purchased as slaves four of seventy-two convicted rebels who were transported to Barbados following the Bloody Assizes of Judge Jeffreys.

Many of the facts set out above, including the correct year of Ferdinand's death and the terms of the Pomfrett and Rebecka Beale wills, were teased out of the Barbados archives at Adams's urging by a fellow soul in the island, Eustace Maxwell Shilstone, who was to become a distinguished historian of Barbados. The two antiquaries struck up a postal friendship in the 1930s which continued throughout the war years and beyond. It was one of the pleasant tasks of researching this book to piece together the two halves of their correspondence from the Adams papers in Cornwall and the files of the Shilstone Memorial Library named after the rector's pen pal, now housed in the Barbados Museum at Bridgetown.

An appealing image emerged of these two middle-aged bespectacled scholars as each settled down in the evening to write to a comrade 4,000 miles distant. Picture Mr Shilstone, a neat, portly, white-suited figure at the mahogany desk of his coral island villa, marshalling his thoughts despite the incessant din of cicadas and courting frogs in his garden; picture Canon Adams, a tall, balding figure in his clerical black, in the cold and draughty study of an old Cornish rectory. In letter after letter, at the height of a world war, the pair swop thoughts on the significance of dusty deeds and crumbling vestry books, the exotic ghosts of seventeenth-century Barbados gathered around them. Add to the picture Canon Adams hunched over a candle, perhaps with a shawl over his shoulders: he was long without electricity after a bomb hit Plymouth's power station in the freezing mid-January of 1941. But from this dogged long-distance correspondence emerged new truths about Ferdinand and his only son.

Shilstone, fifty at the outbreak of war, was a successful barrister. His interest in history was originally sparked by moving office to a street opposite Bridgetown's abandoned Jewish cemetery. There he found some of the island's earliest tombstones, the subject of his first scholarly book. A prime mover in founding the Barbados Museum – a venture demanding steely resolve to take on obstructive commercial interests in the island – Shilstone earned a reputation for being abrupt and dismissive, his temper impaired by ill-health and failing eyesight. Those who knew him best said that after the event he always regretted seeming rude, while freely confessing he was incapable of suffering fools gladly.

Now and then the outside world breaks into the correspondence. On 24 March 1941 Mr Shilstone writes: 'We have nothing but admiration for the stout-hearted English people in their great trial, but are confident that victory will be ours in the end.'

Adams in the meantime was witnessing the worst privations suffered by Plymouth, a key target for the Nazi war effort because of the royal dockyards, with relentless night attacks by the Luftwaffe. Like the Plymouth folk, he endured the mounting losses of supplies – gas, electricity, coal, milk, newspapers, eventually even water. A direct hit on the power station silenced the sirens and the loss of the water supply rendered the fire engines useless. But Adams knew about hardship. He was seventeen at the outbreak of the Great War and had immediately volunteered for the front as a private.

On 28 April that year he writes to Shilstone:

We have been very fortunate so far in our parish. We are only a few miles from Plymouth but so far have escaped unscathed. We have had a few bombs fortunately in fields or in the river mud and have had one dose of some scores or perhaps a hundred incendiaries, but they luckily all fell in fields.

Plymouth had a terrible time for three days in succession last week. I fear the destruction was appalling and the loss of life very heavy. From our garden and house we look straight across at Plymouth, though a low hill lies between and prevents a direct view of it, so we get a wonderful sight of the raids, and if one could forget what it all means it would be (and in fact is) a most beautiful display – brilliant flares slowly coming down and breaking up into streams of silvery fireworks, red tracer bullets trying to put them out, searchlights all around, the vivid flashes of the AA guns and then the shell bursts in the air, the terrible red glow over the burning town … During the last 'blitz' shrapnel came pattering down round the rectory for the first time. It has amazed me that we have not had any before. I picked up a small piece just outside the front door.

An attractive target for Hitler's Kriegsmarine, Barbados too suffered severe hardship in the early years of the war and was virtually cut off from the outside world. Adams and Shilstone were always conscious that the correspondence sharing their discoveries might end up at the bottom of the sea. The battle for the Atlantic was not the first time the Axis had interfered with Adams's research into the Paleologi, however, as he had encountered constant obstacles to extracting further information from Italian authorities ever since the rise of Mussolini. The worst time for Barbados was September 1942 when five ships heading for Bridgetown were attacked by the submarine U-514, the major casualty being the SS *Cornwallis*, a merchant vessel sunk in Carlisle Bay. In eighty-seven days at sea the U-boat sank 17,000 tons of Allied shipping, while a second foray sent a further 15,000 tons to the bottom. U-514 was eventually sunk in July 1943 by rockets fired from an RAF plane.

The French writer Andre Savignon, a winner of the *Prix Goncourt*, was caught in England at the fall of France. He spent much of the war in Plymouth, marvelling at the passive courage of the people as the nightly death toll mounted and each raid wiped out landmark after landmark. 'Gradually, Plymouth lost substance,' he wrote in his wartime memoirs. 'How, though, to make those who have not known it understand the almost physical impression that a city is slipping away under one's very feet, *departing*?' In a few hours over two nights the centre of Plymouth was swept clean away: the streets lost their identity so completely that signboards had to be put up because life-long inhabitants lost their way in the blackened and smoking ruins. 'They pass by, these English, silent, with shakes of the head but never a protest, never a spasmodic jerk of rage,' wrote Savignon. 'Their calm, that is what strikes me: it is stoical and splendid.'

The highest casualties of the Plymouth Blitz came in seven night raids spread over March and April that year. In all, the bombing attacks killed 1,172 civilians and injured 4,448. Almost the entire city centre was gone and Adams was deeply saddened by the catastrophic loss of life and destruction of Plymouth's heritage, writing to Shilstone of the loss of so many beautiful churches and hoping that Landulph would continue to be spared. Especially tragic, he said, was the near destruction of ancient St Andrew's, the largest parish church in Devon. Though Canon Adams did not know it, this was where Ferdinand Paleologus was christened and his mother buried.

But he must have heard of the inspiring scene amid the smouldering ruins of the church when a defiant parishioner, a headmistress, nailed a wooden sign over the door bearing the single word *Resurgam* – I shall rise again. Many years later, at St Andrew's re-consecration, a granite plaque with the same inscription was raised over the church entrance.

❖

A sense of déjà vu is unavoidable as we move on to the opening of Ferdinand Paleologus's coffin a century and a half after his burial. His father's coffin had been opened in Cornwall after very much the same stretch of time; the coffin of his brother Theodore II had been dug up by the 'body-snatcher' dean of Westminster after a period of nearly 200 years. At least Ferdinand's coffin was uncovered by an act of God rather than human inquisitiveness, in the great hurricane of Barbados which laid waste to much of the island on 13 October 1819. It was, however, the same old irresistible curiosity which supplies the rest of the story. Graphic accounts of the scene were written by two nineteenth-century historians of Barbados, Henry Bradfield and the German-born explorer Sir Robert Schombergk.

Writing in *The Gentleman's Magazine* in 1843, Bradfield describes a ramble with a friend among the rocks and cliffs near St John's. As they strolled into the old abandoned churchyard, his companion spoke of the dreadful hurricane, 'the fatal effects of which were yet visible to us, in the shape of ruined tombstones when the dead had been, as it were, torn from their graves like chaff before the devastating winds'.

Standing by a vault belonging to his friend's family, Bradfield was told that on the removal of the disturbed bodies to a new burial ground the body of Paleologus was discovered:

> in a large leaden coffin with the feet pointing to the east, the usual mode of burial among the ancient Greeks. On opening the coffin, which was partially destroyed from the action of the air on the metal, it was found to contain the perfect skeleton, which impressed all present with the idea that he must have been a man of extraordinary stature, and this, as a local octogenarian observed, was known traditionally to have been the Greek prince from Cornwall.

The parsonage and vestry were destroyed in the hurricane, but with the permission of the rector, the Revd John H. Gittens, Bradfield rummaged about among remnants of papers in the ruins – 'much to the discomfiture of sundry scorpions, cockroaches and centipedes, who probably considered the manuscripts as "heirlooms" in the family' – and discovered the old vestry book which detailed Ferdinand's appointments from 1649 to 1669.

Schombergk's account is somewhat different. In *The History of Barbados* he dates the discovery of Ferdinand's body to a later hurricane in 1831 when the original church was destroyed. The coffin was found when the ruins were cleared, not in the churchyard but in a vault under the organ loft. Schombergk writes that the curiosity of the rector – the same Revd John Gittens[74] – was aroused by the fact that it was lying in the opposite direction to all the other coffins in the vault, with head to the west and feet to the east 'according to the Greek custom'. The coffin was opened on 3 May 1844 'to test the truth of the tradition'. Schombergk agrees the coffin was of lead and contained a skeleton of extraordinary size imbedded in quicklime, which the author asserts to be 'another proof of the Greek origin of Paleologus'. Canon Adams remarks in his notes that it is odd both writers believed that burying a body with the feet to the east is a peculiarly Greek custom when in fact it is the usual practice

in England. Schombergk goes on to say the coffin was finally depos-
ited in a vault owned by a local landowner. Another account said that
Ferdinand was buried with an icon of the Resurrection on his breast
while yet another declared the body 'was buried upside down'.

It became apparent to Adams on comparing the various stories that
Ferdinand's coffin was actually opened twice, Schombergk's date of
1844 for its opening being one year after the publication of Bradfield's
article. Adams's Barbados chum was soon on the case, and Mr Shilstone
discovered that the same vault had been unbolted again in recent days,
presumably for a new interment. As described to him, the coffins inside
were piled up almost to the roof, but at one end of the vault was one
very old lead coffin by itself, undoubtedly containing the much-dis-
turbed remains of Ferdinand Paleologus. Shilstone also discovered that
the vault had originally been owned by Sir Peter Colleton, a friend of
Ferdinand and owner of 180 slaves.

The description of the body is a reminder that quicklime was commonly used during plagues and other epidemics as it was thought to
speed up the disintegration of the corpse to prevent the spread of disease. In some Balkan cultures, including the Greek, it was employed to
destroy the body of a suspected vampire. Yet despite a generous layer of
quicklime Ferdinand's skeleton was found in excellent condition. As an
aside it may be worth noting that quicklime was a major component of
Greek fire, the secret incendiary weapon used by the Byzantines in naval
battles. On at least two occasions in Constantinople's history Greek fire
was credited with the salvation of the city from Muslim conquest.

The Paleologus tomb and the story of 'Prince Ferdinand' is still a
regular feature in Barbadian tourism publicity. Holiday brochures refer
to the monument as one of the oldest in Barbados, and the visitor to
St John's Church is immediately confronted by a sign pointing to its
location. But we have learnt that things are not always as they seem in
the Paleologus story, and the truth is the St John's monument is neither
old nor in the place where Ferdinand was first buried. In fact it was
erected as recently as 1906 when the then rector of St John's raised the

necessary funds by public subscription. It was ordered from the less than exotic source of Wippell's, a long-established clerical supplier of Exeter, so at least there is a West Country connection.

Yet oddly enough, the very first note of incredulity sounded over the English family's imperial descent was by John Oldmixon, author of *The British Empire in America* (first published in 1708 and now regarded as a pioneering work on colonial history). Oldmixon therefore visited Barbados when contemporaries of Theodore III would still be alive and quite possibly a few who knew Ferdinand. He refers to a tradition of a scion of the Byzantine dynasty residing in the island 'with a small plantation near the top of the cliff', and voices his personal scepticism about the lineage without stating any reason. It is, however, remarkable that the first reference in print to the imperial descent is one of doubt, putting Oldmixon at odds with the general run of historians for the next 200 years and more.

The inscription on Ferdinand's headstone, clearly based on the brass of Theodore I in Landulph Church, has the incorrect date remarked on by Canon Adams, and runs:

HERE LYETH YE BODY OF
FERDINANDO PALEOLOGUS
DESCENDED FROM YE IMPERIAL
LYNE OF YE LAST CHRISTIAN
EMPERORS OF GREECE
CHURCHWARDEN OF THIS PARISH
1655-1656
VESTRYMAN TWENTYE YEARS
DIED OCTOBER 3 1678.

Present-day holidaymakers in the island have no difficulty in finding attractions to occupy their time, but a lack of things to show to well-heeled visitors from cruise ships was a persistent concern to commercial interests in the interwar years, and it was an enterprising Italian travel agent based in Barbados who realised that the impressive tombstone of the legendary 'Greek prince from Cornwall' could be drummed up as an attraction for tourists, especially if no one mentioned that the monument with its quaint inscription and ancient date was actually a recent import.

One such visitor in 1932 was Evelyn Waugh. The novelist had just published *Black Mischief*, one of his most popular works, but he arrived in a miserable frame of mind following a stormy crossing from Tilbury and his recent divorce from his first wife. When the SS *Ingoma* dropped anchor at Bridgetown on 17 December, Waugh went ashore on a day of intermittent rain and quickly decided 'very little to see in town' besides the statue of Nelson in Trafalgar Square and the memorial tablets to victims of yellow fever in the cathedral. He heard of Paleologus's tomb, however, and with a fellow passenger was driven through never-ending sugarcane fields to St John's. There he viewed the grave – with his thorough knowledge of architecture Waugh would not have been deceived that the stone was seventeenth-century work – and tersely noted in his diary that the church was '1830 gothic of best pre-Ruskin kind'. His stay in Barbados ended that evening with an amateur dramatic performance of a play by P.G. Wodehouse, cocktails and dinner at a hotel, then 'back to ship in pouring rain'. Six years later Waugh gave the name Paleologue to a wily Mr Fit-it and pimp character in his comic masterpiece *Scoop*, a man with two wives and 'countless queer-coloured children'. Waugh later wrote the historical novel *Helena*, the story of how the mother of Constantine the Great found the True Cross.

❖

The graveyard of St John's as I saw it in late April is an unforgettable place and there can be no better view than that enjoyed from Ferdinand's tomb. Yellow sugar birds hopped along the gravestone as green and purple hummingbirds darted amid the orange blossom and geranium trees. My approach startled a blue-faced lizard from the shady side of a neighbouring vault. Close to the grave stands a Barbados Ebony, commonly called the Woman's Tongue Tree because its pods rattle with a loud persistence, and an Oriental *Thuja*, known as the Tree of Life. A constant warm breeze ruffled the palms overhead and the hum of an antiquated mower came from immaculate lawns behind the sprawling rectory. The fine church noted by Waugh might have been transported from the heart of some favoured English village, perhaps the scene of a Miss Marple mystery. But take a few steps and you are on the edge of a cliff. Eight hundred feet below is the dazzling blue Atlantic, its white waves breaking soundlessly on a deserted beach.

The churchyard is a most remarkable sight, for a venerable hamlet of mausoleums to the early planters is all around you. If the dead here are indeed to see a joyful resurrection of the just, Ferdinand will step from his grave to face the sunrise in the east, the direction also of England and Constantinople, as from the ancient coral vaults around emerge the men he knew in life, Colletons, Fosters, Walronds and Hothersalls, those early masters of the island whose plantations we see marked on the decorative old maps with their tiny drawings of spouting whales and galleons, wild hogs and windmills, and horsemen chasing runaway slaves. Beyond the graveyard still stretch the cane fields which made these people rich, for after more than three centuries sugar remains a staple crop of the island.

The 'Greek prince from Cornwall' continues to figure in island lore. During my stay it happened that Clifton Hall came on to the market, glowingly described in the estate agents' brochure as 'a magnificent plantation home which boasts a unique historical legacy as the Great House of Prince Ferdinand Paleologus, a descendant of Greek royalty who named his home from his birthplace in Cornwall, England'. Needless to say, Ferdinand would not recognise the present spacious mansion built of solid coral stone, with its magnificent suite of reception rooms, marble-floored galleries, six bedrooms, three bathrooms and powder room, surrounded by orchards of guava, breadfruit, lime, mango and avocado, all yours for US $3 million. The oldest part of the house dating from Paleologus's time is now the kitchen and staff quarters except for two small rooms used as changing rooms for the swimming pool. Much of the fabric of the main house dates from 1810, however, and is designated as of historic and architectural interest by the Barbados National Trust.

The brochure states that 'the property harbours no other insects than the firefly which light up tranquil evenings that can be spent lounging outside', so the resurrected Ferdinand would look round in vain for the mosquitos that plagued him in life.

✥

We are left with Ferdinand's brother John Theodore to account for. The absence of further record of him in Barbados after 1644 indicates his stay was not a long one. Perhaps he failed to get on with the influential Balls relations and lack of money prevented him from establishing himself as an island worthy like Ferdinand. Returning to Cromwell's England was not an appealing prospect, and the likelihood is that John was among an exodus of disenchanted settlers and indentured servants – and there were lots of them – who left Barbados to try their luck on the American mainland, or headed for neighbouring Dutch and French islands in the West Indies.

Many of these turned to piracy of one kind or another. One enticing possibility is that John fell in with the most famous of the indentured servants to escape from Barbados, the notorious buccaneer Henry Morgan. Forging a new career as an officer of the Royal Navy, Morgan quickly rose through the ranks and took full advantage of the regular wars between England and her enemies, plundering the Caribbean for the enrichment of himself and his crews. A number of unsuccessful settlers left Barbados to enlist with Morgan at Port Royal in Jamaica. But unless further evidence turns up, John's destiny remains a matter for pure conjecture: the fact is that the most elusive of the English Paleologi simply disappears from the record.

# 19

Now and then we had the hope that if we lived and were good, God would permit us to be pirates.

Mark Twain, *Life on the Mississippi*.

Ignorant of any further record of Ferdinand's son, Bradfield and other historians of the day believed Theodore III had died in youth and as a consequence the whole St John's property had devolved upon the widowed mother Rebecka. Canon Adams himself believed this for many years, writing in his guide to Landulph Church that Theodore died in 1680 and was buried in Barbados. Adams's indefatigable friend Mr Shilstone discovered otherwise, unearthing a previously overlooked entry of Theodore's marriage in the register of St Michael's Church near Bridgetown on 14 October 1684. His bride was Martha Bradbury, daughter of Christopher Bradbury of St Michael's.

Within a year Martha's father was dead. By his will signed on 14 August 1685 and recorded a month later Theodore and Martha were left £20 to be laid on in plate on the birth of their first child. On a visit to St Michael's Church I noted the tombstone of a Captain Christopher Bradbury in the porch, this time a genuine seventeenth-century monument. By tying these facts together Adams and Shilstone established that a *Theodorus Palaeologey* who was known to have been buried at Corunna in Spain – previously thought to be an unrelated individual of the same name – was in fact Theodore III, only son of the planter Ferdinand. This Theodore made a will on 1 August 1693, appointing as executor his wife *Martha Paleologua*.

Theodore III was a sailor serving on a ship called the *Charles II* in the reign of William and Mary. This much became clear. He is described in the Probate Act Book as 'recently of Barbados, afterwards of Stepney' and his stated rank of gentleman means he was almost certainly an officer. But his last known address was neighbouring Wapping, which we have heard the London historian John Stow call a 'filthy strait passage' inhabited by sailors' victuallers. It was also the site of Execution Dock where pirates were hanged from a gibbet close to low-water mark and left dangling until submerged three times by the tide.

Theodore's unfamiliar name gave trouble to the clerk who copied out the will as in addition to various spellings of Paleologus he renders his given name as *Theodoxes* in several places. Theodore authorises Martha to demand and receive 'from the Right Honorable the Treasurer or Paymaster of their Majties Navy' all such wages, pay, bounty money, prize money and all other sums of money which are due to him and to convey or let 'all or any of my Messauges Lands and Tenements'. This suggests that Theodore was a man of some substance. The will, evidently made at sea, was witnessed by the ship's commander, Charles Gibson, and three others, presumably officers. It was not proved until 15 March of the following year at London.

By some historians – and also, as will be seen in a later chapter, by writers of fiction – Theodore III has been presented as an officer of the Royal Navy. Canon Adams went part way to the truth by establishing that his name was absent from contemporary Admiralty records; nor was there an officer named Charles Gibson, nor indeed a Royal Navy vessel called the *Charles II*. Adams spent a fruitless four days in further searches of the Public Record Office before concluding that Theodore must have served on a hired ship, but never arrived at the reality. In fact Theodore proved himself a true chip off the old block: he was a buccaneer and very likely a slaver as well.

With his Barbados background and share in the family plantation, it is most probable he learned his trade as a seaman on a slave ship and left the sugar business in the hands of his mother and stepfather. We do not know his date of birth, but there is nearly a decade to account for between his marriage and his embarkation on the *Charles II*. The move to Stepney fits well with this premise as the Thames was a vital stage in the triangular trading system which carried cash crops from the New World to Europe, from there carried manufactured goods to West Africa, and from Africa transported slaves to the New World. In the case of Barbados this generally meant carrying sugar and molasses to London, whence the profits from the sale – often in the form of weapons and ammunition – went to African chiefs in exchange for slaves. Cheap Barbados rum was also used for barter. The slaves were then transported back to the starting place and the cycle was repeated. For a plantation business it made sense to be involved at each phase to maximise earnings.[75] It was also a sensible precaution to guard against fraud and misappropriation by agents at any stage during a round journey of maybe eighteen months.

These were hellish voyages. To add to the unavoidable hazards of sea-faring at the time – gales and tornadoes, freezing cold and intolerable heat, rotten food and lack of water, rampant infectious diseases, pirates – the transportation of slaves added a new dimension of horror because of the grotesque overcrowding of the captives in the hold and the constant threat of revolt. A slaver needed an iron constitution to habituate himself to the cruelty of his trade and commonplace scenes such as dead slaves being used as bait for sharks, so the shark meat could feed the slaves still living. Theodore III had to be as much a stranger to our modern-day sensibilities as was his grandfather.

Following the suggestion of a leading historian of the Royal African Company, the enterprise set up by King Charles II which long monopolised the slave trade, it was possible to trace a slave ship called the *Charles II*. The only record I found of the vessel in the database of transAtlantic slave trade voyages was a tantalisingly brief report of its last known passage in 1704. Much of the information often given of such ships – tonnage, year of construction, number of guns, and so on – is absent, but it is confirmed as a property of the Royal African Company flying the British flag. The *Charles II* began its voyage from Barbados on 1 April 1704 and embarked 273 slaves at Cape Coast Castle in what is now Ghana. Cape Coast Castle, which changed hands several times in the wars between the English and Dutch, was one of the notorious prisons built to house enslaved natives, up to a thousand at a time.

Sometime after its departure for Barbados on 28 July the *Charles II* is reported as captured though the captor is unspecified. A total of 236 slaves are recorded as disembarked, indicating a fairly average death rate on board during an Atlantic crossing. Whether the slaves were captured along with the ship or for some reason disembarked earlier is not clear. Pirates preyed on slave ships both in African waters and in the Caribbean and all but heavily armed vessels were at risk of seizure.

More often encountered in the trans-Atlantic archives from the 1660s is a slave ship named simply as the *Charles*, the property of the Company of Royal Adventurers which was the forerunner of the Royal African Company. This vessel regularly transported slaves from Africa to Barbados. For a voyage of 1665 we have more details of the vessel including its displacement of 130 tons and the captain's name, Nicholas Pepperell, with a recorded landing at Barbados of 165 slaves out of the 238 embarked in West Africa. A ship of this size would typically mount six or eight guns. An added comment is 'voyage completed as intended'. With its sister ship called the *James*, the *Charles* had less luck on another occasion when they were prevented from buying slaves on the Gold Coast by Dutch men-of-war.

Could the *Charles* and *Charles II* have been the same ship? This was the focus of my thoughts when a documentary reference to a Captain Charles Gibson caught my eye and I realised I might have wandered off in the wrong direction. The *Charles II* of our Theodore's time turned out to be not a slaver but a fast, up-to-date and formidably armed warship, and one which was to play a sensational role in what is called the golden age of piracy. On board the *Charles II* as its recently promoted first mate was a Royal Navy veteran and former slaver called Henry Every, reputedly a Plymouth man. He was soon to find worldwide notoriety as the most successful buccaneer in history.

At this time England was allied to the old enemy Spain as a counter to the rising superpower France. Ambitious English investors commissioned a small expeditionary fleet of ships led by the forty-six gun *Charles II* – a warship named not after the dead English monarch but Carlos II, the king of Spain. The once mighty empire was now in sharp decline with its future prospects hampered by an unstable and prematurely senile monarch and a court riven by internal dissent. Destined to be the empire's last Hapsburg monarch, Carlos II had already presided over the loss of much of the Spanish Netherlands and of Portugal and the Portuguese colonies, and the vilest *auto-da-fe* of the Spanish Inquisition. But he still ruled over a domain of nearly five million square miles.

The English expedition was to have a letter of marque from Madrid – in effect, a licence to commit piracy against certain nationals. This would authorise the force to sail to the Spanish West Indies where it was to plunder French possessions, provide arms to Spanish residents and raise treasure from wrecked galleons. Headed by the prominent London merchant Sir James Houblon, the speculators promised excellent pay in advance, and indeed all monies due to the crews were paid up to 1 August 1693 – by a curious coincidence, the date Theodore Paleologus made his will. The exact date of Theodore's death is unclear though we know it was either on the voyage out from England or when the fleet had reached 'le Groyne', the contemporary term for Corunna. He did not live to face the dilemma of either opposing or joining a memorable lawless escapade, the kind of challenge few of the Paleologi could have resisted and which his grandfather and namesake would surely have relished.

At anchor at Corunna, the idle crews of the English ships fretted as problems piled up one after another. Months went by but the promised Spanish document failed to arrive. As their money ran out, the crew of the *Charles II* petitioned Captain Gibson for another advance. The request was refused and rumours quickly spread among the increasingly desperate sailors that they had been tricked into slavery by the Spanish. Chief of the rumourmongers was the first mate Henry Every. Around 9 p.m. on 7 May 1694 a gang of about twenty-five conspirators, joined by men from another of the English ships called the *James* – again, an interesting coincidence – seized the *Charles II*. Captain Gibson was sick and confined to bed in his cabin, though by other accounts he was helplessly drunk: either way, the mutiny was bloodless. As darkness fell the captain of the *James* grasped that something was amiss and called across to the *Charles II* that men were deserting, whereupon Henry Every – unanimously elected the mutineers' leader – made a run for the open sea under fire from the *James*. Once at a safe distance from land, Captain Gibson and all who refused to join the mutiny were put in a boat to row ashore.

Under Every's command the *Charles II*, now renamed the *Fancy*, was the terror of the Indian Ocean for the next two years. Its most famous exploit was the plunder of a convoy of twenty-five ships of the Grand Mughal of India on pilgrimage to Mecca. Now the flagship of a small pirate squadron, the *Fancy* captured a treasure-laden galleon and its escort ship after hours of hand-to-hand fighting on deck. The loot was estimated by insurance assessors to be worth the astounding figure of £600,000 – the value then, not today's equivalent – in gold and gems. It has been claimed to be the richest haul in the history of piracy. But the lasting ill-fame of the action rests on the horrific rape of the women on board. Among those violated was a close relation, possibly granddaughter, of the Grand Mughal himself, though later legend held she was a young princess who willingly joined Every and became his wife. Other women stabbed themselves or jumped overboard to thwart their attackers. The outrage posed such a serious threat to English trade with India that the English government put an unprecedented £500 bounty on Every's head, a sum doubled by the East India Company.

Many of the pirate crew were later captured. Six were convicted of conspiring to steal the *Charles II* with piratical intent and on 25 November 1696 five of them were hanged at Execution Dock at Wapping, the last home of our Paleologus dynasty. John Sparkes, one of the condemned, was the only crew member to admit taking part in the rapes on board the Indian treasure-ship, repenting the 'horrid barbarities he had committed, though only on the bodies of the heathen'.[76] But Every himself was never run to earth. One story says he lived out a life of ease under an assumed name, another version says he was swindled out of his share of the loot and died in poverty close to his birthplace, by tradition Plymouth or one of its neighbouring villages.

The fate of the former *Charles II* is unknown, though it was last positively heard of in the Bahamas where the pirates tried urgently to dispose of the most incriminating piece of evidence of their criminal career before making their separate escapes. Though one account claims Every gave it to the governor of Nassau as a bribe, others say the vessel was lost after being deliberately driven onto rocks. Or could it have been the slave ship of that name, by some means sold on to the Royal African Company with the original name restored, only to fall victim to an act of piracy itself a few years later?

The sensational exploits of Henry Every inspired the publication of many semi-factual and fictional versions of his story over the following decades, among them Daniel Defoe's *The King of Pyrates*. A highly popular play called *The Successful Pyrate* was performed at the Theatre Royal, Drury Lane. Captain Every has featured in the majority of factual books on piracy ever printed. And as in the case of Theodore Paleologus, in modern times the captain has become a fantasy figure with ever more fanciful fictional forms of him appearing in novels, TV dramas and films. A sanitised Every was played by Guy Stockwell in the 1967 film *The King's Pirate* and he has appeared in three episodes of *Dr Who*, in 1966 and twice in 2011. On the last occasion Captain Every was resurrected as a 'space pirate' who assisted the Doctor in his epic battles.

As a last word on Theodore III, it should be noted that 1683 was the turning point in the Ottomans' centuries-long drive to conquer Europe. Their long march west, watched with foreboding by all our generations of Paleologi, ended in the failure of the Siege of Vienna. Young Theodore had the satisfaction of knowing that their empire suffered the rapid loss of much of the European territories they had overrun. Yet from the little that can be pieced together about him, one senses that the third Theodore saw himself as a colonial Englishman, a pragmatist, a pioneer of the new British Empire. He owed more to his Balls family than to any forebear who might have dreamed of returning to Constantinople.

❖

At Canon Adams's instigation, a researcher named Cregoe Nicholson searched the registers of St Dunstan, Stepney, in 1946 and found a record of a christening: *1693/4 January 24 Godscall daughter of Theodore Paleologus of upp. Wapping Gent: and of Martha uxor. 12 days old.* Given the date of Theodore's will in August the previous year it is almost certain the child was posthumous, though Theodore may well have known of his wife's pregnancy before his death.

The unusual name Godscall has been the subject of much speculation over the years. Canon Adams believed it was a surname, probably derived from Martha's Bradbury forebears, though no evidence to support this has been found. Many others have seen in it the seventeenth-century Puritans' fondness for eccentric godly names such as Fear the Lord, From Above and Sorry for Sin, along with more durable choices like Faith and Charity. Yet there is no record of Puritan leanings among the Bradburys or on Ferdinand's side of the Paleologus family. Or is the explanation the most obvious of all, that the baby was so sickly from birth that the mother feared her imminent death even at the christening and stoically accepted that God was calling her? The chances are the child was dead within hours or days, yet she was to be resurrected in the romantic imagination three centuries later.

I found nothing to contradict the traditional view that Godscall was the last representative of the English Paleologi, dying in infancy like so many children of the time. Despite the remarkable given name and surname which would surely leap out at anyone delving into London's old records, nothing further has been unearthed of Godscall Paleologus. So the journey which began many centuries earlier in Constantinople, taking us to Renaissance Italy, to Shakespeare's England and the newly settled tropical colony of Barbados, must come to a bathetic end in Wapping.

From this moment the English Paleologi will live on only in works of ever more elaborate fantasy. On the wilder shores of fiction they will inhabit alternative worlds: Theodore I will elope with Mary Balls and become the ancestor of the rightful, black-skinned queen of England; Theodore II will swop sides in the Civil War and die for king rather than Cromwell; the privateer-cum-slaver Theodore III will be a dashing hero of the Royal Navy; one of the Paleologus brothers, unnamed, will be the masked executioner of Charles I. Even the dead baby Godscall will rise phoenix-like from the grave, a deathless empress in another dimension.

# 20

I am fond of history, and am very well
content to take the false with the true.

Jane Austen, *Northanger Abbey*.

As precious little has been known of the true story of Theodore
Paleologus and his posterity, novelists, playwrights and poets have
allowed themselves carte blanche with the legend and thereby begot
much weird and wonderful fiction. This rich vein of invention can be
linked to the appearance of the original gothic novel, *The Castle of Otranto*,
in 1765. Horace Walpole's lurid romance set a fashion for supernatural
tales of wicked nobles, exiled princes and droopy maidens, customarily
opening on a dark stormy night and played out against a background of
crumbling castles and yawning crypts illuminated by flashes of lighting.
It seems fitting that the fearless, handsome young peasant who figures
in this first book of the genre should be named Theodore and that in
the final pages he is revealed as the rightful prince who will replace the
tyrant of Otranto.

Works of this sort were famously ridiculed in Jane Austen's *Northanger
Abbey*, published in 1818, in which the ingénue Catherine Morland
declares she would like to spend her whole life reading *The Mysteries of
Udolpho*, an extravagantly plotted tale of 1794 by Mrs Radcliffe, queen of
the gothic genre. As a guest at Northanger Abbey, Catherine's overactive
imagination allows her to mistake a washing-list for an ancient document
bearing precious secrets and to suspect her blameless host of murdering his
wife. As we have seen, the histrionic style of Nathan Drake's ballad *Mary
of Hadleigh* follows the pattern popularised by Walpole and Mrs Radcliffe,
as illustrated in these last lines describing William Balls's discovery of his
daughter at the Paleologus tomb in Cornwall:

Groans, as if life its inmost seat forsook,

At length escap'd the pilgrim's tortur'd breast;

And Mary, rising, turn'd with ghastly look,

'My father!' shriek'd, and instant sank to rest!

Near Falmouth lies a village called Constantine, though historians derive the name from a petty king of ancient Cornwall rather than Constantine the Great or the Paleologus line. However, Constantine is the alias adopted by a race of Cornish squires descending from Theodore of Landulph in a novel by the prolific Edwardian writer Sir Arthur Quiller Couch, commonly known as 'Q'. His novel *Sir John Constantine*, published in 1906, purports to be a memoir penned in 1756 by Sir John's son, Prosper Paleologus Constantine, the manuscript having been discovered and edited by 'Q'. The farrago of a plot concerns the Cornish knight's colourful adventures abroad which include rescuing a beautiful princess and being held hostage by Corsican brigands. The Constantines are introduced as impoverished gentry living in a wing of their once-great mansion, 'with its portraits and tapestries, cases of books, and stands of antique arms'. Sir John stands six feet five inches tall and has an aquiline nose, hollow cheeks and shiny white hair, an appearance clearly based on Jago Arundell's description of Theodore I's marvellously preserved corpse.

'Q' was captivated by the Paleologus legend. An earlier novella of his, *The Mystery of Joseph Laquedem*, dates from 1900 and seems to be the first work of fiction to add paranormal or uncanny elements to the story. Arguably the weirdest tale of all, it borrows heavily from the mythology of the Flying Dutchman and the Wandering Jew. It takes the form of a letter written during the Napoleonic Wars by a scholarly vicar, a figure clearly based on the historical Jago Arundell. A mysterious Jewish stranger appears in a Cornish village and becomes the lover of a beautiful imbecile called Julie Constantine, supposedly the daughter of a local labourer but in fact the descendant of Theodore of Landulph. The clergyman shows the stranger a brass plaque bearing the Paleologus coat of arms and an ancient fresco of the Crucifixion, both newly discovered under whitewash in his church. The Jew identifies a figure on the fresco as Joseph Kartophilius, the legendary servant of Pontius Pilate who mocked Christ on the road to Calvary and was doomed to go on living until the Second Coming. The stranger then reveals himself as none other than Kartophilius and explains that only Julie – now in the latest of many reincarnations over centuries – can save him from everlasting life. Possibly the story's most risible line begins: 'When she was a princess of Rome and I a Christian Jew led forth to the lions...'

A play performed during the First World War, *The Emperor's Ring*, added a topical twist to the Paleologus story. The central theme is the familiar one of a delegation of foreign dignities descending on a humble cottage in Landulph to bend the knee before Theodore's living descendant, identified here as an aged miner called Simon Paleol. The visitors are envoys of a group of Balkan states rather than Greek freedom fighters, though they too wish to persuade the heir to lead them against the old foe the Ottoman Empire, now the ally of the Kaiser. Their hopes are dashed when a War Office telegram arrives announcing the death in the trenches of the miner's only son. Appropriately for its vintage, there are many grandstanding speeches from Paleol and patriotic assertions of his family's Englishness. 'He died, like many a Paleol afore him, fightin' for his King an' country,' says the old man brokenly on reading the telegram, tears trickling down his weather-beaten cheeks. In the final scene Paleol scorns every blandishment of his would-be subjects and bawls: 'Make me desert King Jarge an' my country in wartime, would 'ee? Turn me into a furrin pagan, would 'ee?' With that he seizes Theodore's signet ring, the priceless heirloom kept in a teapot on the dresser, and rushing outside flings it far into the Tamar.

The author, William Price Drury, was a high-volume playwright and novelist who enjoyed a distinguished wartime career in the Royal Marines, and it must have been during his time in Plymouth as garrison intelligence officer that he first picked up local folk tales about living descendants of Paleologus. He later settled in the area and in 1929 became mayor of Saltash, the closest town to Landulph. *The Emperor's Ring* play was later reworked for Drury's collection of short stories, published in 1919 with the title *All the King's Men*. Described in the story is the opening of Theodore's coffin as recorded by Jago Arundell, though with the added refinement of the body instantly crumbling to dust like

Christopher Lee in the film *Dracula*. I have found no record of where or when the stage play was performed, though the author himself referred to its production during the war years.

Drury has two modest claims to fame. According to Admiralty records from his time in Devon, he was the first official ever to report sightings of UFOs. He is also said to have been the first writer to use the expression 'Tell it to the Marines' – generally assumed to be an Americanism – as the derisive response to an unlikely tale.

From Walpole and Mrs Radcliffe the gothic imagination moved on to works like *Frankenstein*, *Dr Jekyll and Mr Hyde* and *Dracula*, eventually giving birth to the Magic Realism genre. The sight of Ferdinand Paleologus's tomb in Barbados had a profound effect on the Cuban novelist and essayist Alejo Carpentier, generally recognised as the inventor of Magic Realism, a term encompassing stories in which a character breaks the rules of the real world. Characteristically, events in a magic realism novel go beyond the confines of the rational or natural, drawing on fable or folklore while retaining a down-to-earth or mundane style. Writers in English associated with magic realism include Angela Carter and Salman Rushdie, but the school originated and remains strongest in Latin America. One critic has defined the genre as 'what happens when a highly detailed, realistic setting is invaded by something too strange to believe.'[77]

Carpentier has written of coming across Ferdinand's gravestone unexpectedly on a visit to St John's and reflecting that if the last descendant of the Byzantine emperors could end up as a Church of England vestryman buried in the Caribbean, life was a good deal odder than people realised. Carpentier went on to coin the term *lo real maravilloso*, the marvellous reality, in a novel of 1949. This was several years before the expression first appeared in English. (I like to think that if someone had informed the Cuban intellectual that the quaint seventeenth-century tombstone that so impressed him was actually put up when he was two years old, he might have decided that life could be a sight queerer than even he imagined.)

In recent years the Paleologus story is repeatedly conflated with legends surrounding the Knights Templar, Holy Grail, Rosicrucian Order, the Day of Judgement and the hidden bloodline of Christ theories, while another of its recurring themes – the exiled scion of a deposed dynasty who struggles to recover his rights – has firmly taken root in modern fantasy epics set in fictional worlds. Escapist entertainment of this sort includes *Game of Thrones*. Yet the apocalyptic nature of many of the themes we find in Paleologus fiction may have a deeper source in the psyche.

Robert Goddard's *Days without Number*, published in 2003, is a thriller with supernatural overlays. Set in present-day East Cornwall and Italy with excursions to Tintagel Castle and the Rosslyn Chapel – locations with strong magical associations – its chief characters belong to a Cornish family of Paleologus descended from Theodore I who battle against assorted Bond-style villains. Car and speedboat chases, murders and seductions punctuate a search for a lost stained glass window which bears a cryptic inscription concealing the date of the Second Coming. The secret has been confided to James, brother of Jesus, and preserved by the Templars through the ages. In an end-piece to the book, the scene shifts from the present to the time of the Civil War in Cornwall. With the approach of a Roundhead army bent on wholesale destruction, church stalwarts set about dismantling the precious window to bury it under the Paleologus homestead.

A modern fantasy and science fiction author, M. John Harrison, resurrects various members of the Paleologus family in a 1992 novel called *The Course of the Heart*. This comes close to being a contemporary version of Quiller Couch's novella, mingling a plot about a group of present-day Cambridge students who are affected by a magical experiment gone wrong with the chronicles of a mysterious other world glimpsed in an epileptic woman's visions, the time and location constantly shifting. The offspring of Theodore are a garbled form of the family we know but are confusingly introduced with different names. Thus it is an Andrew who serves the House of Orange in 1600, 'perhaps as a soldier of fortune, perhaps as a diplomat or spy', but who changes his name to John when employed by the Earl of Lincoln.

Another son, called Constantine instead of Ferdinand, returns to England from his pineapple plantation in Barbados and fathers a daughter called Godscall, born in the year of the Great Fire of London. 'Whatever happened to her,' writes Harrison, 'she carried in her bones the cup, the map, the mirror – the real heritage of the Empress and the real Clue to the Heart.' The little girl we saw dying in infancy in Wapping has another-worldly existence here as a deathless armour-clad empress. The visionary epileptic is finally revealed as Godscall's descendant or reincarnation, the Heir to the Heart, the Empress who cannot die. Theodore II also appears in the book but seems to have chosen the royalist cause instead of parliament's, falling at Naseby with the cryptic words 'Oh, the shiny armour'. This may signify a dying glimpse of the Empress Godscall in all her splendour as she hovers over the battlefield like a Valkyrie. Harrison's novel also introduces us to a magical speaking version of the head of St Andrew, the Despot Thomas's gift to the pope.

Theodore I and his progeny are recurring characters in a series of works by Jane Stevenson, who skilfully weaves historical fiction in a set-ting between fact and legend. In *The Pretender*, published in 2002, we meet Lieutenant Theodore Paleologue in Restoration London. This is our Theodore III, son of the Barbados planter – in Stevenson's tale promoted to Sir Ferdinando – but instead of being a privateer he is a valiant officer of the Royal Navy. A well-made young man with olive complexion, aqui-line nose and small pointed beard, he first appears in a scene on the banks of the Thames declaring, 'If all had their rights, I should be emperor of the world', while flinging insults at the passing low-life.

A long section of the book set in Barbados is enlivened by a slave revolt and a hurricane. The Paleologues are portrayed as uncommonly lenient slave-owners, with Lady Paleologue never quite recovering from the discovery that a favourite slave is implicated in a plot to overthrow white rule. The story has Theodore marrying a native Carib woman rather than the historical Martha Bradbury.

Stevenson's Paleologus fiction is further embroidered in *The Empress of the Last Days* published in 2003 and set in the present. In this novel the young Oxford don hero falls in love with a young black Barbadian academic called Melita Paleologue and together they trace her lineage to a clandestine seventeenth-century marriage between the daughter of James I – Elizabeth Stuart, the Winter Queen – and a dark-skinned physician who is really the heir of a deposed African king. This book refers to Theodore III dying a hero at the battle of Corunna rather than on board the privateer *Charles II* and has his daughter Godscall marrying the black offspring of the Winter Queen. Melita is conclusively proved to be the rightful queen of England with all the requisite Anglican marriage rites authenticated over the centuries. Stevenson uses the motif of a Greek delegation travelling to Barbados to offer the crown of Greece to a descendant of Theodore of Landulph, but the proofs presented by Melita's forebear are discounted because of his colour.

Here again the Rosicrucians and prophetic visions of the Day of Judgement are worked into the plot and there is the innovative appearance of the black king who bears the gift of gold to the Christ Child. The learned genealogist in the novel, the Oxford don's Uncle Harold, traces Melita Paleologue's bloodline not only to the emperors of Byzantium and Rome but to the union of Jesus and Mary Magdalene.

A much earlier fictional work linking the Paleologi with the Stuarts is a curious short story by the Scottish novelist John Galt, the friend of Byron. In his autobiography of 1833 Galt describes his fascination with Theodore and his brood: 'I sketched a tale once on this subject by supposing one of them to have been the executioner, in mask, of Charles I, whom I represented as having inspired him with vindictive feelings by insolently treating the fallen fortunes of his house. The manuscript of the tale is preserved.' Whether it was ever published, and whether the manuscript still exists, I do not know, yet it strikes me as of more than passing interest that a fiction writer as far back as Galt discerned a decidedly sinister side to our English Paleologi. Their menacing character was intuited long before Canon Adams unearthed the first evidence of Theodore's career as an assassin.

A related American work of historical fiction published in 2010 is Ken McClellan's *The Last Byzantine*, subtitled *Confessions of a Would-be Messiah*. I have not read the book but in the publicity material its author, a former

US Air Force war planner, points to the 9/11 attacks on the World Trade Center and Pentagon as the catalyst for the novel. Its hero is the young orphan John Palaeologus, rightful heir to the Byzantine throne, who is captured and enslaved by the Turks and forced to become a janissary. He later falls into the hands of the Spanish Inquisition. According to the publicity blurb, Palaeologus hopes to 'pass on the baton of civilisation to the heirs of Rome along with a prophesy of what is yet to come'.

The best novel of Theodore Paleologus never written was Thomas Hardy's. A regular visitor to East Cornwall from the 1860s, when the then apprentice architect was courting his future wife Emma Gifford, Hardy almost certainly heard local tales of how humble descendants of the imperial heir still lived along the banks of the Tamar, either in Landulph or in the neighbouring village of Cargreen; and we know Hardy visited Landulph Church because he made a careful copy of the inscription on the Paleologus tomb in the notebook, begun in 1883, in which he jotted ideas for his future novels. Whether consciously or not on Hardy's part, the motif of the vertiginous fall in fortunes of a great family which is the backstory of *Tess of the D'Urbervilles* mirrors the persistent stories about Paleologus first recorded half a century previously by Jago Arundell, and the rector's much-quoted speculation that 'the imperial blood perhaps still flows in the bargemen of Cargreen'.

It is not hard to see how this dramatic story would lodge in the mind of a writer preoccupied with the malevolent workings of destiny. The memorable opening of *Tess*, published in 1891, has an antiquarian parson hailing the feckless wagoner John Durbyfield as the true heir of the ancient family of D'Urberville, an incident which turns the poor man's brain: 'Under the church of that there parish,' he cries, 'lie my ancestors – hundreds of 'em – in coats of mail and jewels, in gr't lead coffins weighing tons and tons. There's not a man in the county of South-Wessex that's got grander and nobler skillentons in his family than I.' Delusions of grandeur soon have Durbyfield declaring his line 'kings and queens outright at one time', but a fateful claim of kinship with a rich local family calling themselves D'Urberville – a bogus lot who made their money from trade – eventually leads his daughter Tess to the gallows while 'the D'Urberville knights and ladies slept on in their tombs unknowing'.

The stories of humble living descendants of Paleologus did not die in Hardy's day. Among the Adams papers I found notes recording Cornish families of recent times who harbour an unshakeable conviction they are of Theodore's blood. One of the rector's correspondents, writing in 1925 from an address in Plymouth, recalled that in her former parish of Lanreath were two farming families named Cossentine – a corruption of Constantine – who claimed descent in direct line. 'And indeed they look very princely,' she added, 'one of the families especially, four handsome sisters who have a regal poise of the head and beautifully formed hands and feet! Some of them are still living in St Veep parish.'

The works of Sir Patrick Leigh Fermor hardly qualify as fiction, but Theodore Paleologus and his brood haunt a number of these celebrated travel books. In his first work, *The Traveller's Tree*, an account of the Caribbean islands published in 1950, a lengthy section which begins with the author at the graveside of Ferdinand draws heavily on papers lent to Leigh Fermor by Canon Adams, and the imperial descent of the English Paleologi is described in detail. Musing on what strange adventures ended in this obscure churchyard on a tropical island, Leigh Fermor recites a prayer in Greek over the tomb. The history of the Landulph family is repeated in *Mani*, a book of 1958 covering a journey through the South Peloponnese, a place boasting its own folklore of imperial heirs – though the tradition is far shakier there, according to Leigh Fermor, than that belonging to far-off Cornwall. More wistful ruminations on the Paleologi occur in a work of 1966, *Roumeli: Travels in Northern Greece*.

In a remarkable passage in *Mani*, the author is lulled into a pipe-dream in which, at some distant future time, the process of Westernisation persuades an enlightened Turkish people to abandon the lands of the old Byzantine Empire and go back to where they came from. Thereupon begins a frantic search for the true heir to Constantinople – an echo of the Greek independence fighters' quest in Cornwall and Barbados – ending

with an ecstatic vision of a Paleologus once more ascending the imperial throne to a joyous fanfare of trumpets. Surrounded by all the pomp
of the Orthodox Church 'in vestments of scarlet and purple and gold
and lilac and sea-blue and emerald green', the heralds proclaim the new
emperor King of Kings, Most August Caesar and Basilius, Autocrator
of Constantinople and New Rome.

Half a century after Leigh Fermor wrote these words, his flight of
fancy resonated faintly inside Landulph Church when the cream of
Britain's Orthodoxy gathered in sumptuous vestments at the grave of
Theodore Paleologus.

# 21

That the rejection of fabulous pedigrees, the exposure
of spurious records, and the substitution of fact
for fiction in the realm of family history will,
in some quarters, prove distasteful is only what
one must expect. Poor, ill-clad, shivering truth
stands pitiful by the way; for men have ever passed
her by in search of that which they desire.

Horace Round, *Peerage and Pedigree.*

We touched earlier on a number of supposed descendants of Theodore
Paleologus local to Cornwall and Barbados and on the claims of the
great Victorian mountebank Demetrius Rhodocanakis, but claimants
to Byzantine imperial blood – and indeed to the imperial honours –
remain a global phenomenon to this day. Pretenders still pop up in every
corner of Europe, in the United States and elsewhere, and are especially
thick on the ground in England.

Persons already possessed of a crown are no longer anxious to press
a claim to a throne which vanished over 500 years ago: the Romanov
czars were probably the last royals to brood seriously on their
Paleologus blood, speaking of Moscow as the Third Rome and dream-
ing of an absorption of Byzantine lands into the Russian Empire, failing
which they would no doubt have settled for a port with access to the
Mediterranean for the Russian fleet – Constantinople, say.

Along with other inter-related European royalty, Queen Elizabeth II
and Prince Philip can each lay claim to imperial ancestors, albeit by
tortuous routes. Her Majesty's line of descent goes all the way back

to Michael the Crafty and is traced through James I. James inherited Paleologus blood twice over, from his mother Mary Queen of Scots by way of the counts of Savoy – whose pedigree embraces the Paleologus marquises of Montferrat – and from his maternal grandmother Mary of Guise. The Duke of Edinburgh's descent via his Russian forebears is traced back to Zoe, daughter of Thomas the Despot, and her marriage to Ivan III, Grand Prince of Muscovy. Their grandson was Ivan the Terrible. It was on account of this union that Russia adopted the imperial double-headed eagle which has re-emerged in post-Soviet days.

Landulph, the early focus of our research into the English Paleologi, remains a property of the Duchy of Cornwall. The Queen and Prince Philip visited Landulph in July 1962 and according to the local newspaper the royal party 'viewed the interior of the church and was greatly interested in the Paleologus memorial', as well it might be; the royals also met twenty-three tenants of the manor of Landulph.

The Maltese genealogist Charles Gauci is one of the best-known researchers of imperial pretenders, and he and Professor Peter Mallat, an Austrian authority on Byzantine culture, have compiled genealogical tables of twenty-eight lines of supposed descent from the Paleologus dynasty, though they prudently decline to vouch for the authenticity of any. These pedigrees appeared in a handbook printed in Malta in 1985. The chart labelled 'the Cornwall Paleologi' shows the English family's descent from John, but instead of being the son of Thomas the Despot this hazy figure is shown as the offspring of Manuel, the son of Thomas who returned to Constantinople and became the fanatical Moslem known as *El Ghazi*. The table describes our Theodore Paleologus I as 'of Landulph Castle', an imposing address which regrettably has never existed. The later family tree is derived in the main from the Landulph brass and ends, as does my own research, with the death in infancy of Godscall, daughter of Theodore III.

However, this Gauci-Mallat pedigree includes an additional name, one Ricardus Paleologus, supposedly a younger brother of the Theodore born in Pesaro in 1504, the great-grandfather of the Theodore buried in Cornwall. This Ricardus allegedly found himself in the Isle of Wight in 1524 and married a local heiress; we are then referred to a separate genealogical table, 'the Isle of Wight Paleologi', which traces thirteen generations from Ricardus to arrive at 'Prince Petros Paleologus, Duke of Morea, Grandmaster of the Order of St George (English branch). Residence, Isle of Wight, UK'. A second glance at this table shows that the father of Prince Patros was born in 1927 with the rather less glamorous name of Peter Francis Miles.

We are then cross-referenced to yet another chart labelled 'Jaloweicki-Palaeologus' which again originates with Thomas the Despot's son Manuel Paleologus, the one who returned to Constantinople. This pedigree shows Peter Francis Miles as the grandson of Colonel the Baron Joseph Miles – no provenance of the title is offered – of Wakefield, Yorkshire. This Joseph, the descendant of *El Ghazi*, supposedly married a Countess Mary d'Authume-Palaeologina and their son was plain old Peter Francis Miles, father of Prince Petros. What happened to the barony is not indicated, though it may be too piffling to mention in the company of these heady princely and ducal titles.

His Imperial Highness Prince Patros was one of the more engaging figures among the multitude of claimants to the imperial honours. Until his death in 1988 he was a familiar sight in the streets of Ventnor, striding along in a fetching uniform of his own design, 'with long flowing white hair, sandals but no socks, and some sort of order or military award around his neck', as the local paper reported at the time. The vast array of ancient documents which proved his descent seems to have been seen by nobody but the prince himself. *Debrett's Peerage* ridiculed this stellar pedigree but both *The Times* and *The Daily Telegraph* printed obituaries headed with his fabulous title. His widow continued to call herself Her Imperial Highness the Despotina Patricia, *aka* Empress of the Romans, but their son Nicholas now felt free to pour scorn on the fantasies which he said had shamed and embarrassed the family all his life.

At the heart of Prince Patros's claim was that his maternal grandfather, a plumber with the curious local name of Colenutt, inherited his Paleologus blood from the mysterious Ricardus of Tudor times, whose full name was said to be Ricardus Kolenneat Paleologus, the middle name being derived from a Byzantine province and corrupted over the years to Colenutt. According to Prince Patros, the extinction of the line of Theodore of Landulph left the Colenutts as the true imperial heirs.

Yet another branch of this remarkable Jaloweicki-Palaeologus pedigree begins in the early nineteenth century with a Prince Miecstav, nationality unstated, son of Prince Fedor Jaloweicki na Perejastawo who married a Paleologus daughter of the Isle of Wight lot. This junior branch of the junior branch reaches modern times in the person of Sean Patrick O'Kelly de Conejera born in 1957, son of Lt Col Patrick O'Kelly, Baron de Conejera, 'Head of the Isle of Man branch of the family'.[78]

Among other wonderfully named genealogies set out by Gauci and Mallat are the Paleologue-Crivez, the Tocco Paleologo, the Paleologo-Oriundi, the Vassallo-Paleologo, the Schmidt von Launitz Comnene Paleologue, and the Dolgorouky-Palaeologus. Portraits and photographs of the heads of these august families show court dress with knee-breeches, tails and white tie to be much in favour, along with quasi-ecclesiastical robes and flowing capes with elaborate decorations sporting the double-headed eagle. A taste for handlebar moustaches and monocles is also in evidence.

The de Vigo Aleramico Lascaris Paleologo family tree is a remarkable Italian one, confidently setting out the family's direct descent from the Emperor Nero in AD 54. The Paleologus forebears come in with Thomas the Despot – the most popular ancestor among the pretenders – with regular infusions of royal blood from the likes of the kings of Serbia, Jerusalem and the Two Sicilies. The pedigree descends in the present time to the personage known as Prince Enrico Constantino de Vigo Aleramico Lascaris Paleologo, Grandmaster of the Constantinian Order of St George and of the Order of the Cross of Constantinople.

His Imperial and Royal Highness Prince Enrico, who died in 2010 at the ripe age of ninety-one, was never slow in coming forward to proclaim his imperial lineage. The prince felt the hand of destiny on his shoulder in 1967 when King Constantine II of Greece was deposed in the wake of the colonels' *coup d'état*, whereupon Enrico got on a plane to Athens and put himself at the disposal of the Greek people. Representatives of the new government did indeed hold talks with the prince, who pointed out his credentials as heir to the last Byzantine dynasty, but the colonels failed to take up his offer to step in for the departed king. Disappointed but undaunted, Enrico returned to his tireless work collecting money for the many charities associated with the imperial orders, which appear to have come into being only when he declared himself their grandmaster.

There was a different story told about the prince, however. In this he was a fantasist and brazen conman. Branded the son of an unmarried Italian woman of humble origin, Enrico (sometimes calling himself Prince Henri) was claimed by detractors to be a bigamous ex-hairdresser with convictions in various European courts for slander, fraud and theft – in 1953 he was charged with stealing, of all things, 9,464 crates of tinned tomatoes – and in 1972 was pursued by the law for non-payment of support to an abandoned wife and children. He always hotly denied the claim he was once a hairdresser in Genoa. His pedigree was dismissed by a number of worthy authorities as a total fabrication but there were repeated reports of the sale of Byzantine honours and of prestigious plots for the cremated ashes of favoured applicants at the prince's chateau in France. A company in the Cayman Islands was the alleged destination of various funds handled by Enrico. In the 1990s Palm Beach in Miami and Caesar's Palace in Las Vegas were the prince's preferred stamping grounds for organising glittering charity balls from which he garnered handsome fees. At one Las Vegas event he was said to have pocketed $42,000 for conferring titles and coats of arms on gullible aspirants. At a charity ball in Tokyo in 2003 it was claimed those honoured with a seat at the princely table had stumped up 50,000 yen for the privilege.

Since the prince's death the doings of his followers continue to be announced on the webpage of the noble orders, as are plans for future Byzantine balls to further Enrico's selfless efforts for world peace. The recently appointed vice chancellor of the orders is Madam Dewi Sukarno, widow of the deposed Indonesian dictator and noted collector of designer shoes, who states she is dedicating the rest of her life to the betterment of society.

The small medieval town of Viterbo north of Rome has a prominent place in other Italian pedigrees. A large quantity of dubious papers turned up suddenly in Viterbo in modern times which had gone unrecorded for centuries but which conveniently supported certain disputed genealogical claims. Many of these colourful claimants attach their family tree to that from Thomas the Despot to the English Paleologi, so you would think our Theodore of Landulph would at the very least be recognised as *primus inter pares* of the pretenders. But there are other pedigrees which insist on a common lineage with none other than Demetrius Rhodocanakis, and their imperial pretensions rest on a claim that Theodore's marriage to Mary Balls was bigamous.

Prince Enrico's pedigree boasts a grand total of thirty-three named generations from Nero to himself, though there is an unfortunate gap of some 900-odd years between the fiddle-playing emperor and the next identified forebear on the chart. Compared with this, some of the other pedigrees compiled by Gauci and Mallat seem pitifully threadbare, resorting to lots of dotted lines between ancestors separated by hundreds of years. The Syros Palaeologi, for instance, muster only two named individuals between the death of Despot Andronicus of Thessalonika in 1428 and Marcos Palaeologos, temp. 1762. Or take the Mourtzinos-Palaeologos, with just seven names separating a fifteenth-century progenitor from the present day representative, or the Demetraki-Paleolog of Cracow, who name a mere seven ancestors between Michael the Crafty who died in 1282 and Richard Demetraki-Paleolog, born 1949.

Another English claimant, a postman calling himself Archie White-Palaeologus, failed to make the grade for the Gauci-Mallat pedigree collection, but in the 1970s he declared himself to be descended from the imperial family. He said his great-grandfather had travelled to Greece during the war of independence to claim his rightful throne but the provisional government gave him the cold shoulder. Archie claimed a number of Paleologi were still living quietly in England and they got together from time to time to dress in imperial robes and call each other prince and princess.

The Greek cemetery at West Norwood in South London contains the gravestones of a number of individuals claiming imperial blood, though their pedigrees do not appear among those listed by Gauci and Mallat. There is, for instance, a Theodore Attardo di Cristoforo de Bouillion, Prince Nicephorus Comnenus Palaeologus, described as 'hereditary claimant to the Grecian throne 1863', and a 'Princess Eugenie Nicephorus Comnenus Palaeologus' who died in 1934 and whose tombstone proclaims her 'descendant of the Grecian Emperors of Byzantium'. A medical officer of the name Paleologus sailed with the British army to serve in the Crimean War, though where, if anywhere, he fitted into the general picture of claimants I have not established.

The name Paleologus is uncommon but not exceptionally rare in present-day Greece. At the time of writing the national telephone directories list 1,135 subscribers under the traditional Greek spelling, usually transcribed as Palaeologos in our alphabet, with a further 1,149 under the alternative and more modern spelling of Paleologos. As the current population of Greece is estimated at ll.3 million, possession of the name is still noteworthy, and one must wonder how many of these telephone subscribers could also speak of an oral tradition of imperial descent.

✢

The case of Victor Paleologus is very different to the exotic examples outlined above. More people in the United States would associate the name Paleologus with a notorious murder in Hollywood rather than the Byzantine emperors, if indeed there are Americans in any number who have heard of the imperial dynasty. The age-old obsession with exalted bloodlines and titles has largely disappeared nowadays leaving the general public intoxicated by celebrity in all its manifestations: a star of sport, film or television will trump any royal except the most personable and photogenic. It is a sign of the times that the imposture of which Victor Paleologus stood accused at his trial was not of seeking to impress girls with talk of a glorious pedigree, but of posing as a Hollywood producer involved in a James Bond movie.

In February 2003 the body of a beautiful twenty-one-year-old aspiring actress named Kristi Johnson was found by hikers on a steep under-growth-covered slope below a wealthy suburb in the Hollywood Hills. Three years later Mr Paleologus, a failed restaurateur, was convicted of strangling Miss Johnson after luring her to a fake photo shoot. The pros-ccution described him a master conman who repeatedly used the ploy of auditioning young women for a non-existent Bond movie, dangling the prospect of acting roles, $100,000 fees and parties with the likes of Sean Connery, before subjecting them to sexual assault. The district attor-ney called for the death penalty though the case was considered weak by many observers due to the lack of forensic evidence. *The People versus Paleologus* took a sensational new turn when Mr Paleologus unexpectedly changed his plea at the eleventh hour from not guilty to guilty of first-degree murder. He quickly tried to withdraw the guilty plea on the basis of being given flawed legal advice by his attorney when he was tired and confused, but the judge refused to alter the plea a second time.[79]

So far as the focus of this chapter is concerned, there is no suggestion Victor Paleologus ever tried to gain benefit from his name, but he tells me of a strong family tradition of descent from the imperial dynasty and remembers the double-headed eagle proudly displayed in the family's New Jersey home. In his life before prison he paid no attention to ancestry but since his incarceration has begun to research his family's history with the aid of his prison mentor, a former police officer. However, unlike the remarkable individuals whose claims are described above, in this case Paleologus is his real name and not assumed: the immigration papers of his father, who arrived in America from Mytalini in the Aegean, show he was previously registered with both the –os and –us spelling of the name, the latter most unusual in Greece, and Mr Paleologus tells me the family used this form in earlier generations.

As the latest phase of his genealogical research programme, Mr Paleologus is studying the recent advances in mitochondrial DNA fin-gerprinting which famously allowed the identification of the murdered Romanov family following the exhumation of their bodies in Russia in 1991. He has also been excited by the positive DNA identification of the skeleton of Richard III, who was born the year before the fall of Constantinople, following its discovery on the site of Greyfriars Church in Leicester in 2012. Richard's genes were positively matched to two samples taken from descendants of his sister, Anne of York, in the seventeenth generation.

Among descendants of the Russian imperial dynasty whose gene samples provided proof that the remains found at Ekaterinburg were those of the last czar and his family was the Duke of Edinburgh, and Mr Paleologus tells me he is writing to Buckingham Palace as part of his efforts to assemble the DNA information of known descendants of the Paleologus dynasty to compare with his own.

Nowadays it is possible to subscribe to one of many websites worldwide which have sprung up to sell DNA testing kits, from $119 skywards. This promises a new lease of life to claimants to the imperial blood, though it may not be welcome to some existing pretenders. Within a few minutes of beginning an internet search, I discovered one which tempts customers by offering tests to establish a link with various famous figures in history, such as 'Discover your relation to Czar Nicholas II'.

# Epilogue

At the end of our examination of the life, careers, ancestors and descendants of Theodore Palcologus, how close are we to deciding whether he was the genuine article or an imposter?

We know that the credentials set out on the Landulph brass were accepted at face value by generations of eminent historians, with the one exception of Oldmixon. There was, however, a marked predisposition in former times to repeat the assertions of earlier scholars without further investigation. This explains the longevity of mistaken or even fraudulent statements such as Theodore's two non-existent marriages in Chios and Suffolk, to mention only the most obvious. There are other endlessly repeated elements of the traditional story, such as the Greek deputation travelling to Cornwall and Barbados, which we might treat with some scepticism but which would not affect the question of authenticity.

This rests essentially on what we can glean from the archives and allowing for the question mark over the paternity of John, the rest of Theodore's ancestry seems amply borne out by the documents at Pesaro.

My own view is that the century-long association with their patrons the Rovere dukes of Urbino is the most persuasive fact we have before us. This dated back to a time when memories of the imperial refugees were, if not fresh, not beyond recall.

Have present-day historians cast an objective eye over Theodore? Hoaxers like Demetrius Rhodocanakis have left a stain on the name of Paleologus and the outlandish claims of later pretenders may well have made the entire subject beyond the pale for academic research, at least for the present. Steven Runciman was the doyen of Byzantine studies in his time and since the publication of *The Fall of Constantinople* in 1965 no one referring to the man buried at Landulph seems to have queried the new orthodoxy that he was an imposter: this despite the fact that Runciman makes a clear error of fact in the single reference to Theodore he committed to print. His case for the non-existence of a son of Thomas called John was grounded on the writings of Sphrantzes, the contemporary of the last emperor, but this supposedly contemporary chronicle has been undermined by historians since Runciman's death.

It is true that the bulk of the work we rely on to flesh out the story was undertaken by clerical amateurs like Jago Arundell and Adams, but their perseverance cannot be faulted and their labours rooted out a great deal of evidence unnoticed or ignored by professional historians. Runciman himself said that as an historian he added to his writings 'the qualities of intuitive sympathy and imaginative perception', and perhaps our Landulph antiquaries should be allowed the same latitude.

The paucity of ascertainable facts led to much scholarly speculation which was later shown to be misguided. And indeed many of the abiding myths must be laid at the door of Jago Arundell, who despite his groundbreaking research was not immune to the romantic susceptibilities of his day, a kind of osmosis from the gothic novels. There is no doubt he ardently desired that Theodore should be *de stirpe Imperatorum*, to a point where he may well have been inclined to turn a blind eye to any contrary evidence. It is surely significant that after so many years absent from England he returned to be buried beside Theodore, the misappropriated coat of arms of Arundell fixed to the wall below Theodore's imperial eagle. Canon Adams himself, despite decades of forensic investigation, took up ideas which have since proved to be mistaken; no doubt there are many conjectures in this book which will suffer the same fate.

The last question to ask on the matter of descent is whether it really matters. Until fairly recent times there was a generally shared veneration for old names and old titles which has largely disappeared. Few today would lose sleep over the extinction of an ancient name, as few of us care for a concept of nobility which rests exclusively on heredity: these days we are probably more enthralled by charlatans and pretenders. This is a huge cultural change that would have astounded and horrified most educated people throughout history.

Canon Adams reflected that whatever the truth might be, Theodore was surely no upstart imposter, and sportingly added: 'He was certainly no saint but compared to most of the imperial family he almost deserves a halo.' For my own part, years of studying Theodore Paleologus have led me to conclude he was indeed of imperial stock, though probably a bastard. I am also inclined to think his ancestor was from the refugee generation following the fall of Constantinople rather than a related branch from an early time. John was most likely a son of Despot Thomas, but probably illegitimate. Alternatively, the shadowy ancestor may well have been the son of one of Thomas's undisputed offspring, the feckless Andrew or the apostate Manuel. As I speculated earlier, in the former case Theodore's great-great-grandfather and namesake, the Theodore born in 1504, would therefore be the legitimate if extremely embarrassing child of Andrew's Roman wife Caterina. Small as the possibility is, I am loath to abandon it entirely. Emperor and prostitute: if I were a writer of fantasy fiction, I could desire no better heredity for my hero.

The debate over Theodore has kept scholars busy for centuries, spawned generations of charlatans and dreamers, and propelled his dynasty into realms of ever more fantastic invention. With a theoretical pedigree stretching back to the Caesars, he already belongs to a world closer to fable than to history. And however many of his different faces we glimpse – scholar, bigamist, master of horse, assassin, spy – the real Theodore always manages to slip back into the shadows. He may continue to intrigue and entertain us in after lives still undreamed of.

I cannot end with a great revelation, but it is perhaps more appropriate that what remains is an enduring mystery rather than a cast-iron certainty. A final consolation is that if Theodore Paleologus was indeed an imposter, the fraud itself is now of a respectable antiquity.

# Appendix A

## The Joust And The Changing Face Of Warfare

The tournament was still a living tradition at Elizabeth's court, though the primary purpose was now to shine in an elegant spectacle rather than to beat the living daylights out of an opponent. Taking their cue from the royal example, great nobles erected tilting barriers at their country properties, as the first Earl of Lincoln did at Tattershall. His son Earl Henry respected the tradition.

Introduced to tilting in his youthful days at Urbino, Theodore Paleologus belonged to the last generation who saw the trappings of the tournament as an indispensable part of courtly life in England.[80] Following a pattern set by French and Italian courts, the lists at Westminster had increasingly taken the form of the *carrousel*, a spectacle in which knights could show off extravagant armour and costume, enact emblematic scenes and display enigmatic *imprese*, usually to do with undying love for an unfeeling lady or devotion to the Virgin Queen. The most admired feats of horsemanship came to resemble an equestrian ballet. Theodore might have recognised this as a vestige of the world of Castiglione, though the great Italian arbiter of manners warned his perfect courtier to beware taking part in a tournament unless he was splendidly equipped as to horse, weapons and armour, and to keep in mind that it was unbecoming for a gentleman to deign to appear at 'some country show' where spectators and participants were common folk. This may have caused some heart-searching at Tattershall.

Already an anachronism because of the changing face of warfare, the tourney was to be effectively supplanted under the Stuart kings by elaborate court masques, pageants and play-acting which carried minimal threat of physical harm. A new perspective on chivalry was signalled by the publication in 1605 of Cervantes's *Don Quixote*, the tale of a ridiculous knight-errant who tilted at windmills. The author was an old soldier who had been maimed at the battle of Lepanto and endured five years as a captive of the Barbary pirates.

But the military value of the lists had not disappeared. Aggressive energies were still channelled in a disciplined manner in side attractions to the joust, such as running at the ring and the quintain, which helped develop practical eye-and-hand skills for use in warfare. Most of all, the coordination of horse and rider were increasingly important because of the rapid increase in the use of handguns by light cavalry. By the late sixteenth century the fast-moving mounted pistoleer had largely displaced the lumbering heavy cavalryman in full armour, notably in the wars of the Low Countries in which Palæologus had fought under Prince Maurice.

The new breed of light cavalrymen were armed with wheel-lock pistols – there might be several of these weapons, attached to belt and saddle and even stuffed into boots. These mounted soldiers were known in German as *reiters*, in French, *reitres*, in Italian, *raitri*, in English, riders. Riders had to be consummate horsemen as their effectiveness in battle depended on moving fast in tight formation towards the enemy's infantry, firing their weapons at close range, then wheeling away to make room for the following rank of the squadron. One of the prominent English soldiers fighting in the Netherlands, Sir Roger Williams, was an enthusiastic supporter of the new tactic. In his *Briefe Discourse of War* published in 1590 he declared: 'Without a doubt, the Pistoll discharged hard by, well charged and with judgement, murthers more than the Launce.' Speed and manoeuvrability came at the expense of personal safety, however, since riders necessarily dispensed with much of their armour. It was in such a charge of riders at the battle of Zutphen that Sir Philip Sidney received a deadly Spanish musket ball in his unprotected leg.

There seems a paradox in the fact that the high-born Englishmen most closely associated with the romance and old-world spectacle of the Elizabethan tournament – the likes of Sidney, Leicester and Essex – were eager proponents of the new-style warfare, as demonstrated by the many portraits in which they pose with the latest handguns. The Earl of Lincoln's gentleman rider was surely of the same mind. His long service in the continental wars, coupled with his famed equestrian skills, almost certainly point to Paleologus as a rider in the contemporary military sense, with the pistol as a key item in his private armoury.

The kind of education in the military arts Paleologus gave to young John Smith was summarised by Sir Charles Cornwallis, an early biographer of Henry Stuart,[81] who would become Prince of Wales on the accession of his father James VI of Scotland to the English throne. Prince Henry hero-worshipped Maurice of Nassau, who sent Henry with his compliments 'a Dutch captain … a most excellent engineer in all manner of Things belonging to the Wars'. We read that the prince 'did also practice Tilting, Charging on Horseback with Pistols, after the manner of the Wars, with all other the like inventions. Now also delighting to confer, both with his own, and other strangers, and great Captains, of all Manner of Wars, Battle, Furniture, Arms by Sea and Land, Disciplines, Orders, Marches, Alarms, Watches, Stratagems, Ambuscades, Approaches, Scalings, Fortifications, Incampings.'

# Appendix B

## Paleologus's Letter To The Duke Of Buckingham

Monseigneur

L'honneur & La courtoisie qu'il vous a pleu me tesmoigner a vostre dern-
iere venue en ceste Ville de Plymmouth, me donnent la hardiesse de vous
remercier par ceste ci, n'estant pas capable assez de Le Vous tesmoigner
par discours, plustost par effect, estant un gentilhomme, né de bonne
maison & adonné a toute sort d'honnesté Exercise digne du Nom que ie
porte, mais malheureux au reuers de Fortune que mes Ancestres & moi ont
senti. Vous priant Monseigne de croire que s'il vous plaist de m'employer
suiuant vostre promesse, Vous trouuerez en moi, fidelité & suffisance assez
(si ic l'ose ainsi dire) & prendrez pitié d'un poure gentilhomme qui peut
& desire seruire le Roy en ce qu'il professe. Je dis Monseigneur qui peut,
Ayant vescu & respandu son sang a la guerre depuis sa Jeunesse, comme il a
pleu au feu Prince d'Orange, & autres djuers Seigneurs Anglois & Francois
qui m'ont veu & cognu, du rendre tesmoinage. Que s'il plaist a Vostre grandeur de m'employer au seruice du Roy, & commander a Sir James Back
qu'il lui plaise de me donner de vostre part quelque chose pour m'aider
a passer le reste de ma vie, Il ne sera pas Ingratement employé & esper-
ant vous donner toute sorte de contentement, apres auoir prié Dieu pour
Vostre Sante & prosperite, Je demeurai a Jamais

Monseigneur
Vostre treshumble & tres obeisant Serviteur
Theodoro Paleologe
De Plymmouth ce seix Mars 1628

# Appendix C

The Archdiocese of Thyateira and Great Britain is a Greek Orthodox authority established in 1922, the year of the Smyrna massacres. It covers the UK, Isle of Man, Channel Islands, the Irish Republic and Malta. It takes its name from one of the Seven Churches named in the Book of Revelation.

Known in classical times as a great centre of dyeing and the indigo trade, Thyateira was located in what is now the modern Turkish city of Akhisar. In Revelation, Thyateira is where Jezebel entices the Christians into sexual immorality. In the Acts of the Apostles, a woman called Lydia, 'from the city of Thyateira and a dealer in purple cloth', was baptised by St Paul and is honoured by the Orthodox Church as the first known European Christian. The ruins of Thyateira were explored by the Revd Jago Arundell during his pilgrimage to the Seven Churches.

Elected as head of the Orthodox in Britain in 1988, Archbishop Gregorios is a Cypriot born near the now Turkish-occupied city of Famagusta. In 1994 he established the only Orthodox church in Cornwall, a former Methodist chapel at Falmouth.

There are an estimated 300,000 Greek-speaking residents of the United Kingdom.

# Notes

1 Casson, Sir Stanley, *Greece and Britain*, Collins, 1940.
2 Runciman, Steven, *The Sicilian Vespers*, Cambridge, 1958.
3 The Pope was quoting from *Twenty Six Dialogues with a Persian*, translated by Professor Theodore Khoury, in an article for *Sources Chretiennes*, n 115, Paris, 1966.
4 The numbering of the emperors sometimes differs depending on whether an individual was recognised as legitimate or not. Thus Constantine XI may be referred to as VIII, as on the tomb of Landulph.
5 The head was enshrined in St Peter's in Rome, where it remained until 1964, when Pope Paul VI sent it back to Patras as a gesture of goodwill to the Orthodox Church.
6 Most present-day historians say Sphrantzes's major chronicle was an expanded and much elaborated work, possibly outright forgery, by the sixteenth-century priest Makarios Mellisserios, 'the Pseudo-Sphrantzes'.
7 Emperor Justinian I had set a precedent nine centuries earlier. According to the contemporary historian Procopius, Empress Theodora was the daughter of a bear-trainer and a circus acrobat, and prior to her marriage enjoyed a long career as an actress-courtesan of unparalleled depravity.
8 The duke's murder has been seen as the inspiration of the play-within-a-play in *Hamlet*.
9 *Magna Britannia: Cornwall*, Cadell and Davies, London, 1814.
10 Intriguingly, in 1568 Queen Elizabeth's great spymaster, Sir Francis Walsingham, regularly employed a Protestant ex-soldier from Lucca, one 'Tommaso Franchiotto' alias 'Captain Francois', as a double agent. Franchiotto, while simultaneously in the pay of the French crown, alerted his English patron to an alarming plot hatched in France – then at war with England – to poison the queen. The name, city of origin and occupation may all be coincidental but the failed assassin Franceotti could well have been a relation of Walsingham's spy.
11 Lucca's later efforts to eliminate Salvetti included a 1620 plot which failed, as reported by the would-be assassin, because 'every citizen is a policeman' in London.
12 Kurz, Otto, *Fakes*, Yale University Press, 1948.
13 Rhodocanakis, Konstantinos, *A Discourse in the praise of Antimonie* and *Alexicacus Spirit of Salt of the World*, both published in London, 1664.
14 *Letters and Papers, Reign of Henry VIII*, Vol. xi, 463.
15 British Library, BM, 27/41.
16 Historical Manuscripts Commission, Salisbury, 312.
17 Historical Manuscripts Commission, Salisbury, 332.

18  State Papers, Domestic, 1581–90, 176/12.

19  *The Complete Works of Roger Ascham*, published by White, Cochrane, London, 1815.

20  Peynel, *De Guajaci Medicina*, 1540.

21  I have found no record of Earl Henry risking his own person in the lists but his father, the first earl, was a respected jouster.

22  Rye, W.B., *England as Seen by Foreigners*, John Russell Smith, London, 1865.

23  Dugdale, *The History of Drayning and Embanking*, London, 1662.

24  Letters and Papers of Henry VIII, Vol. xii, part 1, February 1536.

25  Acts of Privy Council, xxv, 517, 519.

26  Acts of Privy Council, xxiii, 339.

27  Acts of Privy Council, xxv, 407, 411.

28  State Papers Domestic 1581–90, 177/41.

29  Ibid., 201/40.

30  The Fair Geraldine was herself the subject of colourful gossip. Soon after her marriage to Lincoln the Archbishop of Canterbury, Matthew Parker, accused her of 'frailty' and 'forgetfulness of duty'. Parker went so far as to say the countess should be chastised in Bridewell, a notorious gaol of loose women.

31  Lord Norreys was the son of the Henry Norreys who was executed for high treason by Henry VIII as one of the alleged lovers of Queen Anne Boleyn. Elizabeth's staunch support of the Norreys family was tantamount to an assertion of her mother's innocence.

32  Star Chamber Records, 5, C19/36.

33  British Museum Harleian Papers, 6995/77.

34  Ibid., 6995/109.

35  State Papers Domestic 1595–7, 18, 143.

36  Chancery Records, 2 Ff.1, No. 4.

37  Thomas Bird, *Memoirs of Queen Elizabeth*, London, 1754.

38  Acts of Privy Council, xxvii, 1597–8, 506.

39  Parry, C.H., *A Memoir of Pereguine Bertie, Eleventh Lord Willoughby De Eresby*, Murray, 1838.

40  Willoughby family legend may exaggerate the privations of the duchess and Mr Bertie in exile. The couple left England in 1555 with a considerable number of servants and retainers including a fool and, by a curious coincidence, 'a Greek rider of horses'.

41  John Dowland's *My Lord Willoughby's Welcome Home*, with a setting by William Byrd, remains one of the most frequently played compositions of the Elizabethan age. Among modern recordings for lute or keyboard instrument is a version by the pop singer Sting.

42  Stow, John, *Survey of London*, reprint of 2009, The History Press.

43  A discussion of contemporary jousting and the changing face of warfare is at Appendix A.

44  Barbour, Philip L., *The Three Worlds of Captain John Smith*.

45  *Captain John Smith* by Dorothy and Thomas Hoobler, John Wiley and Sons, New Jersey, 2006.

46  Historical Mss Commission, Salisbury, x, 146.

47  Ibid., 332.

48 Chancery Records, 24, 379/63.

49 To the present day the family of Bertie, Earls of Abingdon, retain the style Lord Norreys of Rycote as the courtesy title of the heir.

50 Historical Mss Commission, Salisbury, 11, 184–5.

51 The neglect of Sempringham Church continued under succeeding earls and it remained in a ruinous state until restored by Victorian zeal. Daniel Defoe, visiting the site around 1725, noted 'the full decay' of the mansion where the Clintons had once lived 'in the upmost splendour and magnificence'.

52 Star Chamber Records, 5, L1/29.

53 Ibid., 5, L13/33.

54 Ibid., 5, L1/29.

55 Ibid., L34/37.

56 Windwood, R., *Memorials and Affairs in the Reigns of Queen Elizabeth and King James I*, London, 1725.

57 Historical Mss Commission, Salisbury, x, 38.

58 According to folklore, the daughter of the king of Spain, Archduchess Isabella, vowed not to change her underwear until the city fell. Curiously, there are legends of other historical Isabellas swearing a similar oath, beginning with Isabella of Castile at the siege of Granada in 1492.

59 State Papers Domestic, 1601–3, 91, 91i.

60 Much of the Tattershall glass ended up at Burghley House and St Martin's Church in Stamford, where Elizabeth's chief minister is buried.

61 Chandos, John (ed.), *In God's Name: Examples of Preaching in England, 1534–1662*, Hutchinson, 1971.

62 A further mystery about the tomb is the number of sons and daughters. The first earl had four sons, not three, and four daughters, three by Bessie Blount and one by his second wife, yet there are seven female mourners on the monument. All seem to be by the same hand and of the same material, so the thought they might have been relocated from another tomb – as sometimes happened when church interiors were rearranged – can probably be dismissed. So along with the question of where the missing sons went to, and why the fourth was not represented, is another: where did the extra daughters come from? One might fleetingly suspect that the countess, whose marriage to Lincoln was childless, had enterprisingly sneaked offspring of her own onto the monument, but by her first husband Sir Anthony Browne she had only two sons, both of whom died in infancy. So we may never know who all these mourners are supposed to be or what kind of musical chairs they have been playing.

63 Another page of the Plymouth records shows the charge against Paleologus at one halfpenny a month but this is thought to be a clerical error.

64 Various sensational accounts of Fludd and his secret order can be found on the internet.

65 That Sir Nicholas was a stickler on matters heraldic is demonstrated on his wife's brass, where the impaled arms of Lower are carefully differenced by a mullet, or five-pointed star, the sign of a third son. The detail of this monument would have been supervised by the knight himself. By contrast his own brass by the same hand, completed after his death, omits this mark of cadency.

66 His title of Archbishop of Thyateira and Great Britain is explained at Appendix C.

67 The title archimandrite marks a superior abbot and is nowadays bestowed as a mark of great respect.

68 Arundell, Jago, *Archaeologia* article.

69 Extract from the diary of Henry Whistler, quoted in *The Narrative of General Venables, 1654–1655*, edited by C.H. Firth, London, 1900.

70 After his surrender Willoughby was twice imprisoned by Cromwell's Protectorate. At the Restoration he returned to the Caribbean as governor and in 1666 commanded a fleet sent against French forces which had seized St Kitts. He was lost when his flagship sank in a hurricane.

71 Still known as Balls Plantation, the estate near Oistins in Christ Church Parish is now the home of the Barbados Horticultural Society. Remaining relics of the old days include a boiling house and a windmill used to grind the sugar cane.

72 Campbell, P.F., The Barbados Vestries, 1627–1700, *Journal of the Barbados Museum and Historical Society*, Vol. 37, 1983.

73 Codrington enlarged his fortune by smuggling slaves into the island at night after the Royal African Company was granted a monopoly in the transportation of slaves. In 1710 his son bequeathed the family estate of 800 acres and 300 slaves to the Society for the Propagation of the Gospel.

74 By coincidence, on my visit to the Paleologus grave I met a Canadian tourist who was at St John's to research a Barbadian ancestor: none other than Rev. John H. Gittens.

75 The captain of the *Charles II* may have played a similar role himself. The surname Gibson appears frequently in the Barbados archives: a Quaker family of that name were major plantation owners, though unpopular with contemporaries because of their efforts to Christianise their slaves. Whether Captain Gibson was of this clan I could not establish. The apparent contradiction of Quakers dealing in slaves seems not to have troubled the Society of Friends at the time. A Quaker slave ship was infamous for conditions on board even by contemporary standards, and on one voyage landed only twenty-two slaves alive in Barbados out of 250 embarked in Africa. The ensuing scandal was about the wasted profit rather than the extreme inhumanity entailed.

76 Grey, Charles, *Pirates of the Eastern Seas (1618–1723)*, Sampson, Low, Marston, 1933.

77 Stretcher, Professor Matthew, 'Magical Realism and the Search for Identity', *Journal of Japanese Studies*, Vol. 25, No. 2, 1999.

78 Gauci and Mallat, *The Palaeologos Family*.

79 Currently in Chino State Prison, Mr Paleologus writes to me insisting he is innocent of murder and continues his attempts to have the conviction overturned. He was previously an inmate of Corcoran maximum security prison, where high-profile fellows included Charles Manson, Juan Corona – convicted of twenty-five murders – and, until recently, Sirhan Sirhan, assassin of Robert F. Kennedy.

80 The Western-style tournament had reached as far as Byzantium during the Paleologan era. Emperor Andronicus III learned the sport from Italian knights who escorted his bride, Anne of Savoy, to Constantinople in 1326.

81 Cornwallis, *Discourse of the Most Illustrious Prince Henry, Late Prince of Wales*, first published London, 1641.

# Bibliography

*Books which are highly recommended to the general reader are marked with an asterisk.

Ackroyd, Peter, *The Life of Sir Thomas More*, Doubleday, 1988; *Shakespeare: The Biography*, Chatto and Windus, 2005.

Acton, Harold, *Three Extraordinary Ambassadors*, Thames and Hudson, 1983.

*Alford, Stephen, *The Watchers: a secret history of the reign of Elizabeth I*, Allen Lane, 2012.

*Andrews, Sue, and Springall, Tony, *Hadleigh and the Alabaster Family*, Andrews, 2005.

Arber, Edward (ed), *Captain John Smith of Willoughby: Works 1608-1631*, Constable, 1895.

Ashton, Robert, *James I by his Contemporaries*, Hutchinson, 1969.

Barber, C.L., *Shakespeare's Festive Comedy*, Princeton University Press, 1959.

Barber, R. and Barker, J., *Tournaments*, Boydell Press, 1989.

*Barbour, Philip L., *The Three Worlds of Captain John Smith*, Macmillan, 1964; *The Complete Works of John Smith, 1580-1631* (three vols), University of North Carolina Press, 1985.

*Barrett, John, and Iredale, David, *Discovering Old Handwriting*, Shire Publications, 1995.

Bates, E.S., *Touring in 1600*, Constable and Houghton Mifflin, 1911.

Bond, Shelagh M. (ed), *The Monuments of St George's Chapel, Windsor Castle*, published for the Dean and Canons, 1958.

Bossy, John, *Giordano Bruno and the Embassy Affair*, 1991; *Under the Molehill: an Elizabethan Spy Story*, Yale Note Bene, 2001.

Bracken, C.W., *A History of Plymouth*, Underhill, 1931.

Browne, Sir Thomas, *Hydriotaphia or Urne-Burial*, 1658.

Burke, Sir Bernard, *Vicissitudes of Families*, 1869.

Burton, Elizabeth, *The Elizabethans at Home*, Secker and Warburg, 1958.

*Burton, Robert, *The Anatomy of Melancholy* (first published 1621), New York Review Books, 2001.

*Carew, Richard, *Survey of Cornwall* (first published 1602) Tamar Books, 2000.

*Castiglione, Baldesar (trans Ball, George), *The Book of the Courtier* (first published 1528), Penguin, 1967.

Chynoweth, John, *Tudor Cornwall*, Tempus, 2002.

Coate, Mary, *Cornwall in the Great Civil War*, Bradford Barton, Truro, 1933.

Cockerham, Paul, *Continuity and Change: Memorialisation in the Cornish Funeral Monument*

*Industry 1497-1660*, British Archaeological Reports British Series, 2006.

Cook, Judith, *Dr Simon Forman*, Chatto and Windus, 2001.

*Cressy, David, *Bonfires and Bells*, Weidenfeld and Nicolson, 1989; *Birth, Marriage and Death: Ritual, religion and the life-cycle in Tudor and Stuart England*, Oxford University Press, 1997.

Crowley, Roger, *Constantinople: the Last Great Siege 1453*, Faber and Faber, 2005.

*Cruickshank, C.G., *Elizabeth's Army*, Oxford University Press, 1966.

*Dalrymple, William, *From the Holy Mountain: A Journey in the Shadow of Byzantium*, Flamingo, 1998.

Darvill, Giles, *Little Sir Hal Killigrew*, CRM and Dysllansow Truran, 1994.

Dent, Anthony, *Horses in Shakespeare's England*, Anthony Dent, 1987.

Du Maurier, Daphne, *Golden Lads: A Study of Anthony Bacon, Francis, and their friends*, Victor Gollancz, 1975.

Dunkin, Edwin, *Monumental Brasses of Cornwall*, 1882.

*Dunne, Richard S., *Sugar and Slaves: The Rise of the Planter Class in the English West Indies*, University of North Carolina Press, 1972.

Elliott, J.H., *Europe Divided, 1559-1598*, Fontana, 1968.

*Evans, Helen C. (ed), *Byzantium: Faith and Power, 1261-1557*, Metropolitan Museum of Art, New York, 2004.

Finlay, George, *History of Greece*, Oxford, 1877.

Forbes-Lindsay, C.H., *John Smith, Gentleman Adventurer*, Lippincott, 1907.

*Fraser, Antonia, *Mary Queen of Scots*, Weidenfeld and Nicolson, 1969.

Gainsford, Thomas, *The Glory of England*, London, 1618.

Gant, John, *Autobiography*, London, 1833.

*Gauci, Charles A., and Mallat, Peter, *The Palaeologos Family: A Genealogical Review*, Publishers Enterprises Group, Malta, 1985.

Gibbon, Edward, *The Decline and Fall of the Roman Empire* (first published 1776–88), Wordsworth edition, 1998.

Gilbert, C.S., *The Historical Survey of the County of Cornwall*, 1817.

Gomme, A.H. (ed), *Jacobean Tragedies*, Oxford University Press, 1969.

Grey, Charles, *Pirates of the Eastern Seas (1618–1723)*, Sampson, Low, Marston, 1933.

Hadfield, Andrew (ed), *Five Jacobean Tragedies*, Wordsworth Classics, 2001.

Hammond, Peter, *Dean Stanley of Westminster*, Churchman Publishing, 1987.

*Handover, P.M., *The Second Cecil: The Rise to Power 1563-1604 of Sir Robert Cecil, later first Earl of Salisbury*, Eyre and Spottiswoode, 1959.

Harrison, William, *The Description of Britain*, London, 1577.

*Haynes, Alan, *The Elizabethan Secret Services*, History Press, 1992.

*Head, Constance, *Imperial Twilight: The Palaiologos Dynasty and the Decline of Byzantium*, Nelson-Hall, Chicago, 1977.

*Herrin, Judith, *Byzantium: The Surprising Life of a Medieval Empire*, Penguin, 2007.

Hill, Christopher, *The Century of Revolution, 1603-1714*, Nelson, 1961.

*Hill, J.W.F., *Tudor and Stuart Lincoln*, Cambridge University Press, 1956.

Hodgett, Gerald A.J., *Tudor Lincolnshire*, History of Lincolnshire Committee, 1975.

*Holmes, Clive, *Seventeenth Century Lincolnshire*, History of Lincolnshire Committee, 1980.

Hoobler, Dorothy and Thomas, *Captain John Smith: Jamestown and the Birth of the American Dream*, John Wiley and Sons, New Jersey, 2006.

Hoyos, Sir Alexander, *Barbados: A History from the Amerindians to Independence*, Macmillan Caribbean, 1978.

Hutchens, Fortescue, *The History of Cornwall*, Penaluna, 1824.

Hutchinson, Robert, *Elizabeth's Spymaster*, Phoenix, 2006.

*Hutton, Ronald, *The Rise and Fall of Merry England: The Ritual Year, 1400-1700*, Oxford University Press, 1994.

Iredale, Eric W., *Sempringham and St Gilbert and the Gilbertines*, Pointon, 1992.

Jardine, Lisa, *The Awful End of Prince William the Silent*, HarperCollins, 2005.

Jones, W.A.B., *Hadleigh through the Ages*, East Anglian Magazine Publishing, 1977.

Kendall, Alan, *Robert Dudley, Earl of Leicester*, Cassell, 1980.

Lacey, Robert, *Robert, Earl of Essex*, Weidenfeld and Nicolson, 1970.

Lack, William, Stuchfield, H. Martin, and Whittlemore, Philip, *The Monumental Brasses of Cornwall*, Monumental Brass Society, 1997 (update of Dunkin).

*Leigh Fermor, Patrick, *The Traveller's Tree*, John Murray, 1950; *Mani: Travels in the Southern Peloponnese*, Murray, 1958; *Roumeli: Travels in Northern Greece*, Murray, 1966.

Lower, Mark Antony, *The Curiosities of Heraldry*, John Russell Smith, 1845.

Machiavelli, Niccolo (trans Bull, George), *The Prince* (first published 1532), Penguin, 1961.

Mijatovich, Chedomil, *Constantine, the Last Emperor of the Greeks*, Sampson Low, Marston, 1892.

Milton, Giles, *Paradise Lost: Smyrna 1922*, Sceptre, 2008.

Miola, Robert S., *Shakespeare's Reading*, Oxford University Press, 2000.

Moule, Thomas, *The English Counties Delineated: Cornwall*, 1838.

*Nicholl, Charles, *The Reckoning: The Murder of Christopher Marlowe*, Jonathan Cape, 1992; *The Lodger: Shakespeare on Silver Street*, Allen Lane, 2007.

*Nicol, Donald M., *The Immortal Emperor: The Life and Legend of Constantine Palaiologos, Last Emperor of the Romans*, Cambridge University Press, 1992; *The Byzantine Lady: Ten Portraits, 1250-1500*, Cambridge, 1994.

*Norwich, John Julius, *Byzantium* (three vols), Viking, 1988–95.

*O'Conor, Norreys Jephson, *Godes Peace and the Queenes: Vicissitudes of a House 1539-1615*, Oxford University Press and Humphrey Milford, 1934.

Oldmixon, John, *British Empire in America*, 1708.

Parry, Charles Henry, *A Memoir of Peregrine Bertie, 11th Lord Willoughby de Eresby*, John Murray, 1838.

Picard, Liza, *Elizabeth's London*, Weidenfeld and Nicolson, 2003.

Pote, Joseph, *The History and Antiquities of Windsor Castle*, London, 1749.

Rogers, W.H., *The Strife of the Roses and Days of the Tudors*, James G. Commin, Exeter, 1890.

Ross, Josephine, *The Winter Queen: The Story of Elizabeth Stuart*, Weidenfeld and Nicolson, 1979.

Rowse, A.L., *The Expansion of Elizabethan England*, Macmillan, 1955.

*Runciman, Steven, *The Fall of Constantinople, 1453*, Cambridge University Press, 1965; *Mistra*, Thames and Hudson, 1980.

Savignon, André, *With Plymouth Through Fire*, Ouston, 1968.

Schomburgk, Sir Robert H., *The History of Barbados*, Longman, Brown, London, 1835.

*Shapiro, James, *1599: A Year in the Life of William Shakespeare*, Faber and Faber, 2005.

Sidney, Sir Philip, *Defence of Poesy*, Macmillan's English Literature Series, 1919 (first printed 1595 as *An Apologie for Poetrie*).

Stanley, Arthur Penrhyn, *The Historical Memorials of Westminster Abbey*, Longman, Brown, 1867.

Steane, J.B. (ed), *Christopher Marlowe: The Complete Plays*, Penguin English Library, 1969.

Stewart, Alan, *Philip Sidney: A Double Life*, Chatto and Windus, 2000.

*Stone, Lawrence, *The Crisis of the Aristocracy, 1558-1641*, Oxford University Press, 1965; *The Family, Sex and Marriage in England, 1500-1800*, Pelican, 1979.

Stow, John, *A Survey of London written in the year 1598*, Sutton Publishing, 2005.

Stoye, John, *The Siege of Vienna*, Collins, 1964.

*Strong, Sir Roy, *Henry Prince of Wales*, Thames and Hudson, 1986.

Stucley, John, *Sir Bevill Grenville and his Times*, Phillimore, 1983.

*Tattersfield, Nigel, *The Forgotten Trade*, Jonathan Cape, 1991.

Thomas, Keith, *Religion and the Decline of Magic*, Penguin University Books, 1973.

*Tindal Hart, A., *The Man in the Pew, 1558-1660*, John Baker, 1966.

Tinniswood, Adrian, *Pirates of Barbary*, Jonathan Cape, 2010.

Vandercook, John W., *Caribee Cruise: A Book of the West Indies*, Reynal and Hitchcock, New York, 1938.

Wedgwood, C.V., *The Thirty Years War*, Jonathan Cape, 1938.

Weever, John, *Ancient Funerall Monuments within the United Monarchie of Great Britain*, Thomas Harper, 1631.

West, Jane, *The Brave Lord Willoughby*, Pentland Press, 1998.

Whetter, James, *Cornwall in the 17th Century: A Study in Economic History*, Lyfrow Trelysen, Gorran, 1974; *Cornish Weather and Cornish People in the 17th Century*, Lyfrow Trelysen, Gorran, 1991.

Young, Alan, *Tudor and Jacobean Tournaments*, George Philip, 1987.

Young, Peter, *Edgehill 1642: The Campaign and the Battle*, Roundwood Press, 1967.

# Articles, Guides And Papers

Adams, Canon John H., *Theodore Palaeologus*, Journal of the Royal Institution of Cornwall,
Vol. VI, new series, 1971; *Landulph Church*, Billing and Sons, Guildford, no date;
*Theodore Palaeologus and his Family*, typescript, no date.

Alabaster, John S., *The Alabaster Chronicle*, Journal of the Alabaster Society, No. 21, 2003;
No 26, 2006.

Archdiocese of Thyateira and Great Britain, *Year Book 2008*.

Avery, Tracey, *Tattershall Castle*, The National Trust, 1997.

Badham, Sally, *The Monumental Brasses of the Collegiate Church of the Holy Trinity, Tattershall*,
Tattershall Parochial Church Council, 2004.

Barrett, Andrew Mark, *A History of the Ancient Parish Church of St Leonard and St Dilph,
Landulph*, privately printed, 2000.

Bierbrier, M.L., *The Palaeologus Family: Fact and Fiction*, The Genealogist 9, 1988.

Bradfield, Henry, *The Last of the Greeks; or, Ferdinando Paleologus*, Gentlemen's Magazine,
Vol 19, 1843.

Chambers, W. and R. (ed), *The Last of the Palaeologi*, Chambers' Edinburgh Journal, new
series No. 419, 1852.

Cope-Faulkner, Paul, *Sempringham: Village to Priory to Mansion*, English Heritage, 2011.

Davison, Frank and Dorothy, *A Guide to St John's Parish Church*, Cole's Printery,
Barbados, 2006.

Done, Roy (updated by Dudley, John), *A Guide to the Collegiate Church of the Holy Trinity of
Tattershall, Lincolnshire*, Tattershall Parochial Church Council, 2005.

Harris, Jonathan, *A worthless prince? Andreas Palaeologos in Rome 1464-1502*,
internet article (Hellenic Institute, Royal Holloway University of London).
(https://repository.royalholloway.ac.uk)

Iredale, Eric W., *Sempringham and Saint Gilbert and the Gilbertines*, Pointon, 1992.

Isom-Verhaaren, Christine, *Shifting Identities: foreign state servants in France and the Ottoman
Empire*, Journal of Early Modern History, Vol. 8, 2004.

Jago Arundell, Revd F.V., *Some Notices on Landulph Church*, 1840.

Mallat, Peter, *The Palaiologos Family after 1453: the destiny of an imperial family*,
The Genealogist 2, 1981; *A Famous 'Emperor in Exile': Thomas Palaiologos and his
descendants*, The Genealogist 6, 1985.

Ronchey, Silvia, *Orthodoxy on Sale: the Last Byzantine and the Lost Crusade*, internet article
(University of Siena).

Round, Stonehouse and Woodward, *St James, Spilsby: History and Guide*, 2010.

Towson, John Thomas, *A Visit to the Tomb of Theodoro Paleologus*, Transactions of the
Historic Society of Lancashire and Cheshire, May 1857.

Williams, Sally, *Grimsthorpe Castle*, Grimsthorpe Castle and Drummond Castle Trust,
    revised edition 2003.

Wilson, Heath (trans), *The Manuscripts of Henry Duncan Skrine: Salvetti Correspondence*,
    Historical Manuscripts Commission, 11th Report, Appendix, Part 1, 1887.

## Some Works of Fiction Concerning the Paleologi of Cornwall

Drake, Nathan, 'Mary of Hadleigh', a ballad printed in *Winter Nights or Fireside
    Lucubrations*, Longman, Rees, Orme and Brown, London, 1820.

Drury, Lt Col W.P., *The Emperor's Ring*, short story adapted from his play of the same
    name, in *All the King's Men*, Rich and Cowan, 1933.

Goddard, Robert, *Days without Number*, Bantam Press, 2003.

Harrison, M. John, *The Course of the Heart*, Gollancz, 1992.

Quiller Couch, Sir Arthur, *The Mystery of Joseph Laquedem*, novella published in *Old Fires
    and Profitable Ghosts*, Scribner's, London, 1900; *Sir John Constantine*, Smith, Elder,
    London, 1906.

Stevenson, Jane, *The Pretender*, Jonathan Cape, 2002; *The Empress of the Last Days*,
    Houghton Mifflin, Boston and New York, 2004.

# Acknowledgements

I am most grateful to the Society of Authors and the Authors' Foundation for the generous award of the Elizabeth Longford grant which made possible research in Italy and Barbados. A grant from the Cornwall-based 'Q' Committee, trustees of the Sir Arthur Quiller-Couch Memorial Fund, helped to fund further researches in England. I must also thank Piers Brendon for his encouragement when few seemed to see the point of a biography of an obscure figure like Paleologus.

Among many distinguished academics who were generous with their time and advice I should mention especially Judith Herrin, Professor of Late Antique and Byzantine Studies at Kings College, London; Robin Law, Professor of African History, University of Stirling; and Professor Jane Stevenson, who combines her educational role at the University of Aberdeen with a successful career as a historical novelist and who kindly tracked down the source of the statement that Ferdinand Paleologus was the inspiration of Magic Realism. Christopher Rowe was an insightful reader of an early draft of sections of this book, and he and Nigel Coulton assisted with the translation of difficult passages of early legal Latin. Two of the country's leading authorities on early handwriting, Dr David Iredale and John Barrett, most generously analysed the handwriting of Theodore Paleologus, and Chris Scott was similarly unstinting in examining the likely circumstances of the death of Theodore II. These and others with specialised knowledge, sometimes of extremely obscure subjects, were unfailingly helpful.

I thank His Eminence Archbishop Gregorios, Father Gregory-Palamas Carpenter, and the Revd Philip Lamb for their patient assistance with many queries. I thank a luminary of the Church Monuments Society, Dr Julian Litten, for his unrivalled knowledge of seventeenth-century burial customs – it has rightly been said he is the best man in England to take you down into a vault – and I am grateful for his informative comments. Andrew Barrett, historian of Landulph, was a fount of knowledge on the church and parish. The Alabaster Society proved a mine of information on the town of Hadleigh and the Balls family, and I offer special thanks to Laraine Hake and Dr Tony Springall for their generous assistance in searching town records for evidence of the Balls family. John Carras of the Anglo-Hellenic League was most helpful in researching records in Greece.

In Barbados, the collections of the Shilstone Memorial Library proved crucial to my research and I was fortunate to have the assistance of Joan Brathwaite, archivist, and Miguel Pena, the museum's researcher. At St John's Church, Angelina Lovell-Johnson was a helpful guide. To Paul Foster, historian of Barbados, serendipitously encountered at the graveside of Ferdinand Paleologus, I am greatly indebted for sharing his encyclopaedic knowledge of the island past and present.

In Italy, the archives of the Oliveriani Library in Pesaro were of central importance and I thank Dr Marcello Di Bella, library director, and his staff, especially Maria Grazia Alberini, for their assistance in identifying documents relating to the Paleologi. Monica Russo was my admirable translator of Italian.

In the United States, I sincerely thank Mr Victor Paleologus for his rewarding and illuminating correspondence composed under the most trying personal circumstances. I always opened his meticulously handwritten letters with keen anticipation. Thanks are also due to Chief Stubbs and Lieutenant Salerno of the Santa Monica Police Department and to Jean Guccione of the Los Angeles District Attorney's Office.

My thanks also to Dr Christine Faunch, head of Heritage Collections at Exeter University; Angela Broome, librarian archivist at the Courtney Library, Royal Institution of Cornwall; Claire Larkin of the Alumni Office, Oxford University; Steve Edwards of the Foundation for Medieval Genealogy; Sue Kauffman of the Liverpool Record Office; Christine Reynolds, assistant keeper of muniments at Westminster Abbey Library; Enid Davies, assistant archivist at St George's Chapel, Windsor Castle; Alan Barclay of the Plymouth and West Devon Record Office; Jon Culverhouse, curator of the Burghley House collections; Ray Biggs of the Grimsthorpe and Drummond Castle Trust; Rachel Lacy, editor of *Orders of the Daye*, the journal of the Society of the Sealed Knot; Mrs Dymoke of Scrivelsby; the Revd Gordon Plumb; Mr Colin Squires of Saltash Heritage.

I am indebted to Dr Garry Tregidga, senior lecturer at Exeter University and assistant director of the Institute of Cornish Studies, and Sarah Jayne of Academic Services, University of Exeter: to Sarah I owe a special word of thanks for unearthing the long-mislaid collection of Canon Adams's manuscripts and letters from a mass of uncatalogued material at the University's Tremough campus. That inspired search saved months of labour.

Kind assistance was provided on many occasions by staff at the British Library (in particular the manuscript reference team), National Archives at Kew, Lincolnshire Archives, Lincolnshire County Libraries, Courtney Library in Truro and the Public Library and Morrab Library in Penzance.

At The History Press, my thanks to Mark Beynon and Naomi Reynolds.

To my wife Lilian, thanks and much love.

Finally I formally acknowledge my debt to the late Canon John Herbert Adams. The results of his investigations provided the early framework for this book and will remain the starting point for any future biographer of the English Paleologi. That indispensable body of knowledge was itself based on pioneering research by his distant predecessor as incumbent at Landulph, the Revd Francis Jago Arundell, who began his enquiries into the mysterious Paleologus before even the penny post was at his disposal. It is humbling to reflect how few are my own discoveries despite such present-day advantages as the infinite archives of the internet and cheap jet travel.

I must, of course, add that responsibility for any errors, mistaken conclusions, misreading of ancient documents and wild surmises is entirely my own.

# Picture Credits

# Index

The immediate family of Theodore Paleologus is marked in **bold**.

Dew

Please return / renew by date shown.
You can renew at: **norlink.norfolk.gov.uk**
or by telephone: **0344 800 8006**
Please have your library card & PIN ready.

| | 8\|15 | | |
|---|---|---|---|
| | | | |

NORFOLK LIBRARY
AND INFORMATION SERVICE
NORFOLK ITEM